. At remembrance ceremonies and services u down the country, these words will be said: 'they shall gr old, as we that are left grow old: age shall not weary them years condemn. At the going down of the sun and in the n we will remember them'. We will take time to remember who gave their today in armed conflict so that we could experience a better tomorrow.

No Thankful Village

No Thankful Village

The impact of the Great War
on a group of Somerset villages
- a microcosm

Chris Howell

Published by

Fickle Hill

Published by Fickle Hill,
Chapel Cottage, Parsonage Lane,
Chilcompton, Bath BA3 4HD

www.ficklehill.com

First published 2002

ISBN 0-947660-04-6

Dewey Classification 940.3

Typeset by Radstock Reproductions Ltd, Midsomer Norton
Printed and bound in Great Britain by
Butler & Tanner Ltd, Frome and London

This book belongs to:

Alex
and
Sam

To my Darling Mum
from your loving son, Neil

Somewhere in France

LOST IN FRANCE

He had the ploughman's strength
in the grasp of his hand:
He could see a crow
three miles away,
and the trout beneath the stone.
He could hear the green oats growing,
and the south-west wind making rain.
He could hear the wheel upon the hill
when it left the level road.
He could make a gate, and dig a pit,
And plough as straight as stone can fall.
And he is dead.

Ernest Rhys

You know, it's a strange thing but all through my life nobody has ever wanted to know about my experiences in the war. Nobody ever asked, and I've never really wanted to talk about it.

Pte. Edward Hurd
1st/4th Battalion
The Gloucester Regiment

Foreword

by

Major Sir Fergus Matheson of Matheson, Bt.
Formerly Coldstream Guards

Chris Howell has invited me to write this foreword as a tribute to my elder brother, Sir Torquhil Matheson - an enthusiast for military matters - for the help he gave Chris. The book is a collection of experiences of men and women, mainly from Somerset, who served our country in the Great War. Chris has done a remarkable amount of research, which has enabled him to capture for future generations not only the horrors of war but also a way of life and the spirit of the nation at a critical time in our history.

My father will have known some of the Coldstreamers whose anecdotes follow, particularly those who served with him in the 3rd Battalion. He was commissioned into the Coldstream Guards in 1894 after service in the Hertfordshire Militia. He took part in the South African War, was present throughout the 1914/18 War - commanding the Guards Division in the final phase - and went on to serve for another 17 years. It was hardly surprising that Torquhil, with such a military background, enlisted into his father's old Regiment at the first possible opportunity in 1943.

Although I share Torquhil's enthusiasm for most things military, I lack the detailed knowledge he had of battles, campaign medals, their recipients and the Regiments in which they served. It must have been a great pleasure for him and Chris Howell when they met and found they shared this interest.

Of the men whose stories are recounted, roughly 30 relate to the Somerset Light Infantry, 13 to the Coldstream Guards and around 18 to other Regiments or Corps. A fine record. In our time, five of our blood relations served in the Coldstream as well as Torquhil's father-in-law and a further five of my wife's family. A few years back my son Alexander was also commissioned into the Coldstream. This is not unusual in the British Army where loyalty and love for one's Regiment is common throughout, and every worthwhile soldier reckons his Regiment is the best.

There are many humorous anecdotes woven into Chris Howell's book as part of the fabric of his patchwork picture of the War. However, most of what he has written about is of a much more sombre nature. The images are haunting and provoking and the few who have read the final draft of this book have been angered, moved and impressed by what they have found. I am delighted to commend his work and pleased that my brother was able to contribute to it.

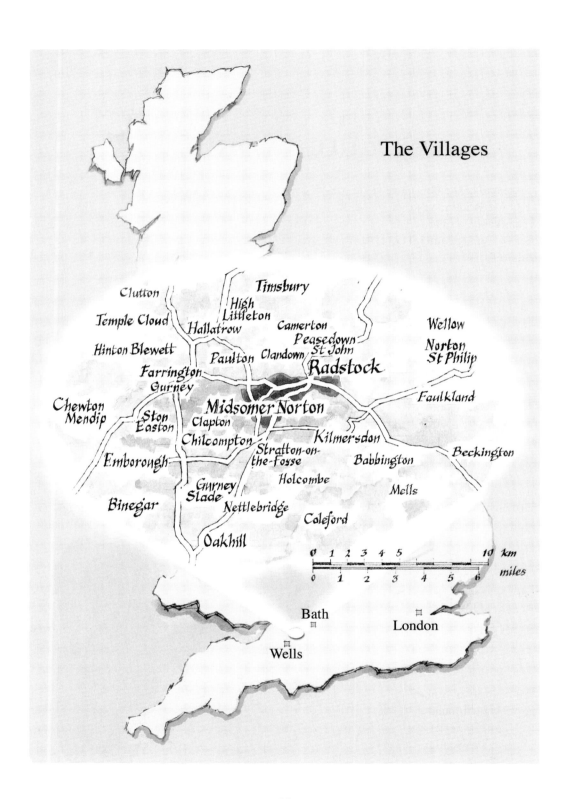

The Villages

Introduction

At the end of the Great War there were thirty two, so-called, Thankful Villages in the whole of Great Britain; villages to which all the young men who went to war returned alive. Remarkably, a quarter of those villages were in the County of Somerset. But there was no thankful village among the mining and farming communities that lie mid-way between Bath and Wells.

This book is a record of what the men and women who lived in that tiny part of the country did during the war. It is not a military history but rather a collage of letters, cuttings and memories, a patchwork picture of the period.

Between 1979 and 1990 I produced a series of oral history and photographic records of life in Somerset around the turn of the previous century. One character, a small-time farmer and horse-and-cart haulier, called Charlie Fry, cropped up in all of them and I was occasionally asked to write a book solely about him. I had a problem with this though, because despite having a great deal of material about him there was one period of his life that few knew about; his service in the Great War. Some who knew him well even insisted that he had not served.

As I continued with research for other books, and with the possiblility of a Charlie Fry book in mind, I usually asked people what they recalled of the war in general and of Charlie in particular. In the process I built up a sizeable resource of notes, tapes and photographs, copies of which I gave to the Imperial War Museum. Otherwise, because I had no time to devote to the book, it lay undisturbed in shoe-boxes.

I have done my best to validate all that I was told. Some was improbable, some unlikely, some wrong and some downright impossible. One former infantryman gave me a graphic account of his part in an action that took place months before he joined his regiment. Another soldier was said to have been killed three miles from his brother, when they were, in fact, three thousand miles apart. Charlie, I was informed, had been in the trenches for seven years during the war - and this did seem unlikely!

The majority of Somerset's soldiers served with the Somerset Light Infantry - the SLI. Rather surprisingly, I found that, the second most likely regiment to recruit the farmers and the miners of North Somerset was the Coldstream Guards, a Regiment founded on the borders of England and Scotland. Charlie Fry had been a Coldstream Guardsman.

Quite early on I had the good fortune to meet Sir Torquhil Matheson - Major Sir Torquhil Matheson of Matheson, Bt. - who was at that time Chief of the Matheson Clan. A former officer in the 3rd Battalion of the Coldstream Guards, who had served in the Second World War, Torquhil was passionately interested in the history of his regiment. He is the only contributor to the book who did not live through the Great War, but his intimate knowledge of its history, his devotion to his Regiment; his enthusiasm for my subject and his constant encouragement to me to 'get on with it', was immensely important to me. Torquhil had promised to write the foreword when I finally finished the book but sadly he died in 1995. I am delighted that his brother, Sir Fergus Matheson of Matheson, Bt., has now kindly agreed to do so.

I was told that Charlie Fry had definitely been in the 3rd Battalion of the Coldstream (which he wasn't) and I was extremely anxious to find anyone who had fought with that Battalion. I would have travelled anywhere in the world to meet such a man. One Guards officer from whom I sought advice was scornful of the notion that I could be successful. Then, somehow, the press picked up the story and one evening I had a phone call from a lady who asked if I would like to talk to her father. Had he been in the 3rd Battalion? Yes. Was he able and willing to talk about the war? Yes. And then - deep breath - where does he live? 'At the top of the village. We can see your house from here.'

The following day I met, for the first time, two of the most dignified gentlemen I have known. In the morning I visited Brigadier Leslie George Pollard, a retired professional soldier of the Royal Signals, and in the afternoon, a former coal miner, 9606 Private Samuel John Taylor of the Coldstream Guards.

We'll start with Sammy.

Midsomer Norton
Somerset
February 1891

Sammy Taylor*

Schoolboy, Coal Miner, Soldier

Mother always useda say the snow were blowin' through the tiles on the roof and on to her bed when I was bein' born. An' I don't reckon as how I've ever been rightly warm since. We useda have a lot of weather in our house. If there were a big thunder-storm we'd be covered up in bed, frightened, and she did open the windows front and back fer to let the lightenin' go straight through and not to strike the house and harm us.

There were always music goin' on somewhere when I were a nipper. Never learnt to read music but I useda play the tin whistle an' the mouth organ. An' my uncle bought a squeeze-box one day an' I learnt to play that when he weren't about. There were a music shop along Radstock Road in the '90s - old Jonah Dando's. I went to'n fer some piano lessons an' when he did go out I did try to knock out a tune on me own - but he did always hear me an' nip back an' rap me over the knuckles. Never 'ad time to learn anything proper, though, 'cos my lovely mother got double pneumonia an' died when I were ten.

Where a person's name is printed in bold type it indicates that his or her story is continued at a later stage

After that the home sorta broke up. Didn't see much of Father any more 'cos he did go off and do other things. I were getting a bit wild and ragged till me half-sister - married to Uncle Ike - took me in. Sometimes a gang on us used to get up on the batch - the old slag heap down in Welton. **Oliver Brooks** - he were always in charge - and his cousin **Jack Britten**, and my cousins the Prangley boys and I were always there. Oliver useda put on his bandolier that his brother Alfred had sent him back from the Boer War - he were out there with the Coldstream Guards, like my Uncle Ike - then he useda take this cannon thing what he'd made and climb up on the batch an' pretend it were a fort. Then the rest of we used to scatter round an' pretend to take him. Sometimes he useda capture all on us, but most times he did reckon to blow us all to pieces before we caught'n. Old Oliver did always win wi' his cannon. He always reckoned he'd get a VC one day.

Other times, when we'd finished our manoeuvres, we did take pit shovels up on the batch and slide all down the side. Useda sit on with the handle out the front to hold on and steer an' then shoot down wi' our legs cocked out. We did fly down there like winkie! We useda have a laugh, mind. Oh, we did have some fun when we were kiddies.

When I left school there was nothing else to do but go into the mines but it were always my hobby fer to join the Coldstream Guards. When Uncle Isaac come home from South Africa he did tell me and me sister about 'em. Uncle reckoned the Coldstream were second to none - Nulli Secundus, he'd say - and that were drummed into we: nothing above us. And they had bearskins. And that's how I come to fancy the Coldstream. Fancied them more than any.

Well, in 1912 I got fed up with being underground and I couldn' stand the under-manager. On the Town Hall they had photographs of the different Guards on a board and I thought t'were time to do something about it. T'were only ten mile to Bath so that same day I walked in to the recruiting place and zed, 'I'm come to join the Coldstream Guards'. 'Oh well, I don't know

'bou that,' he zed. 'I've got plenty of vacancies in the Somersets.' So I zed if it weren't the Coldstream I were off home again. He made me wait while he phoned. I got in the Coldstream.

I got a shillin' a day when I joined, an' had tuh go tuh the shop and buy me shining kit out of that shilling. A tin of Bluebell oxblood polish fer me chinstrap and stuff. They put us through it at Caterham all right! That were strict, mind! The Sergeant Major would come out on the parade ground and give 'ee a good tap in the ribs with his fist. He did say, 'It's no good trying yer hand in here. We duh tame lions!' An' we did believe him, too.

Oliver had joined up before me but I seen a lot of him while I was at Caterham. After me training I went to the 3rd Battalion at Windsor. We were called the Cushy 3rd 'cos we always had such good shots in our lot. An' they always called Taylors 'Cushy' for some reason - so I were always 'Cushy' after that.

That picture were taken at Windsor. The chap what did wear that sash did lend it to me fer the picture, just fer a bit of sport. Smart boy, eh?

* * * * *

Somerset Guardian
1st May, 1914

My attention has been called to a poster issued by the 4th Prince Albert's (Somerset Light Infantry) calling for recruits, by which it appears that some real advantage is at last being given to the Territorial soldier. The bill sets forward the terms of enlistment, that the recruit must not be less than 17 and not more than 35 years of age, that he must engage for four years, and may at the end of that time re-engage for one or more year, if he wishes. The point chiefly emphasised, however, is the amount of pay and allowances granted. It is the plain duty of every young man who is able to bear his part in the defence of the country, and it seems now as though all ought to be able to afford the annual camp, one of the chief difficulties hitherto prevailing.

The unmarried private, who makes himself efficient, receives for his 15 days training 15s pay, 20s bounty and boot allowance 2s 6d, making 37s 6d in all, or nearly 19s a week. This is all clear profit as he is well looked after in the matter of food, which is excellent and well varied, and, of course, clothing and equipment are provided free and railway fares paid. A married private gets separation allowance for his wife and also for his children.

In the case of a married man without any family, he would receive £2 13s 9d for the 15 days, and if he had any children, 2s 6d a head for boys of 14 and under and girls of 16 and under. Of course these advantages are conditional on the performance of drills and musketry, and the bounty of £1 and the separation allowance to married privates are not granted unless camp is attended for the full 15 days.

𝔖omerset 𝔊uardian

15th May, 1914

A movement is afoot to raise a half-company of Territorials at Radstock. At present it is understood there are but four young men living in Radstock who belong to the Territorial Force, and this is not considered creditable for a place the size and population of Radstock.

* * * * *

Lt. Arthur Coombs

4th Battalion, The Somerset Light Infantry
April, 1914

Four, you say. Well, I was one of them. I'd already joined them. At that time the powers that be must have known that the war was coming and they were having great recruiting campaigns all round the country. I thought it was a good idea so I joined and was commissioned that April. My first recollection of the Terriers was years earlier when they had had a show - a field day - up at the Clandown coal pit, all dressed in their red coats. When I joined them as an officer I knew as little as any recruit. I was 18 then, and you can imagine me, looking very young for my age and put in charge of coal miners and knowing less than they did about military matters. Sergeant Ashman used to drill the men in the field opposite Radstock Church and I joined in with them. This is us: G Company of the 4th Battalion of the Somerset Light Infantry - Prince Albert's own - at Norton Hill Station that Summer. They were a grand crowd. I knew them all and where they came from and so on. And they seemed to accept me all right. They nicknamed me 'Our Boy'! By the way, our Company had nine of the 11 in the Battalion football team. I was inside right.

Lt. Leslie Pollard

Indian Army

I always wanted to be a soldier - and I wanted to soldier in India. Father was then Commandant of the 4th Battalion of the Somerset Territorials and it was his view that if Mother wanted me to go, then all well and good, because he couldn't afford to keep me in a British regiment where you had to have two or three hundred a year in order to live. All you got as a second lieutenant was five bob a day. Mother had been born in India, daughter of a Major General, so it pleased her that I should go there.

At the end of my first term at Sandhurst I was made a Lance-Corporal and by the time I passed out I was the Senior Colour Sergeant in charge of all the cadets and all the parades. I put that down to a good upbringing in Midsomer Norton. So, I was commissioned from Sandhurst in January 1911, and left for a year's attachment to the West Kent Regiment in Peshawar.

My father, who was **Dr George Pollard**, happened to know someone - a patient - in Farrington Gurney, who had a relation commanding an Indian Battalion and so it was all arranged for me to join his battalion when I'd finished with the West Kents. And that was that. After my year with the West Kents I was posted to the Hasara. It was all a matter of knowing someone in order to get on - someone in Simla, someone in Delhi.

I joined my Indian regiment at Quetta - though they had nothing to do with India, really. They were Hasarists from Afghanistan. Well, I reported to the guardroom. Second in Command was sent for. 'See those men over there?' 'Yes.' 'Go and take charge.' A curt reception, but no more than I expected. We subalterns were a damn nuisance - conceited young men - we were bottle-washers. Well, by that time I spoke Hindustani pretty well so I went out and started talking. No reaction. They spoke Persian.

I'd been at Quetta about a year when the Battalion had orders to leave. Go out by rail for about six hours - to the end of the railway line, where the desert started. We then had 28 days' marching out to the Persian border, averaging 20 miles a day. All over desert - there was no road. I was acting as Quartermaster at that time so I had to stay behind each morning to see each camp was cleaned up. I had a camel to catch up with the Battalion which marched steadily till it came to mid-day - luncheon time - when I would catch up with them and have breakfast and lunch together.

We were at the border for a year, stopping gun-running. There was a telegraph line which worked occasionally but no other communication except once a month when a convoy came through with stores. That's where I found myself in 1914, when war broke out in Europe.

Cpl. Clifford Jeffery

West Somerset Yeomanry
4th August, 1914

On August 4th we were all mobilised. When I were 15 I'd joined the Yeomanry. They were short of recruits, see? That were the only way I could see to get a bit of hollerday from the farm I were born on. Father were born there and his father came there in 1854. I was bred for farming - couldn't do anything else. I joined as a Territorial and when you signed you had to say if you could supply a horse - if you couldn't they'd find you one. I had me own - Scot's Lad - with a big white face. We had to sign for four years and go to camp every year. This picture were taken in Exmouth in 1912 and there I be - like a great scarecrow, see? I stayed Corporal 'cos I were too good. They couldn't put me higher.

Anyway, there we were on August 4th, all mounted and lined up on the parade ground, and the Colonel made his big speech calling for volunteers. Then another big-wig bloke who were there made another speech. They wanted us to volunteer to go abroad as a unit. The North Somerset Yeomanry went abroad early 'cos they volunteered as a unit, and we'd 'a done the same if we'd all volunteered. So they said, 'Will those willing tuh volunteer ride two steps forward?' Only two of my troop went forward - I and Albie David. Had the officers bloody shitting! Two of us out of about 30. Those bloody officers were cut, suh. They were sure we were going to volunteer as a unit. But our lot never had enough guts.

The gutless sods tried all sorts of wheezes tuh get out of it. They'd parade sick and the doctor'd give them a certificate and they did go home. As the buggers refused to volunteer to go abroad we were used for home defence to begin with. We went over to Winchester and stopped the night in a girls' college there and then we went on up to the East Coast. We travelled by night and crooped down under a hedge by day. Then we were distributed round to different farms.

* * * * *

Somerset Guardian

7th August, 1914

During the past week many men from this district have been called upon to leave their occupations and rejoin the colours. An effort is being made to organise a committee to safeguard the interests of the wives or families or other dependants of those who have been called away. Dr Pollard has kindly taken the initiative in the matter so far as Midsomer Norton and Chilcompton are concerned. If any of the wives or parents of the men serving either in the Army or the Navy would call at the new Drill Hall tomorrow, about 5:30, Dr Pollard would be pleased to see them. It is hoped to make such arrangements in the district that there would be no hardship felt by those who are for the time being deprived of their bread winner.

No. 191

Army Form D. 463A.

ARMY RESERVE.

GENERAL MOBILIZATION.

Notice to join the Army for Permanent Service.

Name _J. Fry_ Rank _L. Sg._

Regimental } _1264_ Coldstream Guards. { Regt. or
Number } Corps.

You are hereby required to join the _Coldstream Guards._

at CHELSEA BARRACKS, LONDON. on **5 - AUG. 1914**

Should you not present yourself on that day, you will be liable to be proceeded against.

You will bring with you your "Small Book," your Life Certificate, Identity Certificate, and, if a Regular Reservist, Parchment Reserve Certificate.

Instructions for obtaining the sum of 3s. as an advance of pay and a Travelling Warrant where necessary, are contained in your Identity Certificate.

If your Identity Certificate is not in your possession and you are unable to proceed to join, you must report at once to this office, either personally or by letter.

COLDSTREAM GUARDS RECORD OFFICE — 4 - AUG. 1914 — BUCKINGHAM GATE, S.W.

Stamp of Officer i/c Records.

Rupert Shepherd
Schoolboy

I knew lads who went pretty well instantly, like that. Before the war our Member of Parliament visited public houses and offered farm workers £1 to sign a paper. Most of them didn't read it - couldn't read it, maybe - but they were most anxious to get hold of his pound. But what that was was a call-up paper in case of emergency - which of course happened in 1914. In August

1914 or just before, they were actually called from their harvest fields to join up. The lads I knew - five of them - were quite surprised to find themselves in uniform. They were Army Service Corps horsemen. Wasn't just the lads who were taken, neither. They used to commandeer suitable horses from farms for hauling guns or officers' mounts and so on. We're told to remember our four legged friends - well those horses died by the thousand in France.

Where I lived then, there were fields used as camps for the first few months of the war, and for a while the soldier boys lived in tents. There were them - the ASC - and various other regiments parked round and about and I used to go there to see them. I was just twelve at the time but no-one seemed to mind me being there.

* * * * *

Hilda Seymour
Schoolgirl

I used to go and watch my father at the blacksmithy he worked at, by the side of the Railway Inn in Chilcompton - he was a blacksmith there with Mr Fred Perkins. All through the First War the Irish horses used to come off the train. War horses - to be shod. He used to do the farrier bit - shoe them for to go off to war. I don't know how they went, but they did. Used to work till twelve at night sometimes to get them all done.

Somerset Guardian

7th August, 1914

There is no doubt that the August Bank Holiday was under a shadow this year. Not only did the sinister shadow of war have its natural effect over things, and keep people from whole-hearted rejoicing, but the rain finished matters off. The downpour at mid-day damped every-one's ardour, and spoilt the attendances at various fetes, while the pelting rain in the evening finally drove all in doors. Naturally enough indoor amusements reaped the benefit. Still, it was a distinctly 'grey' holiday in all respects.

14th August, 1914

I am pleased to see that there has been a general abandonment of flower shows and social functions of a similar kind in this district. The Midsomer Norton Show should have been held yesterday but on Monday the committee and officers wisely decided not to hold it. Last Friday night the committee of the Radstock Horticulture and Poultry Show, which was fixed for Wednesday next, unanimously decided to abandon the event. It is almost inconceivable to think how people can entertain the idea of flower shows, sports and social functions when the whole country is faced with such grave danger. All petty considerations should give way to national considerations.

Many enquiries have been made respecting the local G Company (Territorials) who have been away from the district since July 23rd. I am in a position to state that the men are on Salisbury Plain. The Company, with the rest of the Battalion, left the district for a fortnight's

stay only, and consequently many of the young fellows made no preparation for a longer period. When it was found that they were likely to be away for a much longer time a message was received that the men needed shirts and socks.

The parents or friends of the Territorials who knew of their needs left parcels at the Radstock Rectory to be forwarded. The ladies of Midsomer Norton and Radstock took up the matter immediately at the wish of Col. Pollard and on Saturday and Sunday large sewing parties sat at the Victoria Hall, Radstock, and the Town Hall, Midsomer Norton, where over 200 good warm flannel shirts were made and a large number of pairs of socks were also purchased.

On Monday morning Mr Louis Beauchamp kindly motored Col. Pollard to Durrington to deliver the goods. Parcels addressed to individuals were handed over to them and **Capt. the Hon. Edward Strachey** promised to see the proper distribution of the whole of the goods.

* * * * *

Herbert Caines
Railwayman
August, 1914

Railways were always in my blood. When I was born, in 1888, Father was the station master at Norton Hill Station, in Midsomer Norton, and when I was eight or nine I remember seeing men going off to the Boer War from there. Mind you, Vic Foster was telling me how when his father was a lad he was at the gate of their cottage one day and saw a red coat coming along the road. Then his father saw it and said, 'Here's your Uncle Levi coming back from the war in the Crimea'.

I used to play up at the station and as a ten year-old I used to be able to work the signal box - the telegraph and all. The signalman felt sure I'd go into the railways when I grew up so he'd let me take the trains through with the little needles they used to have on the signal boxes in those days. I used to work those trains through while he sat watching.

Anyway, when I was 16 I'd gone into Bristol to work in the goods offices of the Bristol Midland Railway and then, ten years later, I got married - six weeks before war broke out. Everybody went crazy - crazy to go. 'Kill the Germans! Kill the Germans!' And I said well, yes, but they might kill you. They'd gone mad. And those recruiting concerts they had - I went to them and saw how they worked men up to a pitch. Fellows didn't know what they were doing, they'd just go and sign up and live to regret it. I saw what was happening. It was clear that this war was going to be different. And the enemy was a formidable one. I went to the concerts - but I didn't fall.

Pte. Arthur Fricker
1st Battalion, The Gloucestershire Regiment
29th August, 1914

My Dear Wife,

It was on August 22nd when we came into contact with the Germans and on Sunday 23rd their big guns were pointed at us. The roar was like thunder. All night long we lay in the trenches and the air seemed full of smoke and fire. Towns around were all in flames and men, women and children were running everywhere, in fact some ran towards the Germans' lines.

On the morning of the 26th we were at them again, the Germans being shot down like rabbits. About 12am a German aeroplane, flying the Union Jack and the French colours, was flying down our positions. We thought it was one of our own but whenever she dipped the German artillery took range and as soon as she got up and out of reach they simply poured the shells upon us. Within 10 minutes we had 5 killed and 47 wounded and a number we cannot account for. It was just like hell on earth.

> 27490 Pte. Arthur Fricker
> 14th Battalion, The Gloucestershire Regiment
> Killed in Action
> France and Flanders
> 23rd March, 1918

* * * * *

Somerset Guardian
4th September, 1914

The new Service Battalion of the Somerset LI, (the 6th) has now been raised to the strength of 1,000. In five days 1,000 recruits have enlisted in the Somersets. As a result the 3rd Battalion at Plymouth has been brought up to 1,600 and it is intended to bring it up to 2,000.

I hear that the 4th Somerset LI are fit and well on Salisbury Plain but are short of potatoes and green vegetables. If any have garden produce to spare here is a good use to which it could be devoted. Arrangements have been made to convey it to the command and if any friends of the men could leave any vegetables at the Rectory (Radstock) up to tomorrow (Saturday) evening they would be sent to the camp on Sunday.

Charles Lewin

(Headmaster of Radstock Church School)
Chairman of the Somerset Football Association
addressing the Somerset FA Council
2nd September, 1914

We meet tonight under circumstances little expected when we closed our successful last season. Our gathering is held while over us all lies the shadow of a war that has no parallel in the history of the world, a war whose outcome is fraught with the most momentous consequences to many different nations, and in which England is taking a noble and strenuous part.

Obviously at a time like this our procedure as a County Football Association cannot, and ought not to, follow the lines of former years, when benificent peace held sway, and our sole duty was to promote and control sport. I thought it well to ask our secretary to call at short notice a

meeting of the League's Board of Appeal, that being a small body most easily got together. We met last Saturday, and it is now my duty to lay before you for consideration, and I hope endorsement, the result of our deliberations.

First and foremost we must put patriotism before sport. We must recognise and impress upon footballers that it is more essential to be able to shoot the King's enemies, than to shoot goals; to defend our country's honour is stupendously more important than to keep a rival team at bay, and to fight in England's cause is far nobler than to win points in league football.

Patriotism, duty, nay, even the instinct of National self-preservation, all demand that able-bodied men should obey the Nation's call to arms. It is said that Nero fiddled while Rome was burning. Heaven forbid that future historians should be able to say that the youth of this country was found wanting on the field of play while it should have been on the field of battle. Medals for successful football are good; medals for active service are infinitely more meritorious.

But - it may be asked - do you propose to stop Association Football in Somerset? No, for reasons I shall presently give. We shall carry out a restricted programme, modified from time to time during the season as circumstances require. If we hear that such and such a competition cannot be run, or that certain clubs have disbanded because so many players have joined Kitchener's Army, we shall rejoice and we shall invite clubs to send our secretary the names of any players who have become soldiers, that we may compile what it will be no mere figure of speech to call a roll of honour.

We propose allowing some football to go on because a considerable number of players are too young for enlistment, while a certain proportion of young men were, in the early days of recruiting, rejected on account of some slight physical defect, frequently the condition of the teeth. Surely it is better that these should keep themselves fit and ready for the call that may yet come to them by playing outdoor games rather than by idly loafing about.

We shall indicate a way in which clubs and players can help the Prince of Wales's fund, and we shall ask you to vote, here and now, a sum from the County funds towards the same object. County matches may be abandoned for this year.

* * * * *

To the Editor
Somerset Guardian
2nd September, 1914

Sir,

I attended the meeting held on Tuesday last in the Victoria Hall on behalf of the Prince of Wales's Relief Fund, expecting to see the hall well filled with the young men of Radstock and district. It was rather a wet blanket to find hardly half a dozen young men in the room. This indifference, this apathy, certainly reflects rather badly on our youthful population at a time when our nation is fighting for its very existence as a first-class power. I must say with regret that the severe strictures passed upon the young people of Radstock from the platform were thoroughly well deserved. Let them buck up, shake off this callous indifference and realise that life at a critical hour like the present has its duties as well as its pleasures even for young men . . .

Yours etc.

J A Irvine

Pte. Stan Small
10th Battalion, the Devonshire Regiment
September, 1914

I joined up in 1914. Just a foolish idea. September 7th, it was. I was working down the pit, carting, and there was to be a recruiting meeting in the village and my mate said, 'Let's join up'. But I said no. Then, when I was home at six, Father came in off the farm and said, 'Whatever you do, Stan, don't get joining up'. And I went straight and done it. Yes, I did. It was down outside the inn, a ring of people with miners and farm workers and boy scouts and four or five nurses and so on, and Lord Strachey calling for volunteers. I was 19 and never had no sense and put my blessed name down. And that were that - done. I'd joined the Somerset Light Infantry.

I ended up at Codford, in Wiltshire, in a blessed field full of grass. After we'd been there about a week, young officers - lads, just come from college - come out and formed us into platoons, A, B, C and D and stood in front of us. Then out comes the Colonel, a red-faced man, stocky build in a pair of brown leggings, and says, 'You no longer belong to the SLI, you belong to the Devonshire Regiment. The 10th Battalion, the Devonshire Regiment. It's a fine Regiment to belong to'. Well, you do as they tells you, don't you.

About a month afterwards they came along with two wagon loads of clothes belonging to other regiments - like the Worcesters and the Guards and all that. They bunged it in a field and we could pick what we liked. I shall never forget it. Another outfit we were given was Kitchener's Blue with a piece of cloth on the arm with 79 stitched on to it. That meant we belonged to the 79th Brigade and I was 13752 Private S Small, 10th Battalion, The Devonshire Regiment, 79th Brigade, 26th Division.

* * * * *

From Radstock Church School Logbook
Week ending 11th September, 1914

Events of stupendous national importance have taken place since we closed school. The great European War has broken out; and even our school has been affected by it. The material for our improvements was delayed and we were unable to open on Tuesday Sep: 1st as we intended. **Mr Stephens** *is in camp on Salisbury Plain. The managers have appointed Mr Clifford Gregory, who has recently left Bristol Day Training College, as a temporary teacher.*

Charles Lewin
Headmaster

11th September, 1914

Sir,

As leader of the Paulton Brotherhood Prize Band will you please permit me through your valuable paper to express my astonishment at the rumour which has been going round this district to the effect that this band has been taking collections in support of our alien enemies. As a matter of fact the band was on the Paulton Football field only last Saturday and made a collection for our own countrymen and their wives which amounted to the good sum of £1.1s.

Yours etc

C Williams
Bandmaster

* * * * *

The first public intimation made locally as to the loss of life in the present European War was the reference made on Monday morning at Radstock Police Court when Lord Hylton referred to the bereavement sustained by one of the Magistrates - Mr H S Davey - in the death of his son who had been killed in action fighting against the Germans. The deceased officer was Major W H C Davey.

Messrs Coombs and Co. Ltd. of Radstock and Clandown Breweries have issued a notice to their employees assuring them of their places being kept open for them if they will join Lord Kitchener's Army and promising to pay each man who joins 7s 6d per week during the period of the war.

* * * * *

Alban Chivers
Brewer

Before I went in the army in 1916, I was getting fifteen shillings a week working for Mr Joseph Coombs at the brewery, doing seven brewings a week. That were twice on Wednesdays and twice of a Friday. Thirty five barrels at a time and 36 gallons in each. I'd have liked to have been in the Territorials. Arthur Coombs was in it and he wanted me to be. I got on very well with him and he said he'd have a word with his uncle about it. Reckoned the camp'd be a week off from the brewery for me, but my wife said, 'Oh no you don't! You aren't going in that!' But if I had I'd have been out in India from the time it started till it finished. I wish I had.

Pte. Alfred Dowling
1st Battalion, The Coldstream Guards
September, 1914

Dear Father,

*I got shot through the chest on September 14th.
God knows what we have been through since we left
England.*

*I got through the battle of Mons all right, and after
that I had an idea I should never be hit. We had a bit
of a fight on Sunday, September 6th. We lost
several killed and wounded. After that things went
all right until the 13th.*

*We marched all day and slept almost upon them that night. One of my battalion got shot
just as he got up, but I think it was by a stray bullet. Anyway, we moved off - our regiment,
the Black Watch, and several other regiments and advanced about a mile across a tract of
open country. We tried to charge the Germans out, but that was before we knew what a
strong position they had. Men all around me were falling like sheep, not by the score, but
if you will believe me, by the hundreds.*

*If ever anyone prayed to God to spare them I did, and I was not the only one. We got on to
a road and under a bit of bank. It was then about eight in the morning, and troops kept
coming up until we were three and four deep for about a mile long. I and a man from the
Cameron Highlanders laid for two and a half hours in streaming rain with a dead man on
one side and two on the other side. After that we retired.*

*For dinner I had half a biscuit, one carrot and one turnip raw. We went up and advanced
again in the afternoon, but were driven back, and got the order to retire. I ran about six
yards when down I went. I bled in streams. The blood went right through my shirt and
through my coat and on to this bit of notepaper I am sending you. I have been on my back
ever since.*

> Pte. Alfred Dowling
> 1st Battalion, The Coldstream Guards
> Wounded: 14th, September 1914
> Severely injured: March 1915
> Wounded/discharged: October 1915
> Died: October 1916

𝔖𝔬𝔪𝔢𝔯𝔰𝔢𝔱 𝔊𝔲𝔞𝔯𝔡𝔦𝔞𝔫

25th September, 1914

MIDSOMER NORTON TO HELP THE BELGIAN REFUGEES

NORTON HOUSE TO BE TAKEN AS A HOME

On Wednesday evening, the Midsomer Norton Vigilance Committee, formed at the commencement of the war, has decided to form itself into a committee to consider the Belgian Refugee question and to take what steps they could to render substantial aid in the matter. The committee has decided to acquire Norton House for at least one year and to house and support 30 refugees for that time. Norton House is a well-built, roomy residence and was, until recently, occupied by HH Prince Tchajkowsky.

* * * * *

Ivan Chard
Schoolboy

Caw, he spent some money up there. Nobody down Norton can't tell I nothin' about Tchaikowsky, 'cos he never got in touch with nobody. Not nobody. He come to Norton from London, a couple o' years afore the war but no-one - not no-one - knew who he were or why he were. I used to nip up there across the meadow, night times, and pinch his apples and I know he were there, but I never saw him. Kept hisself to hisself. He used to drive through Norton in his carriage and pair but you'd barely get a glimpse of'n. He did never mix and we could never find him. We could never find out nothing about him - but I've always maintained that he were a spy. And so did my mates. That's my opinion about he. That he were a spy. That went all round the school. A Russian spy do live up there. He were a Russian spy. But our people couldn't bloody see it.

Somerset Guardian
25th September, 1914

A number of young men from Radstock and Midsomer Norton who joined the County Regiment, but who had to return home owing to a lack of accommodation at the barracks in Taunton, left the district on Tuesday for Taunton. Well might other young men, and there are many in this district, follow their example. A few of the villages round here have done practically nothing in this direction. I hope they will awake to their responsibilities and their duty in this question.

* * * * *

Austin Wookey
Schoolboy

Where I lived, out in the country, ever so many men depended on the squire for their living - for their very existence. The squire wouldn't see them harmed but the men were dependent on him. Farmers renting his land were tied down absolutely to him. They could graze their cattle and they could shoot a rabbit but they dare not shoot a pheasant, or a partridge, or a landrail or a snipe. They were the holy things, and if they were caught shooting one they were out. Off the farm and no mercy. No job and no cottage. And it was the same for the women of the village, if they didn't always curtsy to the squire's wife there'd be no work for them.

You can't believe what it was like! Well, in our village, when the war had been going on for a while, the squire's wife took a walk round to every cottage where there was still a man old enough to fight. She rapped on the door and when he answered she gave him a white feather. That was a clear enough message. He had to go. And he went.

* * * * *

Cliff Carpenter
Coal Miner

I tried to go but they wouldn't take me. In the first week of the war three of us went up to the new Drill Hall in Midsomer Norton to join up. They took the other two - the Hyman Lads. At one time there were eleven Hyman cousins in the war. Those two went in the Marines and I wanted to go with them but they asked my occupation and I said I was a coal miner. Well, they reckoned that if I was working underground they couldn't very well take me, not yet, but they'd send for me. It was several months later that they did send and I went to be examined at the Victoria Hall. Dr Pollard did it - in his Colonel's uniform he was - and he found out I had TB. From that day on I was treated in the clinic at Wells Hill. That went on practically the whole war. Later on I'd visit my wife where she was working in Bath, and in Gay Street, where there were soldiers billeted, they'd hang out their khaki clothing and jeer, and maybe throw things. But I never took any notice. I knew I'd tried to enrol.

* * * * *

Reg Jones
Carting Boy

Gilbie Nash were a miner but they took he all right. He were the wife's brother - that's he there, with a whole bunch of other young'uns from Norton, all off to the war. Him with his mate Seward Talbot what worked alongside him at Old Mills Colliery. Seward's in that fancy hat on the right, and Gilbie's standing next to him. T'were a hard life underground and the pair of them and a couple of other fellows just took it into their heads to leave the pit and go off and join the Field Artillery. Gilbie were riding the horses they used to have to pull the guns.

They never knew they were going to have a packet like they got along the Western Front, mind. All Gilbie's crew got killed, bar he, and he were wounded in the left temple - had a steel plate put in the side his head. He were always such a smart fellow before - but he weren't no good fer nothing after. They'd all gone off happy enough from the pit - like a lot of my mates did - but nearly all of them never come back. No, they never come back.

Somerset Guardian
2nd October, 1914

TO HELP THE POOR BELGIANS
NORTON MANOR AS A REFUGEE HOSTEL
SCHEME EXPLAINED AT A PUBLIC MEETING

The Belgian Refugee Committee have decided to take Norton Hall for twelve months as a hostel for 30 refugees from Belgium. With the object of endeavouring to secure support for the scheme, the Committee had proposed, a public meeting was held at the Town Hall on Monday evening.

There was a very large attendance of the general public, including most prominent members of the town. The Chairman, in opening the meeting said they were a detachment of a world-wide army which covered the whole civilised world, excepting Germany.

Mr C H Sunderland, the Secretary, read from the minutes of their previous meeting which stated that the rent of Norton House was £100 per annum but the owner, Mr W Tovey, was prepared to let the Committee have it for the purpose stated for £60 per annum. The Prior of Downside offered to pay half the rent and provide Belgian nuns to teach the children who might be accommodated in the house. Mr John Thatcher offered to pay half the bill, Dr Pollard offered free medical attendance and Mr W R Edwards offered to make up any doctor's prescriptions.

Mr F S Casswell then explained that they hoped by loans or gifts to be able to furnish the house without paying for anything. With certain things they hoped to get given them they hoped to be able to keep the 30 people at a cost of 5s per head per week, which would mean £7.10s per week. After carefully considering the matter they thought they should raise an income of £12 a week. They hoped people would guarantee to pay 5s, 2s 6d, 1s 6d, or 3d each per week and thus secure the income.

They hoped to get half a dozen men who would be prepared to do the work in the garden, so that a proper supply of vegetables could be kept up for the whole year. They wanted people to do the hauling required and hoped to get assistance in many other ways which Mr Casswell enumerated. When the people came they wanted to treat them with great consideration. (Applause) Many of them would probably be in a destitute condition and heart-broken. They must do their best and show every consideration. (Applause) . . .

The Secretary urged that all promises should be made at once, as they hoped to receive the people on October 6.

Lt. Arthur Coombs
1st/4th Battalion, The Somerset Light Infantry
9th October, 1914

After a few weeks in camp on Salisbury Plain we went to Plymouth to guard the bridges and so forth. G Company had the task of guarding Saltash Bridge for three or four days until the Special Reserve was mobilised to take over from us. While we were there, half the company was detailed to go out with Sappers to dig trenches in case we were attacked. Well, word came back to us that our fellows were refusing to dig and the CO told me to go and sort things out. Me! A kid of eighteen! Well, I went out in fear and trembling, and luckily - well I think it was lucky - as I arrived their time was up, and they were falling in. But I still had to make enquiries and I went up to the Sapper officer who was there and it seemed that our lads, who'd only been mobilised for ten days or so, felt that it was the Sappers' job to do the digging but they maintained that they were there to supervise the infantry. Anyway, it all ended peacefully!

People everywhere were quite convinced that it was going to be over soon and that this was the war to end wars. There's no doubt about it. Everybody thought that. It was the general idea that it would be over by Christmas and when we were going down to Plymouth people came out and cheered us as we marched past - and the day we came away the number of girls who came to see the men off was nobody's business.

One thing we had always been told was that we were only for Home Service, but then, in September, the Divisional General of the Wessex Division - a Major General called Donald - was called in by Kitchener and we were being asked to go abroad, to India. I've got his account of it here:

Towards the end of September I received a telegram saying that Lord Kitchener wanted to see me at the War Office next day. I went to the War Office and was taken into Lord Kitchener's room, and you can imagine that I got a little bit of a shock when he said: 'I want you to take your Division to India. Will they go?' You must remember that at that time the Imperial obligation did not apply to the Territorials. I said, 'Well, Sir, I do not think anybody has had much thought about it, but I am perfectly certain that if you want them to go to India they will go there right enough'. He replied, 'Very well, go back to your Division now, get hold of them tomorrow morning on Salisbury Plain, use your personal influence and tell them from me that I want them to go to India and that by going to India they will be performing a great Imperial duty. I have to bring white troops back from India and I must replace them there by white troops from home'.

And we were very lucky that we were sent - if we'd gone to France we'd probably all have been killed.

Charles Smith
Schoolboy

I remember very well when my brother Sydney left home. In the first week in August he and I, and a friend called Stanley, had gone down to Weston-super-Mare for a week's camping. Well, on the Friday war broke out and Stanley was called to go - a telegram came to our tent at two in the morning. Stanley went on back but my brother stayed for the rest of the week. But when we got back Sydney joined up. I think the whole of the village walked to the station the day after their embarkation leave, to see them all off. They went to India. The train pulled out and I could see him leaning out of the window. The band was playing '*God be with you till we meet again*' but that was the last time I saw him. He was shot. And died of his wounds in Mesopotamia. Time hasn't helped in any way at all.

You know, Sydney was a good cricketer. Opening bat for the battalion. Scored 100 not out against the Dorsets and 90 not out against somebody else. They reckoned he'd have played for Somerset if he'd come back. But he didn't come back.

> 2645 Pte. Sydney Smith
> 1st/4th Battalion, The Somerset Light Infantry
> Died of Wounds
> Mesopotamia
> 8th May, 1916
> Aged 19

[13,825 men called Smith from the UK and its former colonies died during the Great War.]

Somerset Guardian
16th October, 1914

The scheme which the kindly disposed and sympathetic people of Midsomer Norton and district propounded for housing 30 Belgian refugees at Norton Manor, is now in full working order and everything is proceeding smoothly. The 30 refugees arrived last Wednesday and are made up of seven families and one single man. Five of the families speak French and two Flemish and one of them understands a few words of the English language. Four French Sisters who have been kindly provided by the Prior of Downside are educating the children in the house. The visitors have suffered a great deal at the hands of the Germans. They are generally quite destitute and have nothing left of their happy homes. In addition to their material goods one of the families has lost two children in the German invasion of their country.

* * * * *

Reg Jones
Carting Boy

Aaah! They Belgians had plenty to eat and drink - more than us. They were all right though. Now and again you'd find an awkward one - but the girls were all right. They were free and easy - and we were kids, just from school. I weren't courting then and every night dree or four of we did go up there, and they'd be waiting fer us, and we'd dance all around the great hall there, to an accordian. Then when we got home our fathers'd give us a good walloping when they'd heard where we'd bin - said we shouldn't go up there no more. But we always did! We'd go up there every night and mix with they girls. Nice girls. Bloody lovely they were. We never had no language problems. We could communicate wi' they all right. Oh ah!

Frickley Hall
Doncaster
29th October, 1914

Dear Mrs Fry,

I am afraid I must write and tell you very bad news.
Your husband Sergeant Fry was killed in action early in
the afternoon of October 23rd near a village called
Langemarck, not very far from Ypres in Belgium. I want
to tell you what a great loss he was to No.2 Coy. I had
known him for a short time at Aldershot before he went
to the Reserve, and was awfully pleased to see him when
he came back to the Company again. He was one of my best section commanders, he did
extremely good work on many occasions, and I had noted him for some time for further
promotion.

We had a great deal of digging to do at the war, and of course, as this was his trade your
husband was specially good at it. It used to be a treat to see him work with a shovel or
entrenching tool, and it was only on Oct: 21st when we were digging trenches that I pointed
out his trench to the other section commanders as an example of what a trench should be.
I remember so well on the Aisne having a long talk with him about the difference between
mining in Yorkshire and Somerset.

We buried him the same night alongside another sergeant of the company under a willow
tree quite close to where he had fallen. I had no prayer book with me, but I did say a few
words over the graves with the meaning of the prayer in the prayer book, though I did not
know the exact words. I send you my very deepest sympathy, and if either I or my wife can
help you in any difficulties, please let one of us know, and we shall be very pleased to do
anything we can.

> *Yrs faithfully,*
>
> *W S A Warde-Aldham*
>
>
> 7267 L/Sgt James Fry
> 1st Battalion, The Coldstream Guards
> Killed in Action
> France and Flanders
> No Known Grave
> 23rd October, 1914
> Aged 26

Major Sir Torquhil Matheson
3rd Battalion, The Coldstream Guards

St Andrew Warde-Aldham would have meant every word of that. St. Andrew was an excellent soldier and a very brave man and he would have had great respect for Fry. Fry had re-joined the regiment from Clandown Colliery *[page 19]* with Alfred Dowling who'd been wounded a month earlier. 'No Known Grave' means that a soldier went missing. Nobody saw them wounded, nobody saw them die. They were either buried by a shell blast or blown to bits.

* * * * *

Joe Ruddock
Coal Miner

That's the Bristol Artillery leaving Radstock. They come out here for a recruiting visit at the start of the war. A pal of mine, Bert Hiscox, were in that - probably him what arranged it. He used to deliver bread for the Co-op and then he joined the police in Bristol. I'd have gone with him but I was a bit short and the police were choosy, with a lot of people being out of work. When the war broke out Bristol formed their own Artillery Company and Bert joined up. After a while they went over to the front.

291128 Sergeant Bert Hiscox
127th Heavy Battery
Royal Garrison Artillery
Killed in Action
France and Flanders
26th September, 1918
Aged 30

Pte. Fred Sainsbury
13th Hussars
3rd November, 1914

My Dear Flo,

. . . I am going to relate a little experience that our troop was in. We were laying in trenches for three nights and days. The first day passed off all right but next day they made a bit of an attack. We killed about eight of them and they left off then but all night we could hear them singing for all they were worth. They were only 450 yards from us all the time.

The next morning, October 30th, they made another attack on us. It was fine sport for about an hour. They came within about 200 yards of us and we were shooting all the time. Goodness knows how many of them were killed but the ground was covered with them. It was awful. They then started to shell us and we had eight men completely buried and I thought my time was up. We had shells all around us and eight of us came back out of 23. The men say the Battle of Mons was nowhere in it compared to this.

We've lost a lot of men but what the enemy's losses are God knows, for no man knows. We saw one ploughfield with heaps of them, I counted 12 in one heap and this is the 18th day of this. Good God, it is awful. It can't last for ever. The African war was nothing to this. We can't move for shells dropping. Some of them make holes in the ground so big you could lay a horse in them.

As I am writing this they are only half a mile from us and sixteen guns are firing at them. We are escort for them, the worst job you can get for they always try to shell the guns. I had a narrow escape the other day. We made an attack on our right flank to deceive them. When we got about 100 yards near them we drew our swords to charge when we found it was useless and our Captain gave the order to retire when we were only 25 yards from them.

My horse got shot under me and I was pitched on my head. I got up half dazed and started to run - which way I was going I didn't know but as it happened I ran the right way and into some trenches occupied by the 19th Hussars. At the same time one of our fellows got hit in the back and came off. Also the Captain; his horse got shot and he did the bravest deed I shall ever see. He cut off his wallets and saddle bag, went back and put the other fellow on his back and picking up his kit he started to bring him in. I wanted to go and help him but the officer in the trench wouldn't let me but he went instead and they carried the man to the trench. I hope he will get the VC or the DSO.

Pte. Laurence Eyres

1st/4th Battalion, The Somerset Light Infantry
November, 1914

Dear Father,

We arrived in Bombay on November 9th and the following day we were allowed to land but not go outside the dockyards. Still, we found a very nice army store within the precincts and bought tea and cake and fresh butter, which were a great treat. None of us were very sorry to set foot on dry land once more, though the voyage was quite enjoyable, if long. It took 32 days.

On Wednesday we marched off the ship and onto a train. We left Bombay dock station and very soon got into the country, so saw little of Bombay. The railway carriages were a pleasant surprise. We had expected to sleep sitting up but instead of that they put 14 of us into a carriage with seating accommodation for 46. There was loads of room for us to put our kitbags and everything and every man could lie full length on a seat.

The railway journey was intensely interesting. At all the stations of any size you could see an Englishman in charge, or rather two or three, sometimes more. Soon we were looking down 1000 feet on either side on rice fields and there was a small river running through them. That was about sunset time and the light was reflected on the river. It was exquisite.

We always got out at a station for our meals. Arrangements were made beforehand by the Indian Government and they had bread, meat, jam and tea waiting for us at various places. We went through Poonah at midnight that night and woke up to lovely scenery. We were glad of our blanket at night, and the early morning from seven to ten was as cool as an ordinary spring morning in England.

We travelled on three railways, the Great Indian Peninsula; The Madras and Southern Manratta; and the South Indian Railway followed by a mountain railway whose name I have forgotten. We passed several troop trains on the way; they were all itching for a scuffle with the enemy after training so long. Some had fought in the Boer War or had been in South Africa or India ever since.

On Sunday morning, November 15th, we reached Metapataiyam and began our climb to Wellington. There is one mountain railway more wonderful and that is in the Himalayas, but this is supposed to be the second in the world. We climbed 5000 feet in two hours. Then at last we reached our destination after 37 hours of travelling. It is 6000 feet above the sea, and a perfect paradise . . .

Lt. Geoffrey Bishop
1st/4th Battalion, The Somerset Light Infantry

I knew Laurence Eyres well - he was an extraordinary chap. I'd joined the Battalion in September 1914, when I was 17. Father was already in it, so obviously I knew G Company - largely Midsomer Norton and Radstock men - very well and a tough company they were, too. Very fine soldiers - nearly all miners. But Eyres was of a different breed. An intelligent man. A Cambridge graduate, I think. He had been going into the church. Used to say his prayers in the barrack room every night and the men obviously respected him. A lot of them used to call him Mr Eyres - but not in any way unkindly. He was in the draft I took with me to Mesopotamia.

* * * * *

Pte. Edward Hurd
1st/4th Battalion, The Gloucester Regiment
November, 1914

You know, it's a strange thing but all through my life after the war nobody has ever wanted to know anything about my experiences in it. Nobody has asked and I've never really wanted

to talk about it. But if you *did* ever discuss it with someone they could find it really confusing if you said you were in the Gloucesters, because there were so many Battalions. You see, ours was a *Territorial* unit. The 4th, 5th and 6th Territorials were pre-war battalions. Then there was the 3rd, they were Militia, and then the 2nd and the 1st, what were regular Battalions. The Militia - the 3rd - were reserves in a way. They were men what'd been in the army before - been to war - and they did a month's training annually and they were commonly known as Saturday Night Soldiers, 'cause they could put on their full dress uniforms and strut about on Saturdays.

Now, in those days the 4th, 5th and 6th were known as the Volunteers but then the time came when they and the

Militia all got their names changed to the Territorial Force. As the war progressed conscription came in, and the 7th, 8th and 9th Battalions and so on were formed. Then the 10th, 11th, 12th and, I know, the 13th Battalions. This makes saying you were in the Gloucesters mystifying to a person.

Anyway, I went in the army when I was sixteen and a half, in November 1914. I volunteered and joined the 4th Gloucesters. Now the Gloucesters is a regiment and a regiment can have a number of battalions. I was in the 1st/4th Battalion. Within a battalion you didn't really know one another with the exception of the 16 of you who stayed together right from when you trained to be a soldier. That was your section and a number of sections made up a platoon and a number of platoons made up a company which consisted of 250 men and a battalion had four companies. I was in C Company.

A full battalion would have about 1,000 men, and there are four battalions to a brigade, and each division has got three brigades. Our Battalion was part of the 48th Division. Now a division is a tremendous thing. By the time you add the Artillery, the Engineers, the Service Corps and all the other men attached you've got the best part of 20,000 men.

Then people get confused about what Kitchener's Army was and what the Old Contemptibles were - and such-like. Well, the first to go were the regular army - the British Expeditionary Force - what were known as the Old Contemptibles, 'cause that's what the Kaiser reckoned they were - contemptible. But in reality they were wonderful soldiers, wonderful. Could fire their rifles so fast the Germans thought they all had machine guns. But there weren't enough of them and so before the war had been going a month Lord Kitchener started getting up his new army, Kitchener's Army - you know the poster, don't you? Kitchener pointing his finger and saying 'Your Country needs you'? Hundreds and hundreds of thousands joined up because of that poster, just left their jobs and went. Jerry reckoned they were cannon-fodder - and that's exactly what thousands of them were.

As things went on there was so much killing, and thousands and thousands of men dead or dying, that even with Kitchener's Army going over they still had to get more men. By that time, though, people weren't quite so anxious to join up. They'd seen what was happening and they knew the way things were going. Too many of their friends and relatives were already dead. Or maimed. Or missing. So the Government cooked up the Derby Scheme so they could see who was *available* to go - if necessary. *IF!* They were needed all right, and they went. But you can see why it is all mystifying to someone what doesn't know, can't you? It can be confusing. So I've never really wanted to talk about it.

Pte. Elijah Mead
1st Battalion, The Somerset Light Infantry
19th November, 1914

Dear Mother and Father,

I am still alive and kicking. I am writing this letter in one of the trenches. We have been in them for five days and nights, and I don't know when we shall get relieved. They call this war but I call it murder. The shells are bursting over us and all around us night and day. They gave me the cold shudders the first night but I don't take much notice of them now - am getting more used to them. I don't mind as long as they don't fall in the trench, for we are well dug in. We don't half bob our heads when these 'Jack Johnsons' come over. They make great holes in the ground and we buried 17 Germans in one of them yesterday. The Germans tried to break through our lines and we gave them what they asked for. My chum beside me got knocked over - poor old chap. If I live to get through this lot I shall think myself a lucky man. I have been through more in the last five days than I did all the time I was in Africa. I live in hopes of getting through. If I die in despair - what will be will be.

* * * * *

Pte. Stan Small
10th Battalion, The Devonshire Regiment
Codford, Wiltshire

In November the rains came. Oh my blessed, that was terrible, terrible. We were under canvas and the field was covered in mud and everybody was wet through. There were so many men falling sick with flu and colds and pneumonia and one thing and another, we had to do something. Couldn't sit on our behinds and do nothing. Well, we got together. 'Let's go home. Let's go home.' So we wrapped our things in brown paper and stuck the parcels under our arms and went out onto the parade ground. But the Colonel put a guard on the gate to stop us going through.

Well, there we all were, all in a heap, ready to go off to Warminster Station - get off home, out the way. But he wouldn't let us go. 'We don't allow this in the British Army. You can't go on strike. I have every one of you in the palm of my hand.' Now, that's what he said. Brute. He saw that we were determined to go home but he wouldn't let us. Well, he couldn't really, could he? He was in charge. But within a week they'd found us billets in Bath - and so off we marched. Rag, Tag and Bobtail.

Somerset Guardian

20th November, 1914

The arrival of the Devon Regiment of Lord Kitchener's Army caused a good deal of interest in Bath on Saturday. Their progress through the city created an excellent impression and the unmilitary variety of their equipment in no way hid the sturdiness and fine bearing of the men. Many of the troops seemed unusually big and strong. Their mud-plastered legs told of the state of the roads round Codford. It has been very rough out there, and they are thankful to come to Bath. The Devons include many young fellows from the Midsomer Norton and Radstock district who endeavoured to join the home County regiment but found the Somersets full up and were drafted into the 10th Devons. Their friends are glad they have come to Bath for the winter.

* * * * *

Pte. Bertram Milsom

Royal Army Medical Corps.
20th November, 1914

Dear Martin and Ethel,

I hope you are in the best of health, as I am glad to say I am. There are still a lot of wounded coming this way which means plenty of work for us to do. On Wednesday there were a lot of Somersets come in and I had a conversation with one of the sergeants. He told me he had a lot of Midsomer Norton and Radstock chaps under him in his company but he was too done up to talk to that night.

I found him out the next day as he was in bed with his left arm broken. He told me the Somersets had had it pretty hot all the time up till now but had done well he was pleased to say. A German was lying in the next bed to the sergeant with a gunshot wound to his back. Last week there were some of the Prussian Guards here, wounded, and they are a pretty big lot of men. I was told they were a select body of men from the Kaiser's troops. I can tell you they are some smart men.

We have here a boy German with a bayonet wound in his arm. He's but a youth - not more than 17 if he's a day. He looked quite brokenhearted as he lay in bed and I know some of our soldiers felt a bit of pity for him. He'd only been in the German army a month and it looks as if his arm will be taken off so his fighting career was short.

Somerset Guardian
20th, November, 1914

I would point out to the many pigeon fanciers in this district that the authorities have decided to use carrier pigeons for certain purposes in connection with His Majesty's Services. No one should attempt to shoot or interfere in any way with carrier pigeons while in passage.

The wife of Pte. G J Coombs, 4th Somerset LI, has five brothers and five brothers-in-law in addition to her husband serving their country at the present time. This is a record which will be hard to beat, certainly in this district.

* * * * *

L/Cpl. Herbert Osmond
1st Battalion, The Somerset Light Infantry
27th November, 1914

My Dear Mother,

I now take the pleasure of writing you a few more lines. I must say that I am still quite well and happy. I am writing this in the firing line with the German lines 150 yards to our front. Of course we take a pop at times when they look up. Our boys wait for the chance to let them have a bit of our lead. Of course the Germans play the same game. Our artillery was shaking them up just in front of us yesterday and it was fine sport to see the shells pitch on their trenches. But we do not think it such sport when their 'Jack Johnsons' pitch on ours. Then again there are always plenty of bullets flying about but one gets used to it and it is no use to get scared as it does not improve matters. It seems funny to be sat down here and see the enemy's shells bursting but as long as they keep away from here for a few minutes it will be all right as I want to finish this before putting it down.

> 7191 Lance Corporal Herbert Osmond
> 1st Battalion, The Somerset Light Infantry
> Re-enlisted Canada
> Killed in Action
> 27th November, 1914
> Aged 28

Somerset Guardian
27th November, 1914

Those who are desirous of sending Christmas puddings to their brave friends with the British Expeditionary Force should not fail to give their orders immediately if they intend to send them through one of the large commercial houses who are undertaking this work. Four weeks today we shall be keeping Christmas in England by our own firesides I hope, happy and secure from invasion and the horrors of war in this country. The circumstances under which the brave sons of the British Empire will spend their Christmas will be anything but pleasant, if the war is still in progress, and there is now no probability of it being over by Christmas. To men situated like thousands of Britain's gallant sons will be this Christmas, it must be very cheering to them to know that their friends at home thought of them, and what could be more acceptable than a gift of plum pudding.

* * * * *

Lt. George Parr
1st Battalion, The Somerset Light Infantry
29th November, 1914

. . . At 7.30am the company marched to a large linen factory, which had been rigged up as a washing place. The men marched into a big warehouse, where they took off their service dress (coats and trousers), tied them together with their identity disc and put them on a red barrow, which was then taken to the fumigator. They then were marched into the bleaching room where there were 15 large vats of hot water ready. Here they took off all their clothes - which were boiled in disinfectant - were supplied with soap and towel and had a thoroughly good wash, ten men in a vat with as much hot water as they want. After they have dried themselves they are supplied with fresh underclothing, shirt, socks, pants, and a vest. When they have put on these they go into the warehouse again, when the service dress is brought in on white barrows, having been disinfected and ironed.

A large number of women are employed, who iron the service dress and the disinfected underclothing (if it is worth it) and mend it ready to be issued out to somebody else. The whole company of about 170 men were washed in about an hour and a quarter. . .

> Lt. George Parr
> 1st Battalion, The Somerset Light Infantry
> Killed in Action
> France and Flanders
> 19th December, 1914
> Aged 24

Radstock Church School Logbook
Week ending 27th November, 1914

Admitted two Belgian boys on Wednesday. They belong to the refugees who have been received in Radstock. The lads are intelligent. At present they speak only the Flemish language.

* * * * *

Somerset Guardian
11th December, 1914

Col. Pollard has been appointed recruiting officer for this district. Intending recruits for all branches of His Majesty's Service can be attested and sworn in at the Drill Hall, Midsomer Norton, any morning at 9 o'clock.

* * * * *

Pte. A G Evans
1st Battalion, The Somerset Light Infantry
13th December, 1914

Dear Perce and Edna,

We have had the flower of the Kaiser's troops hurled against us day and night but they failed again and again to dislodge the Somersets from the positions which we hold. This has been going on for nearly two months. There are French and Indian troops up on the left but the British troops have borne the brunt of the fighting, the Kaiser having brought the best of his troops against us, and they have been literally mown down by our rifle fire and bayonet charges. In the front of our trench and the German trenches there are hundreds of English and Germans lying in heaps for weeks and neither side is able to get about and bury them. They are like that for miles and miles. The slaughter is terrible. I have seen men killed outright on each side of me and there they lay all day for you are not able to take them out till night-time. I have seen many men bleed to death for want of attention. There will be many a vacant chair in England this Christmas for many of those I have seen killed were married men with children. There is nothing more cruel or pitiless than war and may Heaven spare our own country from its horrors. Be of good cheer. I am hoping that the same good luck that has attended me up to now will follow me through.

7350 Pte. A G Evans
1st Battalion, The Somerset Light Infantry
Killed in Action
France and Flanders
19th December, 1914

The History of the Somerset Light Infantry 1914-1918
Everard Wyrall
1st Battalion,
19th December, 1914

At 2.30pm precisely, two platoons of B Company *[moved]* forward, staggering through mud and filth towards the German front line, about 120 yards away. No sooner had *[they]* set foot on No Man's Land than sheets of flame leapt up from the German trenches and bullets from machine guns and rifles met *[their]* advance. The leading platoon had gone forward only about 40 or 50 yards when four 4.5 shells fell amongst the men, inflicting considerable casualties. The terrible condition of the ground, pitted with shell holes, covered with water and deep in heavy clinging mud, made the going extremely difficult. Of C Company, Lieut. G R Parr was well in front of his men when he was wounded in the leg by a machine gun bullet. He fell but immediately endeavoured to rise and carry on with the attack. He was, however, struck by another bullet and killed almost instantaneously. Five officers were killed. The losses in other ranks were 27 killed, 52 wounded and 30 missing.

* * * * *

L/Cpl. Oliver Brooks
3rd Battalion, The Coldstream Guards
Christmas 1914

Dear Alf,

On December 23rd we arrived at a little village and went into some reserve trenches. We stayed there all that night and the following morning. We then went into a farmhouse where we spent Christmas Day and proceeded to the trenches at six o'clock the same night. Everything went well for a time. Of course we had the usual detail from the Germans - continual sniping - which they seem to have made a habit, but we had only been in the trenches for an hour when they started to shell us.

We lay under fire for about an hour and I believe that none of us will ever forget it. It was the queerest Christmas night that I have ever experienced in my life - such a time I never wish to have again. When they had finished we thought it about time that we started to enjoy ourselves. I was sent with six more men along a disused trench to within 30 yards of the Germans to see whether we could find out their intentions, and to see that they did not creep nearer our trenches for the purpose of throwing bombs.

This is a common thing for them to do, especially at night times. We stayed there for a while and then I heard them digging. I may mention that we now have bombs of our own, and to feel more content in my mind after our recent sufferings I decided to let them have one or two bombs. I meant business for I took off my accoutrements and coats and rolled up my sleeves. While I was doing this one of the men held the bomb ready for lighting. It was amusing to see us seven having an argument as to which was the best place to drop it.

At last we decided and I threw it. It dropped nicely into the trench and for that night digging was finished. I threw another bomb which fell close to where the first hit, and then we were contented. All the while this was happening we had been in water and mud that came over our shoe tops. At one point, where the trench was very low, the water was nearly waist deep. We had to go through it just the same. There was no turning back.

1915

L/Cpl. Walter Horler
2nd Battalion, The Grenadier Guards
2nd January, 1915

My Dear Mother and Father,

After 10 days in the trenches we are having another rest and now that I have a little time to spare I will give you an account of what I have seen. We relieved a regiment on the night of December 24th. Next morning (Christmas Day) one of the Germans put his head up above his trench to have a look around and at the same time got a bullet from our man on sentry. About an hour later another German put his head up and we were all astonished to hear him shout, 'A Merry Christmas you English ***!' and was going to shout something else when the same sentry put a bullet through his forehead. Well, for about four hours after that we had a very warm time indeed for they simply poured bombs into us and finally we had to retire into our reserve trenches. No sooner had we left than they swarmed into them in thousands but when they were nicely settled down our artillery shelled them from the rear. Our shells dropped right into their trenches and they must have lost thousands. After that it was quiet and we managed to get some Christmas pudding. The remainder of the time in the trenches passed off quiet but it is very cold and we are up to our knees in water and have to stick it for 24 hours at a time. It is awful and I wish it was all over but I suppose we have to stick it. I will now close, light up a cigar and smoke the health of you all.

Somerset Guardian
8th January, 1915

Midsomer Norton has been selected by the Army authorities as a centre for some 250 or 300 troops of the Army Service Corps. The advance party arrived at the end of last week and the main body was daily expected to follow. The new Drill Hall and the Town Hall have been requisitioned for their accommodation and skittle alleys have been fitted up for sleeping at the old Drill Hall and the Greyhound Hotel.

L/Cpl Oliver Brooks
3rd Battalion, The Coldstream Guards
22nd January, 1915

> When you've drunk your lot of whisky
> And you've smoked your fat cigar,
> And your eyes have twinkled brightly
> At the girl behind the bar;
> Just think of Tommy Atkins
> In his cold, wet trench of clay,
> With nothing much to cheer him
> But his rations for the day.
>
>
> Have you ever thought about yourself
> And the bit that you could do?
> Has Kitchener to shout in vain
> Your country's need for you?
> Put on the khaki uniform,
> And leave your feather bed,
> Let no-one say you shirked it
> When danger lay ahead.

Charlie Maggs
Schoolboy

The Recruiting Sergeant in Norton. Hah! In those days they always had one. Resident in the Drill Hall - always on the look-out for clients. Looks like this one emptied the High Street pretty well! They didn't get their man every time, you know. Uncle Matthew was up having a drink at the Stones Cross pub one day when someone looked out and said, 'Hey! Looks like we've got a new recruiting Sergeant'.

Uncle Matt was an old rascal, he lived on his wits - had to because he was a bad cripple after an accident to his legs. But otherwise he was a big smart lad like his brother who was in the Guards. So they watched the Sergeant making his way up the road to the pub and by the time he'd come through the door, ready to be duped, Uncle is sitting in the corner - ready.

After he'd got himself a drink the Sergeant sauntered over to sit with them and began to talk about life in the army. He obviously had his eye on Uncle and was trying to sell it to him - so how about it? Well, he said, yes he thought he would like to join. And the barmaid played along with it all and said, 'No, Matt. Don't do it'. 'Yes,' he said. 'I shall. I'm determined to.'

'Good lad,' said the Sergeant and then gave him the King's Shilling, which was the way they recruited in those days - a sort of contract, I suppose it must have been. When they'd duly spent the shilling on beer the Sergeant said, 'Well, Matthew my boy, I suppose we'd better stroll down to the Drill Hall and sort out the details'. 'All right, Sergeant,' says Uncle Matt. 'Would you mind just helping me to reach my crutches under the table?' The poor Sergeant nearly burst a blood vessel.

* * * * *

Somerset Guardian
22nd January, 1915

From the Office of the
High Sherriff of Somerset

Numbers of men serving with the colours from the cities, towns and villages of Somerset (National Reservist figures are not included):

	Serving	Population
Midsomer Norton	268	7299
Radstock	163	3690
Wellow	67	2033
Camerton	65	2830
Paulton	48	2732
Timsbury	28	1701
Clutton	24	134
Chilcompton	23	666
High Littleton	15	1008
Cameley	11	403
Ston Easton	11	323
Farrington Gurney	9	693
Litton	6	163

Pte. Tommy Atkins
Royal Engineers
January, 1915

My first job when I left school was working at Ston Easton for Mr Orme, a friend of Commander Hippisley. Mr Orme had a wireless set - a receiving set - with one aerial at Ston Easton and another at East Woodhay, in Berkshire, and he'd take his set from one place to the other. Commander Hippisley used to have a broadcasting set and used to broadcast from Ston Easton and Mr Orme would pick up his message. It was all in code and they'd let me listen sometimes. It was all tink, tink, tink - like Morse code, that sort of thing.

I was at Ston Easton when war broke out and I was there when the Post Office people came round and dismantled his set and put it in boxes and sealed them - Defence of the Realm Act - so he couldn't get in touch with the enemy! Him! Commander Hippisley! In January I left Mr Orme and got a job as a conductor on the trams in Bristol but I quickly got fed up with that so I went up to the depot at Park Road and joined up. Course, the recruiting Sergeant would take anybody as long as you said you were 18. He'd have you 'cause for every recruit they got a shilling, and that were three or four pints of beer. So he says, 'How old are you?' and I said 18. 'That's right. Of course you are.'

So then we met this fire-eating Sergeant - with flashing lights in his eyes - who told us, 'You are not in any Rag, Tag and Bobtail crowd now. You are in the Royal Engineers'. And that's what we were in. And that was that. And I was 16.

Somerset Guardian

29th January, 1915

The Voluntary Aid Detachment Temporary Hospital, opened in Radstock Road, Midsomer Norton, has proved far too small for the requirements of the sick patients from Kitchener's Army located in Midsomer Norton, which now numbers 360. The upper storey of the Higher Elementary School at Midsomer Norton has now been requisitioned, giving accommodation for 50 beds, and at the present time they are all full. A building better suited to the purpose it would be difficult to find, being of modern construction, well arranged and excellently ventilated. Five wards have been fitted out. The domestic arrangements are greatly enhanced by the use of the spacious kitchen provided for the cooking classes. On the ground floor is ample space for the stores. Most of the equipment required to fit out the new premises has been generously loaned by the inhabitants of Kilmersdon, Midsomer Norton and Radstock.

The nursing staff under the supervision of Nurse Burns, is drawn from members of the local detachments; additional help is given by the men's detachments and members of the Army Service Corps who are available as orderlies. The Vice-President, Countess Waldegrave, who is keenly interested in the work, has rendered most valuable help.

* * * * *

Catherine Pollard
VAD Nurse

And Father was Medical Officer in Charge - Colonel George Pollard. He was 56 by then and I can't think how he found time to do everything he did, as well as doing his best for his patients - which he certainly did. That's me standing next to him - got glasses on - and Miss Constance Waugh, Evelyn Waugh's aunt, is standing beside me.

Sgt. George Bray
1st Battalion, The Grenadier Guards
3rd February, 1915

Dear Sis,

Well, I shall never forget February 3rd, being stormed with shot and shell. They captured 20,000 Germans on our right and shelled them last night - put the enemy's ration column out. Blew the horses, wagons and that to pieces. They have some big guns here that can do a lot of damage. It is cold and wet and we are getting a very rough time of it out here. We are digging in all the time and we have lost a good many in the Guards.

We have plenty of men going to hospital with rheumatism through standing in water, but it has took no effect on me yet. We are not in water all the time, of course, men couldn't stand it. We sing very often and we can often hear the Germans singing in their trenches. I cannot tell you where we are, our officers read our letters before they are sealed down. I don't know if there is anything I want more than light and Mr Jack Shearn sent me a nice electric lamp but I shall want some more refills. If you could, please send me out some at once as they are very useful, one of the most useful things out here in the trenches as you can just flash it on and out in a moment.

I could tell you a lot. Will do so later. The war will last longer than you think at home.

* * * * *

Midsomer Norton Church of England Schools
Minutes of Managers' Meeting
9th February, 1915

USE OF INFANT DEPT. BY TROOPS

Reported that the Infant Department was taken over by the Military Authorities for billeting troops on the afternoon of January 21st and the children had been transferred to the mixed Department where the Headmaster had found it possible to share two classrooms. Mr Grindrod, HM Inspector, visited the school on 25th January and 2nd Febry. and his report on the arrangements which he considered unsatisfactory was read. The Secretary was instructed to reply to the Board of Education stating that the Managers were most anxious to take all possible steps to minimise the inconvenience and to state that the Military Authorities had promised to vacate the premises at the earliest possible moment.

Somerset Guardian

19th February, 1915

The management of the VAD hospital at Midsomer Norton, where a large number of sick soldiers have been cared for, are very grateful for the splendid response made to the appeal to 'Pound day' on Saturday last. Four depots are arranged where contributions of articles could be received during the afternoon and the poundage of gifts were as follows: Kilmersdon 320; Midsomer Norton 178; Peasedown 487; Radstock with Clandown 581, making a total of 1.566 lbs, from 334 contributors in addition to £1.17.11 in cash, this including a collection kindly made by Mr Egerton at Mr Albany Ward's Picture Palace in Radstock.

In addition to the men and officers of the Army Service Corps which have been stationed at Midsomer Norton for some weeks, there are now a considerable number of officers and men of the Motor Transport, the Army Service Corps, in this locality. They are quartered at the Old Brewery premises at Holcombe which is now in good order and can afford ample space for the men, but there is insufficient accommodation for the wagons which are parked at the side of the road. No preparation had been made at Holcombe for the reception of these men and it was very surprising to find how rapidly they adapted themselves to their new quarters. By Tuesday evening the whole of the premises were brilliantly lit with electric light which the engineers of the company had installed. The arrangements for feeding this large number are being carried out by the men themselves.

The district of Holcombe offers practically no attractions for the entertainment of the men, while off duty, and they will doubtless find things very quiet in the village. The men have a band of their own and they turned out on Tuesday afternoon and played selections. Perhaps the people in the district would do their best to make the men as welcome as possible during their stay.

Catherine Pollard

While the soldiers were there in Holcombe everyone did everything they could to make them welcome. This was taken by a local chap by the name of Bill Marchant Jones who did his best to amuse them by getting them to pose for various tableaux which he photographed. He called this one *The Traitor's Doom*!

* * * * *

Somerset Guardian

12th March, 1915

HOLCOMBE - THE ARMY SERVICE CORPS

On Sunday the principal Church Parade was at St Giles Church, Leigh on Mendip, one small contingent attended the Trinity Church, Coleford, and a few of the same company attended the Coleford Wesleyan Chapel and the Primitive Methodist Church in the bottom of the village.

On Monday about 50 of the motor lorries and their crews left for Wells during the day where they expected to change the older vehicles for newer ones but only a portion of the contingent returned on the same day.

Pte. Edward Hurd
1st/4th Battalion, The Gloucester Regiment
March, 1915

Our division moved out to France in March, 1915. And we left Salisbury Plain *as* a division. Not in dribs and drabs. When we got to France the trains got us up as far as t'was considered safe from long range shell fire and then we were entirely on our feet and we began to see the roughness of it all. Everything, from the sea coast down, was desolate - been heavily shelled. Where there had been a wood or a bit of a copse, it'd just be sticks poking up. What was once a village might have one habitable house. It was surprising how some of the French stuck there and hung onto their shacks. We'd end a day and find ourselves billeted in cow-sheds, or anything with a bit of corrugated iron over to make a roof. Sleep on cow pats, too tired to trouble what we laid on.

* * * * *

Somerset Guardian
19th March, 1915

Some employers of labour in this district have with commendable patriotism done their best to urge young men in their employ to lay aside their civil occupations for the time being, and respond to the call of their country to join the Army. Though it is not in the employer's personal interest to induce men to leave his service, especially where men are engaged in productive work, yet many employers recognise that at the present moment patriotism comes before profit, and they have been really sincere in their efforts to get eligible young men to join the colours.

Some of the collieries in this locality have lost a number of men from their service and according to the number usually employed some of the smaller collieries in the Somerset coalfield have done well, better after the rate than the larger collieries. As an instance of this I might mention that from the new Rock Colliery, Chilcompton, no fewer than 30 men have joined the Army. The proprietor of this colliery offered all married men in his employ half wages to join the Army for the period of the war, and all single men were offered 5s per week. In the case of single men the money could be banked for them if they desired it, and paid over to them when they returned to their employment, or to anyone they desired it should be paid. No distinction has been made as to the pay, whether a man joined one branch of the army or another, or whether he joined at the beginning of the war or recently.

I would make bold to say that the proprietor of this colliery is a gentleman who cannot hope to be financially benefitted by the war. Personal service by him is beyond the question, but he is sufficiently patriotic to offer a substantial inducement to the men he employs to respond to their country's call, and willingly and cheerfully fulfils the promise he makes.

Gwen Beauchamp

Schoolgirl

Oh, my God! That was Father. Until this moment I had no idea he'd done that. But he never ceased to surprise me by the things he did. We lived in Norton Hall. It was a huge house and estate, with a housekeeper, a kitchen maid and a scullery maid and then there was a butler and a footman. There were eight altogether - and they all slept in. And there were at least three gardeners. Oh, and we had large stables - he owned some race horses and won the Great Metropolitan in 1908. He was also Master of the Wells' Harriers and up to 200 would sit down to breakfast at Norton Hall before the opening meet.

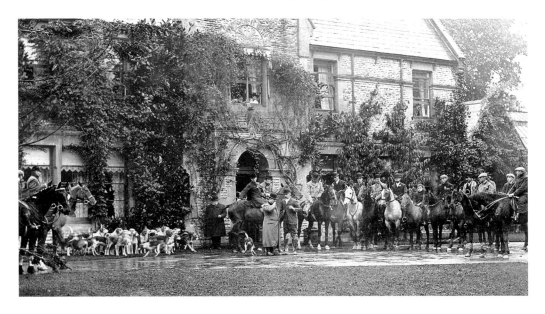

Before the war we used to go to Tenby for our summer holidays. Dad had an old yacht there. Dad and Uncle Frank owned collieries in Somerset and the Forest of Dean, and because the GWR carried most of the coal from the collieries, they always provided us with a lovely private saloon carriage, free, for the journey.

Dad also had a large home farm but his chief interest was in the local collieries. I do think he treated his miners quite well, though. One day, when I was nursing at the War Hospital in Bath, I recognised a soldier with pneumonia. He'd obviously been talking to the other patients about me and then he asked if I'd speak to him. He said, 'I wanted to ask you if the chaps realise who you are, because I don't think you should allow them to chat and joke with you so much'. Just as if. Before the war he'd been one of Dad's miners, and a tenant in one of his cottages at Norton Down, less than a quarter of a mile from my home. This chap gave me a real telling off. I said, 'Look. I am just a nurse like any of the other nurses, and I am taking care of you as I would any other patient'. What on earth did he think?

Pte. Tommy Atkins
Royal Engineers
March, 1915

Soon after I'd joined up in Bristol they moved us to Braintree in Essex. There was a fair thing on when we got there and I remember that the roundabouts were playing *'It's a long way to Tipperary'*. From there we moved to Witham, where we lived under canvas for the best part of the summer, and finally we moved to Wribbenhall and I and two or three other chaps were billeted in a pub. I was still too young to drink.

We were still at Wribbenhall when we heard about the German Zeppelins raiding the coastal towns - Southend and places like that.

* * * * *

Gwen Beauchamp
Schoolgirl
March, 1915

I remember when the first Zep went along the coast while I was at Roedean - there was absolute panic. We all had to run into an underground passage which went under the road to our bathing place. Another excitement was when the first battle cruiser squadron came to Brighton. Quite a large number of us girls were invited to tea and I went to HMS Collingwood. After being introduced to the Captain and various officers, an officer brought a young Midshipman up to me and introduced him as Mr Something-or-Other. He was very quiet and shy and stammered rather badly.

This officer came back at intervals to see how we were getting on and then sat us down next to each other at tea. After tea we danced together. At the time it didn't strike me as being strange that he was the only 'snottie' who was being looked after by an officer, but in the bus on the way back to Roedean, Miss Wraith asked me if I knew who he was. I said I thought he was Mr So and So. But she said 'No, it was Prince Albert!' who later became George VIth.

MOTOR DRIVERS WANTED

For the

Motor Transport Section, Army Service Corps

Pay: 6s per day all found. Separation allowances extra.

A Mechanical Officer just returned will speak on:

MOTOR TRANSPORT IN FRANCE

and will give all information of this most attractive
branch at the capital's barracks, Taunton, on

Saturday next,	April 17th at 2 pm
Bridgwater	16th April at 2 pm
Shepton Mallet	19th April at 2 pm
Bath	20th April at 12 noon

Cliff Latchem
Schoolboy
April, 1914

I remember when my father volunteered. I were six year old. He went in the Army Service Corps - ambulance drivin'. I remember he had a badge on his coat, a Union Jack in a circle with the word 'enlisted' - or 'volunteer' - summit like that. When he left home, Mother stayed in the house an' I ran after him, along this rough path - all made up with ashes an' horse shit in them days - an' I was crying an' saying, 'Don't go Dad. Don't go!' I can remember that as if t'were yesterday. He had to shoo an' drive me back an' eventually I had to give up an' go home an' cry with Mother.

Weren't long before he were made a Corporal an' then up to Sergeant Instructor - that suited he 'cause he were a bloody good boss, he were. The reason why he made it so quick were all the ambulances they had were Model T Fords, an' pretty well all of the personnel were ex-chauffeurs what'd never zid a Model T with bein' used to drivin' Rolls Royces or Daimlers. 'Course, Dad knew all about them through workin' fer the Mattick brothers.

An' that's what he did all the war. Quite a good number apart from him getting bad wi' the bloody dysentery.

* * * * *

Rupert Shepherd
Schoolboy

Tom, my oldest brother - 4054 Pte. Shepherd T - he was an ambulance driver. Got in by accident. At the time there were so many people who couldn't drive - not many drivers in the country really - and they were advertising for drivers. He didn't know what sort of a job it was but he went forward and found himself in uniform and off to France in less than a week. Went there on the 4th September, 1914.

Among the things they had imported into France were London buses - open topped double-deckers and when Tom got there he began by driving one of those. Six shillings a day he got, and he had that all the time he was in, because he had a special qualification - he could drive.

Then he became ill somehow and they gave him a lighter job - but a worse job - ambulance driving. Going up close to the trenches to pick up the wounded. The regiment that he was actually attached to was the 70th Gurkha Rifles.

My other brother, George, was also a soldier - with the Northumberland Fusiliers - the 17th NF. 1257 his number was. He was at Passchendaele, but there again, who wasn't. We had no idea where they were most of the time. Their letters were censored, you know. The first we realised that was when we got a letter from George with a word scratched out - we held it up to the light and could make out *Canadians* - so the Canadians were fighting there with them. Another time he signed himself George Albert, which we couldn't understand because his second name was Arthur. We couldn't figure that one out till an old soldier told Father that he must have been *in* Albert when he wrote it.

I had a sister in the army as well - Pauline. She joined in 1917, when she was 17 - told them she was 18, but there was no problem, they wanted them so she got in. She was due to go to France but my father didn't like that so he contacted her commanding officer and said she was only 17, and she was detained from going over. It was the WAAC - the Women's Auxiliary Army Corps. She was then put on loan to the airforce at a place called Lymm, where one of her jobs was loading bombs into Handley-Page four-engined machines. My other sister couldn't get in. Failed the medical.

Tom went on ferrying the wounded from the front until he got gassed and rendered useless. He was invalided out in 1916. When he came home they gave him this badge thing to wear - just says For Services Rendered - no name on it - for King and Empire, cause we had an empire then. He wore this to stop people abusing him. The women especially used to accost people in civilian clothes and say, 'Why aren't you in uniform?' They could be vicious and for someone like Tom it was awful. He'd already been and gone and done his bit and come home again. He couldn't have done any more.

* * * * *

Mabel Plomley
Shop Worker

When soldiers were discharged they had a discharge suit given them - usually pin stripe - and I made the first sample of trousers that went out of the factory to the War Office. Got the princely sum of sixpence for making them. The year before the war - when I was 14 - I was apprenticed as a dressmaker in Bath. Got the large sum of a shilling a week. One week, when I was ill, I only managed to go to work on the Monday, and the following week, when I went, they gave me my previous week's wages - a penny and a halfpenny for the three quarters of the day I had worked (wasn't I rich?). Then when war broke out I went to Colmers, working on khaki, making soldiers' uniforms.

When the 10th Devons - Kitchener's Army - came to Bath they were billeted close to us, in the empty houses in Sydney Place. They were cold, wet, miserable houses, not been used for years. As we were already working from eight in the morning until nine o'clock at night some of us from Colmers spent the Saturday afternoon making bags - palliasses - for the boys to fill with straw to sleep on so as they shouldn't have to sleep on bare boards.

I got to know lots of army men. One Sunday morning, I was standing at our door, noseying at something or another, and two little boys come down - well, they were about 18 and just joined Kitchener's Army. (I went to Kitchener's funeral service, mind, at Bath Abbey. Got pushed in with the crowd.) Anyway, these lads went to the lady next door and asked if she could darn some socks for them. They said they were clean, and she said, 'You go and ask Mabel. She'll do them'.

So of course Mabel took them in and Mother and I did the darning for them. Used to come to my home and my mother would wash their towels and vests and shirts and pants, and their socks. We would mend everything for them. At first it was for only two, but by the time they left it'd got to twelve or fourteen, coming regular. Mother did charge them four-pence, to cover her soap and everything, 'cause things were scarce in those days. They did all come down on Sunday mornings instead of going to Church Parade - 'cause they were all Wesleyan in those days. They'd come down home instead, bringing their dirty washing and Mother'd sort it all out for them - had to mark it all with different colours 'cause one would claim the others.

They were lovely boys. The last night they were home - before they had to march off to Sutton Veny - we all sat up till one o'clock so all their clothes was clean and tidy. My mother had got very attached to one of those boys and did not like to see him go. She nearly broke her heart when they left.

* * * * *

Pte. Stan Small
10th Battalion, The Devonshire Regiment

When we'd got to Bath we were all put in billets at the bottom of Pultney Street and did our cooking in Sydney Gardens. We spent three or four months there and trained up at Lansdown Racecourse. That was lovely. I certainly liked that. But then in April we marched back down to Sutton Veny to complete our training and a few weeks later we got lined up on the parade ground and marched to Warminster Station. Then Southampton. Set out late one evening. Next morning - France.

𝔖𝔬𝔪𝔢𝔯𝔰𝔢𝔱 𝔊𝔲𝔞𝔯𝔡𝔦𝔞𝔫

23rd April, 1915

DEPARTURE OF THE DEVONS

MAYORAL SEND-OFF

The 10th Devons left Bath on Tuesday morning and not withstanding the fact that by shortly after 9 they were already out of the city on their 21 mile march to Sutton Veny, they received a fitting send off from the Mayor and Corporation, as well as a big crowd of townspeople. The Mayor has never spoken better . . .

'We have gathered together to say farewell to what we know is one of the finest regiments in the British Army . . . Your advent here a few months ago was a very welcome advent and your stay has been satisfactory in every way. During the time I have held the office of Chief Magistrate not one solitary word of complaint have I heard. You have made friends every-where . . .'

On account of the distance to be covered no delay could be brooked and in a few minutes the first half Battalion was gaily setting out with their faces set towards their new camping ground. On all hand there were waving handkerchiefs and people pressed through the crowd to hand out chocolate and cigarettes with which to beguile the twenty odd mile of dusty roads . . .

The History of the Somerset Light Infantry 1914-1918
Everard Wyrall
26th April, 1914

All day long nothing could be done but lie close and make the best of a desperate situation. Throughout the night 26th/27th until 3am all ranks were hard at work improving the defences, which presumably afforded better shelter for the men, for during the 27th, though the hostile shelling continued with great violence, only 18 NCOs and men were killed or wounded.

* * * * *

Somerset Guardian

Private Joseph C Withers of the 1st Somerset Light Infantry, eldest son of Mr and Mrs Henry Withers of Welton Hill, Midsomer Norton was with the Expeditionary Force in the fighting area ever since the British troops took part in the operations. He was in the Regular Army and was just completing his 13th year, some four and a half of which was spent in India. He had distinguished himself in the present war and recently sent home to his parents for safe custody an official card signed by Major-General H J M Wilson, Commanding the 4th Division, with his name, number and regimental particulars written on the top. The card stated, 'Your Commanding Officer and Brigade Commander have informed me that you have distinguished yourself by conspicuous bravery in the field. I have read their report with much pleasure'. No particulars are yet available as to particulars of the brave deed. On Monday afternoon, unhappily, Mr and Mrs Withers received a telegram from the War Office notifying them that their brave son Joseph had been killed in action on April 27th.

Mr & Mrs Withers have had three sons serving with the colours. The eldest of the three, Private William Withers, G Company, 1st/4th Somerset LI, joined the local Territorials in Midsomer Norton when the appeal was made for recruits at the commencement of the war. He is now stationed in Jullunder, in Northern India. Buglar James Withers joined the army since the war began and is now in the 7th Battalion, Somerset Light Infantry, in training at Rolleston Camp, Wiltshire.

> 9808 Pte. Joseph Colborn Withers
> 1st Battalion, The Somerset Light Infantry
> Killed in Action
> France and Flanders
> 27th April, 1915

Somerset Guardian

30th April, 1915

Now that so many people are concerned with the welfare of local men at the front there seems to be an anxiety to discover some method whereby, for a reasonable outlay, accepted gifts may be sent to their friends. Some of the larger business firms of the country are undertaking, for a small outlay, to send various parcels of goods which men on active service would appreciate.

So far as this district is concerned, the only thing of its kind, so far as I can discover, is being done by the Radstock Co-operative and Industrial Society who are booking orders for various classes of goods which can be sent carriage paid to men at the front or on ships engaged in war. Tobacco, cigarettes and cigars at an extremely cheap rate are being sent.

For 2s 6d a parcel containing 1/2lb of tobacco and 1/2lb of cigarettes is sent carriage paid to any address which might be supplied with the order. A parcel containing such things as tobacco, cigarettes, a pipe, biscuits, sweets, fish and meat pastes, soap, candles, medical comforts, writing materials, canned fish, eating raisins, etc., is being sent for 4s 6d.

If the parcel is ordered for a regiment or ship and not for any particular individual serving in either, the charge will be only 3s 8d. Full particulars as to these parcels, on which I might say not a penny-piece profit is made, will be gladly furnished on application to any of the Society's branches, and it is solely in the interest of men serving that I draw attention to this matter.

* * * * *

Midsomer Norton April Fair was held on Monday but for the first time within almost living memory the event was shorn of its attractiveness by the absence of the usual collection of amusements which are generally to be found congregated in the streets of the town. The business side was transacted as usual on Monday morning, when farmers and dealers were present at the auction.

In the evening thousands of people congregated in the Town Hall and Church Squares and the adjacent thoroughfares. There was an entire absence of amusements in the shape of roundabouts, switchbacks, swings, shooting galleries, etc., but the few hawkers' stalls in the streets did a big trade. There was an almost continuous battle of confetti between the crowd, which was practically the only fun of the fair.

The men of the Army Service Corps who have been stationed for some weeks at Midsomer Norton, were expecting to leave on Wednesday. All arrangements were made and everything was packed up and ready but on Tuesday evening the orders were cancelled and the men are still at Midsomer Norton. Their baggage had all been loaded on the GWR at Radstock on Tuesday but on Thursday morning the majority of it was unloaded and taken back to Midsomer Norton. No-one knows when they will depart.

George Taylor
Carting Boy

Now, I'll tell thee a little story. I left Norton afore they Service Corps soldiers did - and I'll tell thee why. My father an' all his brothers were miners - well in them days that's all there were round here - so as soon as I were 13 I went straight down the pit as a carting boy. And that were pretty bad, pretty bad. We did haul about two hundredweight at a time - drag it out, tip it up and back for more. Backwards and forwards and the blood did come out of your ribs and out yer knees. To harden our skin we did rub all our urine into yer legs and body.

We'd go down at half five and start at six and generally t'was five o'clock when we finished. Shillin' a day we got for that, same as in the army, but the army was quite a change. Oh yes, quite a change.

One day, when I were just 16, I'd been into Bath with my mate George Budget what worked with me in the pit. We were cycling back into Norton and we met these four soldiers and a girl. Well, George reckoned he'd shift them and cycled between the woman and the soldiers and knocked the woman down - an' she were pretty bad, I'll tell 'ee.

Well, a policeman came along and these soldiers started hittin' *him* about an' he called to us to help. Well we did, and when t'were over he said for us to get on home - but I wasn' going the way we'd intended. Those men were with the Service Corp what did have billets in the middle of the village.

Next day everybody knew about it - everybody. So I said to George, we'm in trouble, we've got to get away. Less join the thunderin' army. Right, he said and we went up to see Dr Pollard and he give us the shilling and told us where we 'ad to go. In the Somersets.

Next morning, instead of going to work we went to Welton Station and met **Joe Evans** from Paulton and the three of us went straight down to Taunton. Straight to the barracks where the three on us had brush handles gid to us. We 'ad to practice slopin' arms an' stuff with they. After about three weeks our stuff come through an' we had our guns and our khaki and the next day we shifted down to the 6th Battalion, down to Plymouth.

Cpl. Vincent Carter
1st Battalion, The Somerset Light Infantry
3rd May, 1915

Dear David,

We are having rather a rough time of it out here now, and the dirty German shells are dropping round us in fine style. We have had a few of our lads wounded but we hope to pay them back soon. I expect they will soon know a little about us as we intend to give it to them, for they are using those shells with the poison in them. We have had a bit of that and I can tell you it is awful as it makes your eyes burn as if someone had thrown lime in them. But they will be sure to get paid for it. I was out on listening patrol the other day and found a young officer of the Suffolk Regiment who had not been dead long. I volunteered to go out later and bring him in and they gave me consent. I and my chum buried him in a decent grave and put a wooden cross at its head. It made my heart sad to see the young fellow. Our Sergeant is going to inform his parents who are living in Colchester, and his father is a minister.

Somerset Guardian

Official news has been received this week by his parents, Mr and Mrs William Carter, of the Batch, Paulton, that their son Corporal Vincent Carter of the 1st Somerset LI was killed in action in France on May 3rd. The deceased, who was only 24 years of age, joined the Army since the outbreak of the hostilities and enlisted in the Somersets for 12 years. The sad news, when it became generally known, created a painful impression in the village and much sympathy is being extended to Mr and Mrs Carter. Corporal Carter is the first Paultonian to sacrifice his life in action in the present great struggle.

* * * * *

9808 Cpl. Vincent Carter
1st Battalion, The Somerset Light Infantry
Killed in Action
France and Flanders
3rd May, 1915

As soon as the troops which have been stationed some weeks in Midsomer Norton and Holcombe had departed on Friday last their absence was greatly noticed. Both lots took their departure on Friday and in the morning the streets of Midsomer Norton and Radstock presented a very lively appearance.

The Midsomer Norton men - the 168th Company, Army Service Corps - composed of 385 officers and men, who had been quartered in Midsomer Norton for five months, paraded in the Town Hall Square at 10:15. Captain London called for three cheers for the inhabitants of Midsomer Norton who had treated them so kindly and these were heartily given.

The order to march was given by Major MacDonald, the officer commanding and then the company headed by Midsomer Norton Town Brass Band paraded to Radstock. On arrival in Radstock the band played the National Anthem and Auld Lang Syne and the company marched on to Bath. So far as is known there will be no further troops quartered in Midsomer Norton this summer.

The Holcombe contingent was busy in Radstock this Friday loading up goods at the GWR station assisted by a section of the RFA. Later with their heavy wagons they set out for Avonmouth where they embarked.

Ruth Evans
Wife and Mother

Oh, I was so sorry when the Service Corps did leave Norton. In those days my husband worked for Norton Council, where the soldiers did stable their horses. And there was so much food! He did say it was a shame to waste it, so he brought it home. Legs of mutton with only a couple of slices took off. The waste was shocking - it almost kept my family. Oh yes, I didn't half miss them.

* * * * *

Ellen Blake
Wife and Mother

When my husband was called up he had to go abroad after a little while - went to Belgium - that's a bit further on than France, isn't it? That's right. Belgium. And that were awful. Course, I had the children small and I'd just opened this little shop thinking to make a bit. Pay wasn't much from the army and I thought it would help. I did make baked faggots, 'cause my mother done that for years and had a splendid trade in them and, course, I knew what to do.

Well, people did queue up at lunchtimes with their basins to have hot faggots and gravy for dinner. Always a queue at dinner time. Then I'd get a ham and cut it out, quarter pounds and half pounds - however they wanted it. P'rhaps a large tin of corned beef that they could have a quarter from if they couldn't afford the ham. Then I did make dough cakes - quite a selection, you know.

I never went in for sweets and things, mine were more eatables. Eatables that they could have and eat straight away - ready cooked. The bakers did always come round and deliver in them days but I did make my own - didn't normally make it to sell, just for friends, but I did if anyone ordered some. I'd get my flour from Mr Maloney's mill down in The Square and my eldest little boy would go to the brewery in Welton to get barm - that's like liquid yeast - and I would make bread with that.

Then we kept a few fowls in a field and we did breed poultry and sell them and some I did cook and cut out in the shop. P'rhaps you'd buy a wing or a leg, whatever you could afford, or a couple of slices off the breast. And then when it did come to the skelington I did sell that, too, but I'd leave a bit of meat on if I knew someone was a bit poor. There's tricks in every trade, you know.

* * * * *

Pte. Edward Hurd
1st/4th Battalion, The Gloucester Regiment
16th May, 1915

We first went into the line at a place called Givenchy and we soon knew what shelling was about - but then in May we went up the road a bit to Festubert. And that was terrible. We went into the line where the Royal Munster Fusiliers had been slaughtered, virtually wiped out, in the Battle of Aubers Ridge. Eleven and a half thousand men killed. In one day!

Our positions weren't like proper trenches, they were lean-to things without backs. There'd be a bay with about half a dozen men in and then a gap between and then another bay. So there we were, and for some reason the Germans opened up a terrific bombardment and a lot of it fell in our lines. Whether that's what they'd done to the Munsters I don't know, but we lost a lot of men. New chaps were brought in to replace them - men you didn't know - hadn't trained with.

Something happened during that attack that I can't understand. It makes you smile and it makes you cry. Whether it was an act of God or not I don't know. Those German shells came down and we could hear the boys to the left and the right of us shouting, 'Stretcher bearers! Stretcher bearers!' And we could see the bearers scrabbling over men's bodies and over arms and legs and hunks of flesh. And all the time you could hear the screaming of the wounded.

Then the bombardment ceased. And nothing happened, and that was strange, 'cause what usually happened was that they would carry on their shelling, perhaps all day, and then it'd stop. Then, suddenly the Germans would be over and those that'd survived the bombing would be waiting for them. But this time the attack never came. It just went quiet. We weren't touched. And I don't know why. I really don't know why.

After we'd been bombarded we'd have to renovate our positions and then at night we'd have to go up and see to the wire while the Germans were sending up Very lights illuminating everything. Perhaps you might be repairing it or making gaps for some future raid and these lights would go up. When those things turned over and shone everywhere, illuminating everything, you'd stop still, make believe you were a tree stump and pray they wouldn't open up with a machine gun, 'cause they could sweep at random and hit men with a multitude of bullets. But if our Very lights showed up Germans repairing their wire we'd send out a party to do ours and it'd be unlikely that they'd open up for fear of firing on their own men. There'd be two parties out there doing exactly the same thing. Oh, it was all very frightening, terribly frightening.

* * * * *

L/Cpl. George Taylor
6th Battalion, The Somerset Light Infantry
3rd June, 1915

I suppose I'd been at Taunton for six days or so when I were picked out as an NCO fer the rest. Lance Corporal. First thing I had to do were to drill 'em on about an acre of grass. Slope arms, present arms, about turn - stuff like that. One day I had a platoon drilling up and down and when they all should've turned left one on 'em turned right - I knewed him before we'd joined up - didn't live no more than five mile from here.

Well, with that a senior Warrant Officer come round the corner and started bawling out - told me to get the man. He were hard mind. He got down and picked two daisies an' stuck them on the soldier's sleeve - on his left arm - an' shoved his face right up to his ear'ole an'said, 'Next time you hear LEFT, look at the daisies'. This chap looked'n straight in the eye an' said, 'Ah, you've put daisies on my arm now, but I shall *cover* you in bloody daisies the first chance I got'. Well, **Daisy Boy**, as we'll call'n, got 28 days in the glasshouse fer that. But that wasn't the end of the business. Far from it. Quite soon after that we went to France.

73

BLACKSMITHS

Blacksmiths are urgently required for Service in the Royal Engineers, for the
duration of the War. Men desiring to enlist as Blacksmiths in the Royal Engineers
are put through a test at their trade which is less difficult than tests for shoeing-smiths.
They might, for example, be required to cut off a length of 1/2" round iron bar,
bend into a ring of five inches diameter, and weld complete.

For terms of pay and service apply to the nearest Recruiting Officer

RECRUITS WANTED

For Remount Squadron, Army Service Corp

Men between the ages of 25 and 40 are required at once for the

Remount Squadron, Army Service Corp

The ordinary standards of height and chest measurements
may be waived, providing men are organically sound, and
the sight test may be passed with the aid of glasses.

Pay: Ordinary Army Service Corps rates.

For Enlistment: apply to nearest Recruiting Officer

WANTED!

500 recruits to wear Harvey's £2 suits

Made to measure at the special price of 32/6d.
40 patterns to select from.   Fit and style guaranteed.

W Harvey & Co. Welton Supply Stores

11th June, 1915

The first aeroplane known to actually pass over Radstock did so yesterday morning at 12:20. One or two had previously been known to fly over places within a few miles of Radstock but this was the first one to pass over the town.

Some of the scholars of the Radstock Council School have for a few weeks been bringing eggs for the wounded soldiers and these have been handed over to Mr F Wilmott on Friday of each week and Mr Wilmott has forwarded them to the collecting station. One of the scholars, called Leonard Woodland, who placed his name and address on one egg, has received a letter from a wounded Grenadier who is anxious to discover the whereabouts of a friend who was with him in France. The friend was a Somerset man. The letter was as follows:

Dear Friend,

Excuse me writing to you but when I was having my tea I noticed your address on my egg. I am very thankful to you for your kindness to think about the Tommies. My best pal, when I was in France, was a man called Dinwiddie. He was a policemen but belonged to a different company than I did. His home was in Somerset and I was wondering whether you would know him or not. He was in the same bayonet charge as I was in and I should like to know how he got on or whether he is living or not. He was a nice chap. Excuse the scribble as I am writing this with my left hand as I got wounded in my back and right arm at Neuve Chappelle. But I am getting on very nicely and knocking about a bit. My Home is in Lancashire so I will conclude. Wishing you the best of luck I remain

Yours sincerely,

J Regan

* * * * *

Sir,

May I be allowed through your columns to urge for the sparing use of new potatoes in this time of stress? They are a very wasteful luxury. There is, of course, no possible objection to the digging of early sorts on reaching maturity.

Very faithfully,

T J C Gardner
Radstock Rectory

Somerset Guardian
9th July, 1915

The County revenues collected during the March quarter showed a decline of about £800, this being mainly due to the large number of male servants who have joined the Army.

A communication has been received from the War Office by recruiting authorities instructing them to invite men who have been refused by reason of weak eyesight, defective teeth or slight physical defects to submit themselves again for medical examination. In future no man who is organically fit is to be refused.

Nessie Down
Schoolgirl

I was 14 when that was taken, with the feather in my hand, dressed as Peace. We had this carnival on August Monday. Well, you had to keep your spirits up, didn't you? All of us there worked at the Standard Works and there were p'rhaps a dozen other groups and floats. It was quite a big procession - went all up round Norton. One lady turned up dressed as a soldier and they wouldn't let her go out till she'd cut all the buttons off. She wasn't allowed to impersonate a soldier, you see, that was illegal. We were almost all women and girls there. Most of the menfolk were gone - away - in India. Dad was. He was with the Territorials before the war and was sent out there for the duration.

Pte. Arnold Langley
7th Battalion, The Somerset Light Infantry
(Machine Gun Section)

Somewhere in France

(For my Comrades in Peasedown)

Oft in my dug-out I think of poor chaps left at home
And the miseries that surround them no matter where they roam
How awful it must be at night to sleep on feather bed
And find for breakfast daily there is butter on their bread.

Out here the things are different, and life is great and free;
But we don't have butter on our bread, sugar or cow's milk in our tea.
The only thing that worries us are lyddite bombs and shells;
But bully beef and biscuits make us feel fit and well.

To all my pals at Peasedown I send my sympathy
And advise them for their safety to come out here with me.
There are young men in Somerset who can do 'their bit' I'm sure
So let them join the MGC, who are invaluable in this war.

* * * * *

Trench Diary
3rd Battalion, The Coldstream Guards
8th October, 1915

The enemy had obtained a footing in the trench (Big Willy) on my left, held by the 3rd Battalion, Grenadier Guards. The enemy were pouring into the trench near G4 V60 and bombing towards my left. A terrific effort then had to be made. 6738 L/Sgt O Brooks with six men and followed by 7895 Cpl E Barnett and his section, started from my left and tackled the enemy and bombed them back foot by foot along Big Willy until they cleared the whole trench up to Point 60, when the Germans retreated.

Somerset Guardian
8th October, 1915

Three sons of Mr Henry Foster have responded to their country's call and joined the army. Private Cecil Foster joined the Coldstream Guards on August 28, 1914 and went out to France on December 8th, last and was taken Prisoner of War by the Germans at La Bassee on January 25, 1915. Before joining the army he was in the service of the Marquis of Bath. The only one of the three brothers still taking part in the war is Sapper Reginald Foster, 175th Company, Royal Engineers, who is well known in Radstock. Rifleman Leonard Foster has fallen and lies buried on the battlefield.

> S/9304 Rifleman L H Foster
> 7th Battalion The Rifle Brigade
> Killed in Action
> France and Flanders
> 20th September, 1915
> Aged 17

* * * * *

Lieut. Rex Lewin of the Sussex Regiment, one of four sons of Mr C J Lewin, Headmaster of the Church of England School, Radstock, has been officially notified as having been wounded. The official notification was received by his father on Wednesday last week but a letter written to him by a friend was returned to him saying that Lieut. Rex Lewin was missing. On Wednesday evening Mr Lewin received a further official notification stating that Lieut. R Lewin previously reported wounded is now reported wounded and missing.

* * * * *

School Logbook
Radstock Church School
14th October, 1915

On Tuesday a War Office telegram informed me that Lieut. R R Lewin had been killed in action. He was one of our old boys, with a most promising career ahead of him.

A boy named Gardiner was admitted on Monday.

Charles Lewin

Headmaster

Somerset Guardian

15th October, 1915

On Tuesday morning Mr C J Lewin received the following telegram: 'Deeply regret to inform you that Lieut. R R Lewin, 2nd Royal Sussex Regiment, is now reported killed; body found by 2nd Coldstreams, and identified from effects. Lord Kitchener expresses his sympathy. Secretary War Office.' This marks the end of a career of the greatest promise. From his father's school Rex Lewin went to Sexey's School, Bruton, where he gained first a Secondary School Scholarship, and afterwards the Senior County Agricultural Scholarship. He then proceeded to University College, Reading, passed in record time the London Matriculation and Inter-Science Examinations, and gained the College Diploma as well as the Degree of BSc. (Agriculture) at London University. Though only 19 years of age he was at once offered a post on the Reading University College staff, which he accepted and became Lecturer on Agricultural Botany. During his career as a student at Reading he became a member of the College OTC., and gained the A and B Military Certificates. He entered the Special Reserve of Officers, was gazetted as second lieutenant in the Royal Sussex Regiment, and joined up as soon as war was declared. He saw service in the trenches last winter, but was invalided home, suffering from exposure. Some months ago he went out again, became first lieutenant, and was called upon to fill the honourable and dangerous position of Bombing Officer to his battalion. He fell during the advance on September 25-26.

Lieut. Lewin was a keen sportsman, a first-rate shot, rowed stroke in the College Eight, was President of Wantage Hall for a year, and Vice-President of the College Debating Society. Lieut. R R Lewin is the first officer from Radstock to lay down his life in the defence of the honour of his country in this great war.

Lieut. Rex Richard Lewin
2nd Royal Sussex Regiment
Killed in Action
France and Flanders
25th September, 1915
Aged 21

Minutes of the Meeting of the Managers
of Midsomer Norton Church of England Schools
21st October, 1915

BILLETING TROOPS

After considerable correspondence, a payment of £20 had been received from the War Department as rent, being 16 weeks at 25/- a week. A copy of the Secretary's claim for dilapidation against the War Office was presented and approved.

* * * * *

Somerset Guardian
22nd October, 1915

Miss Pollard, of Island House, Midsomer Norton, has recently undertaken to forward once a month, parcels of food and clothing to Midsomer Norton men who are Prisoners of War in Germany, and has made arrangements with the British Legation at Berne, in Switzerland, to supply each of the men with a quantity of bread every week. The cost of the latter is 4s 6d a month for each man supplied, and to enable her to continue her good work during the winter, and perhaps extend it to other prisoners of war, further financial help would be welcomed. The parcels have been received by the men to whom they have been addressed, and Miss Pollard has had letters or postcards thanking her and the subscribers to the fund from Sgt. E G Welch, of the Coldstream Guards, Private Oliver Veale, 1st Somerset Light Infantry, and Private George Vranch of the Coldstream Guards. All three received the parcel in good condition.

* * * * *

Mr and Mrs Henry Carpenter, of Church Street, Radstock, have three sons now serving King and Country. Two of them, **Sapper Henry Carpenter**, who is a married man residing at Wells Hill, Radstock, and **Sapper James Carpenter** who is a single man living at home, only recently joined the Army in response to an appeal from the Army authorities to Somerset miners to join the Royal Engineers for certain duties for which healthy, strong miners were especially suited. These two brothers, who worked at Braysdown Colliery, near Radstock, answered the call among others and left Radstock for Chatham on October 28th. The other of the three brothers, **Pte. Chris T Carpenter**, joined the Coldstream Guards on October 2nd, 1914.

Cliff Carpenter
Coal Miner

Yes, Jim and Harry made up their minds that they would go. (Harry's the one with the white tie on in the picture.) The Army was offering miners six shilling a day instead of one shilling that the ordinary soldier was getting and they went off to become Sappers - Royal Engineers - the poor devils who tunnelled under the German lines to lay the great mines. Jim and Harry and Bill Biddle and three others from Braysdown - Cooper, Button and Tom Rouse - left Radstock one day and were in France the next.

They'd only been digging for a few weeks when the pair of them were blown up. Jim got away without being damaged but Harry was terribly badly shell-shocked and brought home. He was one of the first patients in the new War Hospital in Bath. It was all wooden huts then, and he was in Number Two. I remember the day he came home. I waited down by The Waldegrave pub in Radstock for him to arrive home on the brake from Bath.

Oh, he was so shell-shocked. I got'n back along to my mother's house and Dr Scales came in to see him. The doctor had a hard hat on and Harry must've thought he was a German and set to and attacked him. Doctor reckoned he quite understood and told me to get Harry along to his own home, with his wife and kids. Well, we got him along there and into his bed with his wife and children in another room.

Then Dr Scales said to me, 'Look Carpenter, you're his brother and you're the one who'll have to stay with him tonight'. And I thought, 'Good God! What am I going to do with a mad man?' Well, what I done was to get a brush and jammed it up against his door to give me a chance if he did try to come down.

He got over it eventually but he was always quick tempered where he never had been before. And always aggressive and quick to take offence, where before he had been a gentle, friendly sort of chap. Oh, he was quite mad. And he went totally blind for a time, too. He never got a pension, mind.

Lance-Sergeant Oliver Brooks
3rd Battalion, The Coldstream Guards
27th October, 1915

Dear Brother,

*Just a few lines to say I received your letter quite safely.
I am in the pink and hope that you are also. I must say I
have won the VC and the King is to give it to me
tomorrow 'somewhere in France'. Let everyone know and
don't write again till you hear further from me. I'll write
a longer letter when I have calmed down.*

> *Your loving brother,*
>
> *Oliver*

Somerset Guardian
5th November, 1915

Lance-Sergt. Oliver Brooks Wins the VC - Well Known Midsomer Norton Man's Great Deed

The following announcement was issued by the War Office on Thursday week: The King has been pleased to award the Victoria Cross to No 6738 Lance Sergeant Oliver Brooks, 3 Battalion Coldstream Guards, for most conspicuous bravery near Loos on October 8.

A strong party of the enemy having captured 200 yards of our trenches, Lance-Sergeant Brooks on his own initiative led a party of bombers in the most determined manner and succeeded in gaining possession of the lost ground. The signal bravery displayed by the non-commissioned officer in the midst of a hail of bombs from the Germans was of the very first order and the complete success attained in a very dangerous undertaking was entirely due to his absolute fearlessness, presence of mind, and promptitude.

On Tuesday evening the Press Association published the following details referring to the declaration by His Majesty the King of Lance-Sergeant Oliver Brooks VC. After referring to a serious mishap which befell His Majesty as he was reviewing the troops on active service in France, and the preparations for the King's return to England, the official intimation says:

In the hospital train on the other side there was a very pathetic but stirring incident. His Majesty, though lying helpless in bed, pluckily determined to personally invest the soldier to whom the VC had been awarded for conspicuous gallantry. The soldier was Lance-Sergeant Oliver Brooks of the Coldstream Guards who won his decoration on October 8 last when a strong party of the enemy succeeded with the aid of bombs and grenades in effecting a lodgement in about 200 yards of our trenches.

Lance-Sergeant Brooks gallantly led a party of bombers to the attack under a constant and heavy fusillade and succeeded in regaining the lost ground. The complete success of the operation was very largely due to the Sergeant's coolness, and absolute fearlessness, for the danger of the operations was extreme.

The new VC was conducted to the hospital train and was taken to the side of the bed on which His Majesty was lying. As the King was lying prone and helpless, and yet was bent on personally affixing the decoration, the soldier knelt on the floor of the saloon and bent over the prostrate monarch. Even so His Majesty found that he had over-rated his strength and could not manage to get the pin through the thick khaki. Assistance had to be given before the operation could be completed . . .

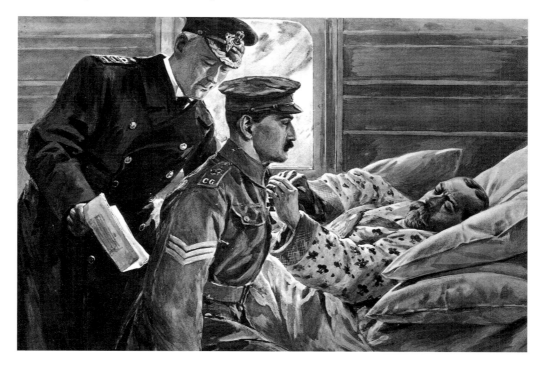

In the Illustrated London News there is a double page picture illustrating the King whilst lying in bed in a hospital train in the act of trying to pin the VC on Lance-Sergeant Oliver Brooks. In the picture is seen Sir Charles Cust who is holding an account of the act for which the VC was given. The picture is headed: *Decorating one of his illustrious Army whilst in bed in a hospital train. The King's fine action.*

An elder brother of the VC, Alfred James Brooks, served in the 1st Coldstream Guards throughout the Boer War and received the Queen's Medal with six engagement clasps and the King's Medal with two. Another brother, the youngest of the family, Pte. Stanley Brooks is in the RAMC and has been out in the Dardenelles.

Pte. Sammy Taylor
3rd Battalion, The Coldstream Guards

Ol' Oliver were for ever tellin' us he were going to win the VC - always told everyone he'd win one or die in the attempt. And he did. He were always very clever wie his hand grenades, mind. He used to dentonate them - put the dentonaters in them. You 'ad to be very careful with those things mind, 'cause once you pulled the pin out they did go off in seconds, you had to look sharp and get rid of 'em - anywhere. But he were good at that. Then, this particular day, he really did get the Victoria Cross. That were a great day for all the local lads in the regiment.

* * * * *

Sergeant Woodland
3rd Battalion, The Coldstream Guards

Dear Mother,

No doubt you have heard about our gallant VC hero, Sergt. Oliver Brooks of Midsomer Norton. Well last night in the village schoolroom and in sound of the guns we had a Sergeants' supper and concert to which all the officers were invited in honour of our comrade who has the honour to be the only VC hero to be decorated by the King's bedside. There were no prouder men at the concert than Sgt-Major Grey and Sergt. Purnell of Bath and myself to think that the first VC to come to the 3rd Battalion should be won by a Bath man, or near enough to be called one. The concert was a great a success and the song of the evening was, 'We all come up from Zummerset'.

* * * * *

Somerset Guardian
12th November, 1915

LANCE SERGEANT OLIVER BROOKS VC - Welcomed home to Midsomer Norton.

On Saturday evening, Lance-Sergeant Oliver Brooks VC, of the 3rd Batt. Coldstream Guards, arrived at his home at Midsomer Norton and was accorded a great reception. The gallant hero had been granted a special leave of 7 days and crossed over from France to London on Friday.

* * * * *

Stuart Brooks
Schoolboy

The army people had told Uncle Oliver to keep his decoration covered up while he walked through Bath to the Somerset and Dorset train. They were worried that he might attract too much attention and get mobbed. In a nice way, of course. I had something to do in Radstock that day,

84

and when the train came in I was over by the market. Well, I raced across to the station and down the platform. And then I could see him in a compartment showing his VC to Mr Simpkins, the surveyor from the mines. He had his hand underneath it, holding it out so's he could see better. As soon as Oliver saw me he pushed the window down and said, 'Where's Dad and Uncle Alf?' 'Oh,' I said, 'They're up at Norton Hill waiting for you. There's a great reception. You'll be all right when you get up there.' He said, 'I'm glad I met you". And then he had to put the window up 'cause the train started moving.

* * * * *

Brian Thatcher
Schoolboy

It was a day I'll always remember. I was coming home from school for the weekend and it was purely by chance that Oliver Brooks got into my compartment on the train from Bath. There were others there and during the journey he told us something about the happenings. At every station there were greetings and people peering through the window. At Midford, at Wellow and at Radstock. Finally the arrival in triumph at Norton. A show had been laid on by the village - as we called it in those days - but my mother wouldn't let me partake. 'Much too young' she said. I was furious. But it was, and still is, one of the red-letter days of my life.

* * * * *

Somerset Guardian
12th November

Long before the time of arrival of the train the approaches to the station were packed by a dense crowd. As Lance-Sergeant Brooks walked into the waiting room he unbuttoned his greatcoat and displayed the much coveted distinction. He was very warmly welcomed and on leaving the waiting room and appearing in full view of the crowd he was received with tremendous cheering. The gallant Sergeant was at once chaired and carried shoulder high in procession to the Town Hall square. The Midsomer Norton Town Brass Band headed the procession and played '*See the Conquering Hero Comes*'. The streets of the town were decorated with flags and bunting, the bells of the parish church pealed out a quarter peal of grandsire triples under the guidance of Mr E Chivers and detonators were discharged upon the railway . . .

On arrival at the Town Hall square the hero had another reception when he mounted the platform accompanied by several of the members of the Urban Council and some of the principle residents of the Parish. Mr G E Delve, on behalf of the Urban Council, and the residents of Midsomer Norton, heartily welcomed Lance-Sergeant Brooks VC to his home.

Sergeant Brooks, in replying to the welcome was received with cheers. He said, 'I am afraid I am too excited tonight to find words to adequately thank you for the hearty welcome you have given me on winning the VC. I should like to say to the young men of Midsomer Norton

85

that I hope they will follow in my footsteps and try to bring similar honour to the town. You will be glad to know that my six bombers have each received the DCM. (Cheers) The Germans tried to drive us out of the trench but we saved the position. I said, 'It's up to us to drive them out. Will you follow me?' They said, 'Yes Sergeant. We will follow you wherever you go.' I said, 'Men. Remember we are Englishmen. We have a great task in front of us and we have to stick to it.' And we did. (Cheers) I took my men into action and we came out all right and won the victory. (Cheers) After the meeting the VC was chaired again and the band played him home to his home in Radstock Road.

* * * * *

Pte. Stan Small
10th Battalion, The Devonshire Regiment
November, 1915

After we'd been in France a day or so they took us to a place outside Amiens called Pissy - well that's what we called it, anyway. And, my goodness, didn't it rain! It didn't bother me because by that time I belonged to the regimental transport and could get screwed down underneath a waterproof sheet, but the other poor devils had no cover. It really bolted down and they had to stay out in the wet mud.

Then off we went to the battle front - into the front line at Cappy, where the Black Watch was. Not to take over, just to get the experience. From there we were just going to join the 1st Battalion in the trenches when they sent us down to Marseilles where we spent three weeks on their race-course it was a beautiful place. Another race-course! Those places seemed to agree with me!

Then, all at once we had to harness up and go down to the docks to go on boats. Most of the Battalion went on the *Hannibal* and the *Ivernia,* but I was with the Lewis guns and the transport on the *Menomony*.

I asked where we were going but the chap I stopped didn't know. But he reckoned the last lot they'd taken out had gone to the Dardenelles. To Gallipoli! Oh, I hoped we weren't going there 'cause that was like certain death. The Australians and the New Zealanders were there and they reckoned the Dardenelles were running red with blood. That was terrible.

I can never understand men coming from Australia and New Zealand and going to an unholy place like that to be murdered. Can you? Why? Why did they land at Suvla Bay? The Turks held all the high ground and those poor men were massacred. Why did those beautiful men go there to lose their lives in a barren place like that? I can't understand it,

Now I'm retired and my family aren't here I sit and think about it. And the Western Front. Men getting up and going over the top at five in the morning. Men hung up on barbed wire. Lose perhaps 1,000 men to the Germans with their machine guns hidden in their concrete posts. Bubububububububub! Men falling like corn before the reaper. I can't understand it. Can you? Having to do it because some general says so? Your life's your own, nobody else's. But the awful thing is that that war was the most exciting thing that ever happened to us.

Anyway, a couple of days after we got on the boat this sailor spotted me and said that we were not on course for the Dardenelles. We were going to Salonika.

* * * * *

Lt. Geoffrey Bishop
1st/4th Battalion, The Somerset Light Infantry
May - December, 1915

I was on detachment at Amritsar when we had a call for volunteers to go to re-inforce the 2nd Battalion of the Dorsets in Mespot. They already had a draft of one officer and 29 men undergoing a month's special training in Jullunder but they had an outbreak of scarlet fever there and they couldn't go, so all the draft came from Amritsar. The Second in Command asked if I would like to go. The next day I got a signal saying that I *was* going.

We left about the second week in May and I took a draft of 30 men, including myself and, as I've already said, Private Eyres. The second draft of 15 arrived about the end of August. The official history says it was a total of 75, which is entirely wrong. Thirty and 15, according to my arithmetic, makes 45. The history books are wrong.

We got there in early June, just before a battle that was called Townshend's Regatta. This was a largely waterborne affair in which General Townshend with a few officers and 100-odd soldiers and sailors captured the town of Al Amarah and a crack Turkish regiment - 'The Constantinople Fire Brigade' - as well as hundreds and hundreds of other Turkish prisoners. Townshend's ultimate target was Baghdad and in September we captured Kut-al-Amarah for the first time in awful physical conditions. The temperature was well over 100 in the shade and the men had no water. They were totally dehydrated and exhausted. But we took Kut.

On November 22nd we again went into battle. This time it was the Battle of Ctesiphon, an indecisive to-do. It was a strange battle which was very nearly won, but in fact we didn't owing to lack of any reserves at all. The battle was a very bloody affair with 4,500 British and Indian casualties, and not unnaturally they were largely infantry. I had six chaps in my platoon killed in about five minutes and more were killed later. There was no-one else to put in and when the Turks came back at us we retreated to Kut, a tremendously arduous march of about 120 miles, which, broadly speaking we did in about three days.

The Turks caught up with us about half way back to Kut and were given a bloody nose. After that affair we hardly stopped. The Turks came closer and closer to us but we got back to Kut on December 5th and they arrived a day or so later. The siege had begun.

* * * * *

Somerset Guardian
10th December, 1915

Mr Alexander Mattick, son of Mr Robert Mattick, Frome Hill, Radstock, has secured a commission in the Royal Army Medical Corps and left Radstock on Thursday to take up his duties. His special knowledge of Chemistry fitted him as very useful for this branch of the service.

Sapper Reginald Foster, Royal Engineers, of Radstock arrived home from the front on Saturday for seven days leave having been at the seat of war for several months. He doubtless holds the local record for being on active service soon after enlisting. Within four days of joining the Royal Engineers he was in France and under shell-fire. He was one of four brothers serving when he joined, but one of his brothers was killed and buried not half a mile from where he was on duty, and he was not aware of the sad event until afterwards.

Information has been received by his friends in Radstock, stating that Corporal C T Carpenter, of the 1st Battalion Coldstream Guards, has been wounded in the arm and leg with shrapnel. His injury, however, is not serious.

Another local man, Gunner William J Lewis, of the 25th Battery, RFA, of Chilcompton came home on Friday for a few days leave. He had been in France ever since the war started and he has two brothers serving. The pleasure of returning home after a long period of very trying work was minimised by the fact that within a fortnight of his arrival his wife had buried their two youngest children, one of whom - a little boy - was born soon after he was called up for active service.

Reg Jones
Carting Boy

Everyone. Everyone knew **Charlie Fry**. You can't never forget a bloke like him - he's someone you do keep in your memory. No-one ever had a bad word to say about'n. He were a character - he were different. Mind you, the whole family were different - Lemuel, Wilhelmina, Arthurina, and Classy Constance were all different - but Charlie were special. T'were a shame that he ever had to go to war, really. It changed him completely. He were the smartest fellow you ever saw when he dressed up on Norton Fair day. He always stood straight as a ram-rod - like a soldier - even before he went, even as a young kiddie. But he was never the same after he come back from the war. He were changed. He were never the Charlie what had gone.

Brother Lemuel had the Smithy in Church Square an' Charlie looked out to the run-down little farm they had at Coombers Grave. We used to go up there pinching his apples - everybody did. He used to cuss we, and oh! he really knew how to cuss. He were a world champion cusser. Oh yes, he could really swear. He was always known for havin' a good swearing vocabulary. Anyway, he always knew we were having his apples. 'I shall catch 'ee, Jonesy, I shall catch 'ee.' But he never did - he wasn't really bothered, anyway.

When t'were haymaking time you could always hear Charlie - you didn't need to know where he was, you could always hear him. He'd yell fer kids to come and help him an' they'd go up an' do it fer nothing, and as one lot got wise to him another lot'd take over the work. Oh, he did shout; my God, he had some lungs. You could hear'n a mile off - cussin' flames a flashin'.

Charlie didn't pick and choose his friends. Didn't matter if you were high or low, he'd pass the time with

everyone just the same. When I were a kid the vicar were Vicar Newlyn - did wear a half top hat and ride a horse - he were pally with Charlie and they'd always pass the time together. An' there were'dn't a policeman he didn't know. He were always in trouble for one little thing or another but never serious - though he did go inside fer waterin' his milk once. But everyone knew Charlie and everyone respected him.

Ivan Chard
Timber Worker

Uncle Charles had to go. Be conscripted I mean. I can mind that as if t'were today. Charlie said to his brother, 'All right, Lem. One of us got to go. You stay at home and look out to the business and I'll go'. Both of them were on useful work, Lem was shoeing artillery horses and Charlie and me were hauling coke and timber to keep the pits going. But that weren't as important as what Lemuel were doing.

* * * * *

Classie Constance Fry
December, 1915

When Charles went to war he did it for my younger brother. They were both as intelligent as their brains would allow them to be but Charles thought that his younger brother had more brain than he did to manage the family's affairs. So he went up for his examination and said to Dr Pollard, 'Please don't take us both, take me. Lem can manage the farm and the smithy and look after Mother and Father better than I can. Please take me'.

* * * * *

Ivan Chard

So anyway, down he went to Dr Pollard an' sez, 'I've got these orders come, an' you've got to examine me or summit'. 'You're the class of man they do want out there,' sez Pollard. 'Yes,' sez Charlie. 'But you won't be one of the bloody ones that d'go, will yer? Why don' you go yerself, you bugger?' He were full blunt and hearty mind. He didn' care how he did slip it out. Anyway, he were passed as fit. Then he had to wait to find out whad'd happen next. I can mind that as if t'were today.

* * * * *

Annie Cleeves

No, Dr Pollard was not like that, he was a kind man. Poor Georgie, my brother, had to go. He was a tiny little thing, no bigger than me, but he had to go to be examined and all the rest of it. Mother was so upset. She had me and my older brother Charlie, who was already in the Field Artillery, but for her there was only one child, and that was George. She did everything she could to stop him from going but he was called up and he went and saw Dr Pollard. Before they went in my father said, 'Take your teeth out, my son. Let's have them'. So he took them out and that made him look worse than ever. When they took him in the doctor looked this little eighteen year old boy up and down and then took him by the forelock and said, 'Come with me'. Then he led him away by his fringe to some other doctors and said, 'I don't think we need *this*, do we?' He wasn't even examined! But when my husband ran away to enlist, Dr Pollard didn't give him away even though he was under age. He went in The Devonshires - says they were the 'Ever Faithful', but I should question that!

* * * * *

Catherine Pollard

Dad always really wanted to be a soldier. Of course he loved his doctoring, but that was never his first love. He joined the Artists Rifles when he was 17, but in the old days his father, who was a Cambridge Don, said to him, 'George, I've got three sons. You must be a doctor, a parson or a lawyer. You're the oldest, which do you want?' And my father thought and said, 'Well - doctor'. 'Very good, then you will be a doctor.' And so in 1883 George Samuel Pollard became assistant to Alexander Waugh - Evelyn's grandfather - in Midsomer Norton. He was 55 when the war started and they simply would not take him. He was heart-broken and did everything he could to go to India with his beloved 4th Battalion, but he was simply too old. But he wore his uniform just the same. There's absolutely no question about it - he'd have jolly well gone if he could.

1916

𝔖𝔬𝔪𝔢𝔯𝔰𝔢𝔱 𝔊𝔲𝔞𝔯𝔡𝔦𝔞𝔫
28th January, 1916

DEATH OF MRS LEWIN

We much regret to record the death of Mrs Sarah
Lewin, wife of Mr C J Lewin, which took place at the
Church School House on Saturday morning, the 22nd
inst. Mrs Lewin had been in failing health for some
considerable time, being subject to a heart weakness
and had not left her room since Christmas Day. The
loss of her gallant son Captain Rex Lewin of the
Royal Sussex Regiment who was killed in action on
September 25 last on the Western battlefield was a
severe blow to Mrs Lewin in view of her marred
health. At the time of her death two other sons were
at the front taking their turn with their regiments in
the trenches viz: **CSM Cecil Lewin** of the King's
Liverpool Regiment and **Lieut. Kenneth Lewin** of
the 7th Duke of Cornwall's LI. The remaining sons
are Master **Claude Lewin**, of the Inns of Court
Officer Training Corps and Master **Roy Lewin** who
is a pupil at Sexey's School, Bruton.

Elsie Hilliar
County Champion Cheese Maker
January, 1916

That's Dad - who was a builder and farmer - paying the workmen one Saturday morning just before the war. We had 50 men working for us then - but the war really knocked the stuffing out of the business. Several of the men were in the 1st/4th Somersets and, of course, they went off to India as soon as war broke out. My brother Will went with them - and died out there. Within two or three weeks a whole lot more joined Kitchener's Army.

After a couple of years of war it slowly dawned on the Government that our chaps were being killed faster than they were volunteering, so Lord Derby drew up this scheme for getting more men - either to go to France or to work in the factories at home. His plan was to persuade men to volunteer on the understanding that they would only be called on if it became absolutely essential.

They were all put into groups according to their personal circumstances and were quite clearly told that single men would be called up before the married ones. Even that didn't do the trick, though, and at the beginning of 1916 they started compulsory conscription. Men who were called up were able to appeal at tribunals if they felt they had a good enough reason not to go. Thousands upon thousand of them appealed - but very few were successful.

It certainly put the kibosh on our business, what with one thing and another, and it wasn't long before poor Dad was down to three men working for him.

𝔖𝔬𝔪𝔢𝔯𝔰𝔢𝔱 𝔊𝔲𝔞𝔯𝔡𝔦𝔞𝔫

11th February, 1916

CALLING UP OF SINGLE MEN UNDER THE COMPULSION ACT

The following notice applies to the Continental system of 'classes' to single men who have no excuse and are now under the Compulsion Act. Each class consists of the men born in one year, and corresponds to the Derby groups of men of one age. But 'group' is to be kept for those who enlist voluntarily and 'class' for those who are taken.

WAR OFFICE, Sunday, 5pm

With regard to the Military Service Act it should be realised that the groups for single men under the Derby Scheme will close on March 1, 1916, as after that date men liable for service are brought automatically into the Army Reserve by the operation of the Act.

Men coming under the Act will be classified according to age into 'classes' as the men attested were into 'groups' and will be called up corresponding with the groups that have been called up. The reason for calling them 'classes' is simply for administrative purposes to avoid confusion.

They are as follows:

Year of Birth	Class	Year of Birth	Class
1897	1	1885	13
1896	2	1884	14
1895	3	1883	15
1894	4	1882	16
1893	5	1881	17
1892	6	1880	18
1891	7	1879	19
1890	8	1878	20
1889	9	1877	21
1888	10	1876	22
1887	11	1875	23
1886	12		

The 12 classes on the left hand side, those aged from 19 to 30, corresponding to the Derby 'groups' already called up, will thus be called from March 3rd, whether in one lot or in four classes at a time is not yet clear.

Herbert Caines
Railwayman

You were a sort of compulsory volunteer. Everybody had to sign on and then be sorted out into groups. People who didn't have special jobs had to go at first and others were put back on reserve - farm workers, railwaymen like me, and others. Kept on reserve until we were needed.

* * * * *

Reg Jones
Coal Miner

Every Friday there were scores and scores of Tribunal appeals in the Guardian, and I went an' saw a few of 'em fer meself. Some of them were awful. Pitiful. Some of the older men who weren't sent to the front were made to go down the mines with us. I can see 'em now. Caw, t'were terrible to see em down there. We had shopkeepers, insurance agents and all sorts come down, but they couldn't do what we did do. We were the carting boys, the cream of the country, and we were used to it. When we started underground we had to rub our own urine into our bodies to harden' em. And we *were* hard. But those blokes what come down from the top were pathetic. You'd never believe a man could be so out of his depth. Some even come down wearing white gloves. I can see them now, the poor sods.

* * * * *

Somerset Guardian
11th February, 1916

A number of single young men in this locality who came in Groups numbered 7, 8 and 9 left on Tuesday, Wednesday or Thursday morning this week to join the Army. From statements that have recently been made it is evident that many people have but a very vague impression as to the circumstances prevailing in the mining district. They seem to entirely overlook the fact that if miners attempt to enlist they are ordered back to their employment. Or even if they are called up under the group system they are, at present, not allowed to leave their employment.

Whether they have grouped or not it is evident we must see very large numbers of strong, well-built young men in the district for some time to come. How they should spare their time having completed their eight hours' shift in the pits each day, I am not prepared to suggest.

* * * * *

Lt. Arthur Coombs
1st/4th Battalion, The Somerset Light Infantry
February/March 1916

Our Company had been in Amritsar since late August - it was always a centre of sedition and a hot-bed of unrest and there had been riots there. We joined the rest of the Battalion here, in Peshawar, about six weeks later. Peshawar in the winter was a delightful spot. Those are the barracks in the picture. It was taken by a man called Lewis, from Bath, who was up on the roof of one of the blocks. That's me at the tip of the Colonel's shadow and our Company is at the back. By that time we'd become a double company, commanded by the Honourable Edward Strachey.

Strachey was a great man - been in the Grenadier Guards. An absolutely delightful man. All the troops loved him. We always thought ours was the best Company 'cause we had him there and he knew what soldiering was. I always remember how he taught us to drill our men properly. There were deep drains - three or four feet deep - all around the parade ground and he'd have us out chatting about our platoon when the men were marching and suddenly he'd say, 'Take command of the Company'. He taught us to think - and quickly!

Geoffrey Bishop is not in this picture, of course. He and his men had left Amritsar for Mesopotamia several months earlier. They could very well have been fighting at Ctesiphon when this was taken, before their incarceration in Kut-el-Amarah. They were beseiged there for three months from early December - in quite appalling conditions - despite two abortive attempts to get them out.

In February, 1916, we sailed up the Tigris from Karachi to Mesopotamia in an attempt to get them out. We were just under 800 strong and our Company went with B Company on Puffing Billy, the steamer in the other picture I've given you. There were two of them with huge barges attached to either side. We disembarked at a place called Sheik Sa'ad and set up a camp at Orah where we stayed for a day or so before setting off.

On March 7th we left Orah on a remarkable night march of about twenty miles. We must have been the leading company because I was beside Captain Strachey - who had the compass - when he was being told that he was going to guide us all out. The regulars who were with us didn't think much of the Territorials and they didn't know that Strachey had been in the Grenadiers. One of the Staff Officers said, 'I take it that you do know how to read a compass?' Pompous ass. Strachey passed it to him. 'You set it.' But he knew perfectly well how to do it.

The march was quite a remarkable achievement - an absolutely astonishing achievement - 20,000 of us, moving over unknown territory counting the turns of bicycle wheels to work out our distances. But it was completely successful, and when we arrived next morning we found ourselves in front of our objective, the Dujailah Redoubt. Ours wasn't the first attempt to relieve Kut but this redoubt hadn't been attacked before. Actually there were very few Turks in the trenches because for the previous few days our people had been moving English troops about on the other side of the river to make the Turks think the assault would take place there.

We had been told the brigade we were with was not to attack but that we would give covering fire when the brigade to the left of us went forward. One didn't hear very much but from what I could gather the people on our left were either late or missed their way and didn't attack. I think we could have gone into the redoubt with little trouble or opposition but presumably the place was mined so we'd have been blown up in any case.

In the afternoon we had orders to move and about four o'clock we attacked, but by that time the Turks had got wind of us and were there in considerable numbers and able to drive us back. As we moved forward we found them just sitting there - waiting, and then they opened up with their rifle fire and shells. They killed three of my own platoon pretty instantly. Woods was one, he was a Midsomer Norton cricketer. Then young Bailey, another Norton man, and Seymour who was a porter on the Great Western Railway station at Radstock. I know there were at least a couple more Norton men who died.

Well, the long and the short of it was that our efforts to get into Kut failed and Townshend's - and Geoffrey Bishop's - awful sojourn continued.

Cpl Arthur Purnell   L/Cpl Thomas Bailey   Pte.T H Seymour   Pte. Frank Woods

1st/4th Somerset Light Infantry
Killed in action on 8th March,1916 at Kut-al-Amarah

* * * * *

The History of The Somerset Light Infantry - 1914-1918
Edward Wyrall
8th March, 1916

A and B Companies of the Somersets were ordered to retire and it was during this retirement, carried out slowly and with great steadiness, that the Battalion sustained severe casualties. Captain E Lewis had already fallen as he was gallantly leading his men to the attack. A little later 2/Lieut. Lillington was also killed. (Capt. Baker had fallen earlier.) In other ranks the Battalion lost, during the day's fighting, 9 killed, 50 wounded and 4 missing. When darkness had set in the whole force was withdrawn a considerable distance from the Dujailah Redoubt to the sand-hills. The following day, after it had been ascertained that it was impossible for the force to maintain its positions, owing principally to lack of water, a further withdrawal was ordered to Orah. The 1st/4th Somersets formed part of the rear-guard, the general retirement beginning in the early afternoon. Thus ended the Second Attempt to relieve Kut - a gallant though unsuccessful effort.

* * * * *

Lt. Geoffrey Bishop
1st/4th Battalion, The Somerset Light Infantry
9th March, 1916

The day after the Somersets' attempt to relieve Kut - which Arthur has told you about - the Turks sent in a flag of truce and I was told to go out and meet this chap. I suppose I was sent because I was last at school and probably spoke French better than anyone else. The fellow was riding with an orderly and had a letter from Khalil Pasha, who was the Turkish C in C. I also had an orderly and sent him in with the message and told the Turkish chap to return the next day, but he insisted on waiting. Our lines were then anything from 500 to 600 yards apart and I was out there in the middle, with him, for a couple of hours. Nice chap - a Captain. He was Kahlil's ADC or one of his junior staff officers. We spoke in French and he gave me a packet of cigarettes which I hadn't had for some time. We talked about the war and the Germans - and he didn't go a lot on the Germans. He said his uncle had a villa on the Bosphorus and he'd like me to go and stay there after the war - that sort of thing. They were good soldiers, good fighters. Not unpleasant really.

We had quite an interesting conversation with the result that the following day, when I'd finished my report, I was seen by my Brigadier and sent in to Townshend to tell him about it. That's his house in the picture, incidentally. I spent about an hour with him, but that was the only time I saw him. Then he sent this chap a message telling him to stuff it. However, rations were steadily being reduced and during the last few weeks we were each down to a quarter pound of bread and some horse-meat. We got relatively more and more hungry as time went on, until we were permanently hungry. Men were getting a lot of dysentery and that unpleasant deficiency disease called beri-beri.

The white flag went up on 29th April - about mid-day, I suppose it was. We went off late the following day and then the officers were taken off to Baghdad, away from the men. I was then a prisoner for the next two and a half years. Of a strength of 15,000 men, 1,800 were killed or died of disease and 1,900 were wounded. Of the 45 men I'd had with me, only four - of whom I was one - survived. I know you'll be pleased to learn that Laurence Eyres also made it. But the rest were all killed in action or died as PoWs.

* * * * *

LOCAL APPEALS TRIBUNAL
10th March, 1916

Charles James Fry, 31 years of age, of Church Square, Midsomer Norton, appealed for exemption as a farmer. The Chairman: You might have put in two or three other occupations. Appellant: I am the conductor. I have two boys and two girls under me and without someone to tell them what to do things would go all wrong. He added that he farmed 90 acres of land and it was good land. He had 30 head of cattle, milked 17 cows and had 10 horses. The Chairman granted a temporary exemption and informed the appellant that he must see what arrangements he could make for carrying on the farm should he have to go.

Somerset Guardian

17th March, 1916

On Monday morning, Mr C J Lewin received a telegram from the War Office informing him that his second son, Lieut. Kenneth P L Lewin, 7th DCLI, had been killed in action on March 9. The deceased officer had had a distinguished career, and his future was full of the highest promise. He was born at Radstock, September 16th, 1889. From his father's school he gained a Junior County Scholarship, and proceeded to Sexey's School, Bruton. Here he won an Intermediate and afterwards a Senior County Scholarship. This, with the Open Science Exhibition which he gained at Trinity College, Cambridge, enabled him to enter the University. In 1908 he gained a First Class in the Natural Science Tripos, Part 1, and the next year became a Major Scholar of his College.

Kenneth Lewin was granted the Peter Leigh Exhibition, and a year later divided the Coutte-Trotter Studentship with the last of the Senior Wranglers. With the aid of a grant from the Balfour Fund he worked on Infusoria (micro-biological research) at Munich under Professor Hertwig. In 1911 he occupied a table at the Naples Biological Station. Several brilliant pieces of biological research were carried out by him, and he published some original papers, read before the Royal Society. After acting as assistant to the Quick Professor of Biology at Cambridge for some time, he was appointed Pronto-Zoologist at Rothamstead, which appointment he held until the outbreak of the war.

Lieut. Lewin joined the colours at the first call, gaining his commission as second lieutenant soon after. Quite recently he was recommended for promotion to first lieutenant. His brother, Captain R R Lewin was killed on September 25 last. Lieut. Lewin was present in Radstock at the funeral of his mother less than two months ago.

Lieut. Kenneth Lewin

7th Duke of Cornwall's Light Infantry

Killed in Action

France and Flanders

9th March, 1916

𝕾𝔬𝔪𝔢𝔯𝔰𝔢𝔱 𝔊𝔲𝔞𝔯𝔡𝔦𝔞𝔫

17th March, 1916

MEETING OF ATTESTED MARRIED MEN

Practically every affected married man attended a meeting held at Midsomer Norton when Mr F Biggs presided. The Chairman, in his remarks referred to the calling up of the married groups so soon, and said it had come as a great shock and surprise to all, and in his opinion was unwarranted and certainly unjustifiable. The Derby Scheme had been nothing more than trickery and deception from beginning to end.

When they attested they were shown literature, which stated that all single men were to go before married, and then the married men, in order of age from 19 to 40, and those who did not respond would be dealt with first. Those facts were urged upon them very forcibly by the canvassers . . . The Government had found loopholes for hundreds of thousands of single shirkers to slip through by the large lists of reserved occupations, into which these cowards had gone to escape serving their King and Country.

The Government had also given the conscientious objector his opportunity to escape, and thousands had suddenly developed consciences. Was it fair or just that they should be called upon to break up their homes and leave their wives and families, while all those single shirkers were left behind, who would no doubt be earning more wages in consequence of their going and be living on the fat of the land? Was it fair that they should have to fight for such cowards and humbugs? They should like it to be thoroughly understood that the attested married men of Midsomer Norton did not for one moment wish to shirk their responsibilities but were willing to do their duty to their country, but they thought that the pledges given to them should be carried out, and that all men, married and single, should be called upon to do their share equally, one man with another, without fear or favour.

The following resolution was passed and was signed by 54 men and copies were sent to Mr Asquith, Lord Derby, and Mr J King, MP: We the undersigned married men of Midsomer Norton, who have attested under Groups 24 to 46, strongly protest against the calling up of married groups until the pledges given by Mr Asquith and Lord Derby to the married men have been fulfilled by calling up all single men first. The large list of certified occupations has afforded an asylum for many thousands who have entered these occupations for the purpose of evading their responsibilities. We join in the universal opinion that most of the single men thus excused would be better employed at this great crisis in serving their country at the front rather than in their present occupation which could be filled by women or older men.

We further strongly protest against the calling up of married men before compulsory service has been introduced for all unattested men of military age. Our attestation was obtained by statements in recruiting literature and on the advice given by canvassers that attested men would be given many definite advantages over those who did not attest, whereas the advantage at present rests with the unattested, who jeeringly tell us that we were very foolish to have attested. Under these circumstances we earnestly appeal to you to suspend the mobilization of married men for a period and to issue a plain statement in the meantime.

* * * * *

Somerset Guardian
24th March, 1916

COMPULSORY SERVICE

Hundreds of letters are being received by the War Office from Attested men, urging the adoption of general compulsory service. There is a disposition in War Office circles in favour of the proposal and, while it is recognised that Labour may oppose it, the general belief is entertained that the country generally would receive a further compulsory scheme without much opposition.

* * * * *

LOCAL APPEALS TRIBUNAL
25th March, 1916

The first case taken was that of **Reginald Maggs**, aged 22, married, of Chapel House, High Littleton, bread deliverer, who was appealed for by Radstock Co-operative Society. Mr Gent stated that Maggs had been with the Society some 18 months.

Mr Gibson: I take it you are making every endeavour to get men over military age for work?

Mr Gent: Yes, we are. We have advertised in six or seven papers.

The Chairman: Would it not be possible for women to do this class of work? If you could get a woman to drive a horse she could carry a loaf of bread.

Mr Gent: We haven't looked at it from that point of view.

Colonel Pollard: Couldn't people come to the shop for their bread? There should be no difficulty. This man goes some 12 or 14 miles with the bread.

Mr Gibson: I take it you serve a number of isolated houses?

Mr Gent: Yes, a good number. If you can get the people into the idea of fetching their bread from the shops we shall be pleased to give up delivering. You must remember we have a very big trade. We baked 182 sacks of flour into bread last week.

The Chairman: We have been living in a very luxurious age, and customers want everything delivered to their homes, even down to a few ounces of pepper sometimes. In town very small articles costing a few pence are often delivered.

The Tribunal granted two months exemption from date.

Elsie Hilliar
Munitions worker
March, 1916

I ran away. I just ran away to be a munitions worker. I was working on the farm in those days - in skirts, mind, girls never wore anything else. Then I said, 'I can't be doing with this anymore. I'd better find some britches or trousers or something and get down to some real work'. So, I had some of my brother's britches. A girl in trousers! There was a real song and dance about that in the village - it was shocking! It was even in the papers! It really was. I'm quite serious. Whatever next?

I worked hard all day long and one day I said I'd worked hard enough here. I'm going away to work in munitions. So I packed my trunk ready to go off to work in a factory in Coventry. First I went to say goodbye to my sister who at that time was working in the hospital and she said, 'I'm going with you'. So we left at eight in the morning, went to the Labour Exchange for a pass and then off up to White and Poppy's factory in Coventry.

I was 18 when we went, and 14 stone - yes I was - couldn't get a gown big enough for me! I was 14879 and my sister 14878 - Foremistresses. I've got three rings on there but she had four 'cause she was a year older than me, so, the senior foremistress. We were working on the AT fuses - I've still got one. Made it myself. Took it out in bits and pieces as I made them. Still got it upstairs.

When we got to Coventry the snow was as high as my knees and, cor, didn't we starve during that war. All's we had was bread with a scraping of whatever we could find. Mustard! And then they put us out of work when they brought Scottish girls down to the factory. Well, I wasn't having that so I arranged for us to move to Filton in Bristol. That's me with some of the trimmers there - me next to the sewing machine. Machines haven't changed much, have they? I know I have!

I worked on the first Bristol Bomber that went up. I was on the linen covering for the wings, and things like that. When the time came for it to fly it went straight up - beautifully - and then came straight down again and crashed straight into the ground. Something wrong with the engine maybe. Whatever it was, it had crashed, and we set to to get another one ready. When that went out they found that someone had slashed through the fabric of a wing. So we had to make another wing. Oh yes, that used to happen. Sabotage.

I used to cycle home for the weekends, clean the house, and then cycle back the 20 miles to my digs the other side of Bristol. I stayed at Filton for the rest of the war and when it was over - or the next day, anyway - I cycled home to the family business. It was my 21st birthday.

* * * * *

Cpl. Clifford Jeffery
West Somerset Yeomanry
1st April, 1916

We hung around the East Coast until September 1915, and then went abroad. We went up to Liverpool and embarked on the *Olympic* - the first time she was used as a troopship. A thousand of us on board and all Yeomanry units from Scotland right down to Land's End. Different units. We went out east, to Mudros, off Greece.

We were stuck on board there in the harbour for nearly a week and when we were finally taken off we were landed at Suvla Bay - we were the first reinforcements after the Suvla Bay landing. We got there in October and stayed until Christmas, when they evacuated Suvla. Suvla'd been a good idea but badly organised. They'd got on the bay with hardly a shot bein' fired. Then they'd stopped on the coast tryin' to find water but the Turks were on the gurt high hills in front of 'em. And they took a hell of a pasting.

When we got there all we had to do were dig trenches. Didn't dare show our heads above ground or they'd pick us off. Then they started evacuating us - they'd take out three fellers and put one back. Thass how they deceived the Turks. They didn' know nothin' about it till we were off - ha! Went back to Mudros and stopped there fer a few days. Had our Christmas dinner there, and then off to Alexandria. I stopped in Alexandria fer two months I suppose - in charge of a mule depot, little Canadian mules, snotty little buggers they were, no bigger than a donkey. An, caw, weren't they contrary devils, too. Bit like me I suppose.

When we had joined up we actually signed that they could keep us one year after war broke out. When that were up you were entitled to come out if you wanned to. Well, that were more than up, and I wanned to go home cause Father were home lettin' the farm go to ruin. So they paraded 30 on us, all time-expired. We all agreed that nobody were gonna sign up - we'd have a bit of fun with the officers. First one they came to were Sgt. Milton and, ha!, he never had the guts to say no, s'nuh. I was down in the middle of the line and when they got to me they said, 'Of course, Cpl. Jeffrey, you'll sign'. And I said, 'No Sur. I've got some duties to attend to at home. I've made up me mind. I'm goin' 'ome'. Huh, he didn' like it. 'You go home an' you'll be called up agen as a conscript.' An' I said, 'If I go home an' get called up I shan't be a conscript 'cause I've served my time an' I'm entitled to be discharged. An' if I do get called up I'll take damn good care I don't come back in the West Somerset Yeomanry!' Ha!

I come out on the fust of April. In the middle of May they brought out an Act of Parliament that all time-expired people should stay in the army. I were just in time.

* * * * *

Somerset Guardian

20th April, 1916

The first hospital train known to have passed through Midsomer Norton and Radstock travelled over the Somerset and Dorset Railway on Monday at about 2 o'clock on its way to Bath. The train was admirably fitted up.

Midsomer Norton Fair, which this year fell on Easter Tuesday, would have, under ordinary conditions, provided an attraction for many hundreds of people during the holiday, but the war and the limitation of the fair to one day by the Charter under which the fair is held, robbed the event of its importance this year. Messrs. Blinman and Miles had but few cattle to offer, and the number of horse dealers bent on business was greatly reduced. The pleasure fair has for years been one of the events of the season, but it will probably never resume its former glory when it was kept in full swing for two, three, and sometimes even four days. On Tuesday there were but a few stalls and one or two minor attractions. A large number of people turned up as usual, but found little or nothing to engage their attention.

* * * * *

Clifford Jeffery
Farmer (and former soldier)

Soon after I got 'ome from Alexandria the buggers tried to call me up again. There were a lot of tribunals an' medicals goin' on here at home. I'd go down an' there'd be three or four officials and army officers an' you had to state yer case. I was put down fer 'substitution', that-do-mean-to-say that if they took me, they'd replace me on me own farm - on my own farm! - with a bloke what waddn't fit fer the front line. Twice I had word that a bloke were actually comin' to substitute me but he never turned up. An' I never went to look fer 'im. I had 155 acres to do. I *had* tuh bide home to work, see? An' we *did* work in them days. Had Land Army girls from the camp come once - to help with the thrashin' - but they were bloody useless.

Poor devils. One girl came wi' a pair o' army boots on. They didn' even fit where they touched, an' before lunchtime her feet was like raw pieces o' beef. I sent 'er to the missus to get fitted wi' summing more suitable. They oughta 'a had more sense than send a girl out like it. She was only about 16. Some of 'em were city girls. They just couldn't cope.

Another time I 'ad orders tuh plough up ground fer corn. Twelve acres, I think. Then t'was another fifteen. Had tuh get rid o' me flock o' sheep 'cos I never 'ad nowhere for them to run. Then they told me to do another twelve, an' that were flood-land, under water half the year - an' I refused to comply. Two army officers and a civilian come up an wanned to look over the farm. In the end one of the officers said, 'Jeffery, I congratulate you on your farming'. About a fortnight later I had a note withdrawing the order. It wen' on fer some time like that an' then I 'ad another note, sayin' 'Total Exemption'. They reckoned I was worth more bein' at home than I was in the army.

* * * * *

LOCAL APPEALS TRIBUNAL
12th May, 1916

Charles James Fry, Midsomer Norton, Farmer, aged 31, single, stated that he had two girls aged about 15 and 17, and two boys under 15 working on the farm. He himself worked 16 or 17 hours a day. - Capt. Mawer urged that the appellant's father was the tenant of the farm, and that the appellant was also a haulier and carrier. Exemption was granted for three months for him to get his crops in.

Somerset Guardian
26th May, 1916

The inception of the new Summer Time Act which came into force last Sunday morning was carried out locally with an entire absence of friction or inconvenience. It was not till the evening that one really noticed that any change had been made, and that when people found that daylight lasted till 10 o'clock at night the full effect of the change was very noticeable and much appreciated.

One curious point arose in connection with the mail train which brings the first morning mail to Radstock and the district from Bath. This train is timed to leave Bath Midland Station at 2:50am, but last Sunday morning there was no 2:50am as at 2 o'clock the hands of the clock had been pushed forward to 3 o'clock. If the train was started at 3 o'clock the Post Office authorities would have been deprived of 40 minutes time in which to get the mails ready. The railway company therefore arranged for the train to leave on this particular morning at 3 o'clock 'or as soon as the mails had been loaded'. The mail was a few minutes late but no particular difficulty was experienced and after Sunday the train left at its proper time: 2:50am.

* * * * *

LOCAL APPEALS TRIBUNAL
29th May, 1916

Grist to the Mill

Mr B C Maloney, of the Town Mills, Radstock, appealed for Clifford Grist, aged 19, single, 4 Mill Cottages, Radstock, miller's carter and second miller. It was stated that the staff had been reduced from seven to two, besides Grist. Mr Maloney said that Grist had met with an accident, being run over by a wagon and was now recovering. His was the only mill in the district. Grist was the sole carter left. Exempted until November 7. The Chairman: Grist can now go back to the mill. (Laughter)

A Colliery Clerk

The Radstock Coal Co. applied in respect of F C Moon, aged 28, married, Clandown, colliery clerk. Mr Harvey, for the company, said it was highly specialised work. An inspector from the Ministry of Munitions had paid a 'combing out' visit to the firm, and it was possible that Moon would be badged. Capt. Mawer: A Wiltshire inspector might have raked Moon out. (Laughter) On the badging question, Major Reilly said the inspectors were going round to see who could be unbadged, and the clerical staffs were the first they were taking. Appeal dismissed.

A Question of Sons

The appeal of **Walwyn Oram**, aged 22, single, milk vendor, Westfield, Radstock, was dismissed. There was an appeal by his brother, Frank Oram, aged 35, single, as cowman and carter to his father. Captain Mawer said that having two sons out of three for the army they agreed to a conditional exemption of Frank. The Father: Can I exchange the sons? (Laughter) Captain Mawer: Only in novels. (Laughter) The Tribunal adhered to the recommendation of the military to conditionally exempt the elder son, Frank.

* * * * *

Lt. Arthur Coombs
1st/4th Battalion, The Somerset Light Infantry
May, 1916

We lost a number of officers and men at Kut. And we lost more a while later at Beit Aisa, and I'll tell you who was wounded there; a chap from Midsomer Norton called Bill Withers. I am given to understand that he had two other brothers - called Pharaoh and Noah. His mother was a wonderful woman who ran the isolation hospital there. I well remember when Withers got hit. He knew it would mean him going home and he called out, 'I've got a Blighty one!' but unfortunately he was a cripple in a wheel chair for the rest of his life. The family had already lost another son fighting with the Somersets in France. After our failed attempt on Kut we'd gone back to Basra and from there went on to Shaiba where we spent most of the summer in training and building up our numbers. One of the first officers to visit us there was Allan Thatcher, from Midsomer Norton, who was out in India with the 2nd/4th Somersets.

* * * * *

Lt. Allan Thatcher
2nd/4th Somerset Light Infantry
May, 1916

Yes, they were at Shaiba when I joined them - soon after their disastrous action at Kut. I'd arrived in Bombay in January '15 and from there I'd gone down to Bangalore where we had to find detachments for different places. When war had first broken out we lived in Silva House, next door to Evelyn Waugh's family. I knew him quite well although he was younger than we were - I remember that he used to wander round the garden in a white smock when we knew him. I knew his brother Alec better than Evelyn - I was at Sherborne with him. When I left there I studied at home for my law finals. And then war was declared and I was launched into the world.

My father had been in the 1st Battalion of the Somerset Volunteers and he thought it would be a good idea if I joined the Territorials. We went up to Borden Camp on Salisbury Plain and saw Lord Strachey who was in command and who knew my father, and I was accepted. I was commissioned on 7th October, 1914, and at the beginning of December went off to India with the 2nd/4th Somersets.

My first trip was to the Andeman Islands. There was a lot of naval activity going on there at the time and I understand that the Germans were filling up boats in Batavia - which was a convict settlement - and arming them and landing them in these islands. I went on one patrol in the islands with my platoon. Went up north on a Royal Indian Marine ship to inspect the bays to see if there had been any disturbance of the sand on the beaches. That took about six days but we found nothing. Quite a pleasant trip, though. Enjoyed it.

Another thing I did while I was with the 2nd/4th was guard the Viceroy of India for 48 hours while he was staying at Government House in Bankipur. I was in charge of an Officer's Guard. Myself and 30 men. I had a tent in the garden of Government House. Dined with him both evenings. I didn't have full dress uniform so I had to send for my tail coat and waist-coat and white tie to dress up for the dinner. He gave me a silver cigarette case for that duty. Still got it. It was quite an interesting thing to do. Quite interesting. I stayed with the 1st/4th and Arthur and Co. for a year or so, and then I joined the 10th Gurkhas in October, 1917.

* * * * *

Somerset Guardian
9th June, 1916

Last week I published a note on behalf of some of the lads who were formerly in the G Company of Territorials and lived in Midsomer Norton, Radstock and the neighbourhood, asking that their friends at home might kindly supply them with some cigarettes. I then stated that the lads were having a rough time with little in the shape of comforts. This is pretty evident as the Captain of the Company - the Hon. Edward Strachey - could not write directly to the relatives of the men who fell in the action on March 8th because he only had one envelope in his possession. He used it to write to his mother, Lady Strachey, and enclosed in it, on bits of flimsy paper, messages he asked her to transmit to the relatives of the men who had served under him. I have seen some of these and they certainly seem to bear out my statement that the men are short of necessities, much less luxuries.

The total number of eggs collected by Mr. F Wilmott for the wounded soldiers and sailors up to the end of April was 19,323. In the months of March and April the number of eggs sent from Radstock was 1,945. Those contributing to this number were: Mrs Callender, Midsomer Norton, 759; Mr Pound, Peasedown, 260; Miss Long, Kilmersdon, 398 . . . The children attending Stratton-on-the-Fosse day school kindly sent the sum of £1.0s.6d towards the fund.

Pte. Harry Cockle
1st Battalion, The Somerset Light Infantry
June, 1916

Yes! We've had our rum and lime-juice,
And we gits our bully beef,
And ferro-concrete biscuits
What's busted up our teef.

We gits no eggs for breakfast,
They send us over 'shells',
And we dives into our dug out,
And gits laughed at by our pals.

Just a tiny bit of bacon,
Well, fer sport we call it 'am,
Four fighting British soldiers
And a one-pound tin of jam.

Sometimes we git some rooty -
Well, you civvies call it bread -
It ain't as light as fevvers,
And it ain't exactly lead.

But we gets it down us somehow,
And we never send it back,
Though it gets smovvered up with whiskers,
What gets rubbed off the sack.

The dust blows in our dixies,
There's dirt upon our mit,
So can you really wonder
That a soldier's full of grit?

But I ain't a'going to grumble,
Cos I'm feeling well and fit,
And I've got one consolation,
That I'm here to do my bit.

Rupert Shepherd
Schoolboy

Their rations were always pretty basic, at best. From time to time Father would send parcels out to my brothers, cake if it was possible, and chocolate when we could get it. They both smoked and sometimes he'd send a tin of 50 or sometimes less in a cardboard box. I preferred the boxes, 'cause I could pinch one before he sealed the parcel. One thing Tom always wanted was for us to send him something to wash his hands with. Grease solvent - called Gre-Solvent - in a green tin about three inches across.

* * * * *

Somerset Guardian
16th June, 1916

Mrs Albert Barnes, of Double Hill, Peasedown St. John, belongs to a family that, in the days of family enlistment, responded nobly to the call for men for the Army. A large number of her relatives are serving in the various branches of the Services, some in the Army, some in the Navy, and some in the Air Service. Mrs Barnes's immediate family, who are all serving in the Army, are her father, Henry Stent, five of her brothers, her husband and two of her brothers-in-law.

* * * * *

Pte. Francis Oakley
4th Battalion, The Gloucestershire Regiment
July, 1916

My brother Charles was a Sergeant with the 1st/4th Somersets in India, but instead of going with them my friends and I decided to join the Gloucesters. We'd seen them training on the beaches at Weston-super-Mare and it seemed a pleasant way to start the war. I'd really wanted to join the Yeomanry but they felt that a few pony rides did not really equip me for their purposes.

In July, 40 of us from the 4th Gloucesters went with men from other West Country regiments that were sent to reinforce the 9th Devons. They had been absolutely smashed at Mametz Wood on July 1st, on the first day of the Battle of the Somme. In 90 minutes, out of the 775 men who went into action, 149 were killed, 55 were missing and 267 were wounded.

After being in France for about a week I found myself near Bazentin le Grand. We'd made our way out of a wood, just as dawn was breaking. We got out into the open and formed up in one long, single line and moved off. The first thing I saw was two dead Germans lying by a howitzer, and as I passed a huge black rat scarpered out from under one of them. Then we crossed a sunken road and saw chaps spread out on each side and I waved to them before I realised that they were dead. Dead men, watching me.

We wheeled round and started to dig in along a road beside a cornfield. A little further along there was an ash tree and underneath it was a dead horse. After we'd been digging away for a while my back was beginning to ache. I eased up and in that moment I got hit by shrapnel. Just a little ball it was, but it smashed away part of my jaw, and all of my front teeth.

* * * * *

LOCAL APPEALS TRIBUNAL
28th July, 1916

The Radstock Co-operative Society appealed in respect of a number of employees. The first of these was Clifford Baker, aged 29, married, bread deliverer. Captain Mawer (military representative) said he would like first of all to give some figures. There had been 59 appeals lodged in respect of the society's employees. One had been given conditional exemption, 30 temporary exemptions, 10 applications were refused, and 18 cases were outstanding.

Mr Tanner: How many do you employ?

Mr Gent, the General Manager: 180.

The Chairman: How many of these are women? - Just over 50. How many are of military age? - Most of our men are eligible. Fifty of our men have joined the colours and we are keeping their places open and making every man an allowance. Our annual turnover is £200,000 a year and we supply 6,000 households. This man is the only original deliverer left.

The Chairman: Anybody can do delivering after a little practice.

Mr Gent said they were on their beam ends for labour.

The Chairman: You would not be in such a position if women in the mining districts would do a little work and rise to the occasion. Their husbands get a lot of money and they are content to stay at home. If you could only instil a little patriotic spirit in the women to come out and help in a time of the country's need, you would not be at a loss for labour.

Mr Swift: Miners' wives work as hard as any other women.

The Chairman: Not for other people.

Mr Swift: They have their homes to attend to.

Mr Gent: No woman could do this work. I would not attempt to put a woman to work this hard district.

The case of Baker was dismissed.

Hilda Seymour
Co-op Delivery Girl

I knew Cliff Baker quite well. Mother always reckoned he was from that Happy Families game - Mr Baker the Baker, you see - but I don't imagine *his* was a happy family when his appeal was rejected and he had to go off to the war. I was in service in Bristol when it all started and I remember, very early on, watching an army band march past and I saw this butcher just put down his basket and march after them - up Blackboy Hill to Durdham Down, to sign up. He was in the army. That's how they got them to go to war in the beginning.

Well, then I came home and in the paper there were advertisements for girls to take men's jobs to let them go to war, so six of us went to the Co-op and I was on grocery deliveries. I was sixteen years old and doing a man's job, delivering with the horse and cart. You carried all your groceries and bread and draperies as well. We worked till midnight.

A man used to go out and take orders for the drapery and you delivered it. Delivered every-thing. And of course you had your jars of jam - might be jam this week or might be treacle - and you had to bring back each jar with a name on it for next week, and you'd fill the empty one yourself from a big barrel. The jar you did take back one week you did return the next. Course everything was rationed.

I started my round and went through several villages, into farms, along cart tracks, on out to a couple of cottages - walked from the roads and down through fields to some places - over the common, do more villages and back home. Ninety to a hundred houses before I'd done. And that was the round I did on Fridays. I stayed with the Co-op till the end of the war. Then one morning the manager told me that the man whose job I'd taken had come back without warning. So I had to go. It broke my heart to give up the horse.

The History of The Somerset Light Infantry 1914-1918
18th August, 1916

THE BATTLE OF DELVILLE WOOD

At 3am on the morning of the 18th August, the 6th Somersets moved to their assembly positions in Delville Wood *[and]* were in position by 6am. At that hour the preliminary bombardment opened with guns of all calibre pouring shell on to Leer Trench and Hop Alley . . . but so difficult was observation for the gunners that some of the 'heavies' fired short and 15 casualties were suffered by the Somersets from our own guns.

* * * * *

L/Cpl. George Taylor
6th Battalion, The Somerset Light Infantry
18th/19th August, 1916

All's we were ever doing on the Somme were goin' over the top somewhere or other. Every month it were somewhere different. And then we had the big one - when we took Delville Wood on the Somme. We got a good hidin' there, but we got up an' took the wood. We lost 53 dead and 227 wounded or missing in less than a day an' a half - an' I'll tell you who one of 'em were. Every Saturday night a chap used to come round Midsomer Norton sellin' oranges, apples, bananals and things. Shearn his name was. Well, I'd just taken four or five new men into the front line and there were Perce Shearn in a dugout and while I was there a German come up an' stuck a bayonet right drew'n. I chucked a bomb at Jerry an' ad'n.

> 19158 Private Percy Raglan Shearn
> 6th Battalion, Somerset Light Infantry
> Killed in Action
> France and Flanders
> 18th August, 1916

The History of The Somerset Light Infantry 1914-1918

THE BATTLE OF FLERS-COURCELETTE

The casualties of the 6th Battalion in this affair were truly terrible. Every officer who went over the parapet (and there were 17) had become a casualty. Three had been killed, 12 wounded and 2 were missing. In other ranks the Battalion had lost 41 killed, 203 wounded and 143 missing. It was a veritable death trap, and here the Somerset men, as they advanced, were shot down in dozens by German machine gunners firing from the north and east.

Major Sir Torquhil Matheson
3rd Battalion, The Coldstream Guards

The Coldstream Guards had an even worse time, if that's possible. Between September 10th and 17th, the Regiment lost 438 killed and 781 wounded. Then, on September 15th, reinforcements began to arrive from England, with Sammy Taylor among them.

* * * * *

Pte Sammy Taylor
3rd Battalion, The Coldstream Guards
August 1916

When we got to the Somme I were shootin' a rifle at first and one day I thought I seed somebody movin' up in a trench an' took a shot at'n - but, come to, t'were one of our machine gunners. I'm glad I never hit'n 'cos he started cussin' when he come out the trench. Uh zed, 'You bugger! Virin' at yer own men!' Caw, he didn' half cuss! But we'd not bin told he were out there - we just had'n bin told.

Soon after that happened one of our stretcher bearers got killed. Well, back in Chelsea barracks I'd passed a course in First Aid, so I were first in line fer the job. We always used to wear a red cross but Jerry never took no notice of that - they did still vire at we when we were carrying chaps out on the stretcher. They didn't worry, not one bit. But I expect our chaps were the same. One of the things we stretcher bearers had orders to do was to see none on 'em didn't doze off. A lot of soldiers useda go to sleep where they were standin' - and that were a Court Martial offence.

Terrible mess it were out there. Terrible. We were carrying wounded back all day

and all night. Blown to pieces some of the poor devils were. Our medical bloke useda say that if we found one out there we couldn't do nothin' for, to leave'n, 'cos t'were no good wastin' good lives on one that weren't gonna recover. Just tend the ones we could get back for medical help.

I were really hardened to the things I saw, but it caught up wi' me later. I remember one pair of chaps we had wi' us whose nerves had gone - they were ever so frightened. Because we were stretcher bearers the officers told I an' me mate to stay behind when we went up to the trenches to make sure these two come up. They weren't fit to fight, though - they didn't know who they were or where they were half the time. They couldn't help it, the poor beggars.

The Jerries were scared witless, too, mind. Once, in the trenches, I seen a German come an' give hisself up. We saw'n comin' with his hands up an' our chaps had orders not to shoot'n. Our officers were glad to have him fer to get information out of'n. He'd had enough of it, adn't he? I felt sorry fer'n. Only a young chap, frightened to death he looked - suh white as a maggot. I reckon he had shell shock. I felt sorry fer'n.

* * * * *

Somerset Guardian
1st September, 1916

Everyone in Radstock and the district who knows Mr C J Lewin will be heartily pleased to learn that his son, Sergt. Major Cecil Lewin, has been awarded the Military Cross. The announcement was made officially in the London Gazette on Friday night and the intelligence was received in Radstock on Saturday with unmixed pleasure. This is the first military distinction won by a Radstock man in the present war.

Sergt. Major Lewin is one of four brothers who freely and voluntarily offered their services to their country at the earliest moment. Two, alas, have made the supreme sacrifice, Captain Rex Lewin who fell while heroically leading his men in the advance on Loos, last September, and Lieut. Kenneth Lewin, who was killed by a sniper last March, within six weeks of his mother's funeral, which he came home from the front to attend. It is an open secret that had Lieut. R R Lewin survived his wounds he would have been recommended for an equal or even greater honour in recognition of his brave and gallant deed that cost him his life.

Sergt. Major Lewin received his early education at his father's school and, having won a County Scholarship, proceeded to Sexey's School, Bruton, where he remained for three years. He became a pupil teacher in Bristol, and next, having passed the examination for King's Scholarships went to Battersea Training College for Schoolmasters. At the end of his career as a student he took up an appointment in Liverpool. Here he was making his mark as a school-master when war was declared. He at once enlisted as a private in the King's Liverpool Regiment, and was rapidly promoted. He was in France for several months, seeing a considerable amount of fighting. How he won the Military Cross is thus officially recorded in the London Gazette of August 25th: 'For conspicuous gallantry and devotion to duty in action. When his Captain was wounded he took command, and, though wounded in the shoulder and arm, continued to encourage his men and direct their fire until wounded a third time in the lung. He even then staggered up again and continued to control his men till he fell from exhaustion.'

Sgt. Major Cecil Lewin, MC, was very badly wounded in the performance of the gallant deed that brought him fame. He is still in hospital in Plymouth and only a few days ago another bullet was found in his shoulder.

* * * * *

Pte. Sammy Taylor
3rd Battalion, The Coldstream Guards
September, 1916

One day while we were on the Somme, me an' my mate come out fer a bit of a break from the trenches an' got on a wagon an' rode back behind the lines fer a bit. Then we come across a shop wi' a little accordion in the window. I thought to meself, I'm goin' in an' zee how much he is. So I zed, 'Excuse me'. But she didn' know what I were on about, so I zed, 'Music. In the window'. An' caught hold of'n. She soon understood when I said summat about money, an' zed it were 15 francs. That were mine!

Then we had to walk back along part of the Somme, where t'were all quiet, an' I were playin' this thing an' a few of the lads were singin' as we walked along. There were some Froggies on the other side the stream, havin' a drink an' clappin' an' dancin' while I were playin'. Oh, it did make a bit o' life, 'cos everyone were strung up with the war. They wanted a bit of summat fer to take their mind away fer a bit, dinnum?

We always got on all right with the French people. We were billeted in one village an' when we come back from the trenches we 'ad tons of tobacco - tins of the stuff - 'cos half the chaps never smoked - so we give it to the French people.

One time, two of us dug out a plot of taters fer a Frenchman's wife, 'cos he were at Verdun, fightin'. We went an' asked her if she'd like 'em dug out, cause t'were the right time then. She said she would, very much, so we went an' done it an' while we were diggin' away, this 'ere Colonel of ours, Johnny Campbell, come by on horseback an' looked across an' laughed. An' we saluted. Nice taters she had there. They don't plant taters like we do, they put 'em in like molehill shapes in the ground, so many in a little ring. We took em back up an' she were very kind - she got some fat from somewhere an' made us all some chips. That were good. The food we had when we weren't in the trenches were bully beef mostly, an' stew - had it all the time.

119

I remember the first time I had the rum ration. I told the officer I never liked it an' he said, 'You've got to have it, it's compulsory'. Said, 'You won't refuse after you've 'ad a drop or two'. T'were bitter cold out there in winter, and I could feel that goin' all the way down tuh warm me feet, an' I thought, no, I shan't refuse that again! You were hungry half the time out there and that rum didn't half burn going down yer belly on an empty stomach. Now, whisky I did like! My mate Georgie Slater - came from Newcastle, I think he were a barman or summit - he used to get some spirits sent out. You know, whisky and that. An' my wife used to send me out tins wi' pasties in, and he did share his whisky wi' me and I did share my pasties wi' he!

When we were in the trenches we got nothin' to eat as a rule, unless it was fresh air. There were never no grub brought up to us - the only thing we ever had out there once were Spanish onions - an' we slung they at Jerry. What we did used to carry on us were them big square biscuits what wouldn't go soft even in hot water. But thou daresn't eat'n. That were called iron rations and only for emergencies. You had to keep'n on 'ee 'cos if they did come and inspect 'ee and 'ed gone, that were field punishment - you might get tied to a gun wheel fer so long. That's the truth.

I seen two darkies get field punishment once. They'd come all the way from Singapore to fight wi' the Coldstream on the Somme. Well, one day they got a bit fed up with it all and reckoned they were the swabs of the British army. D'you know? Somebody heard what they said an' went around and reported it to an officer - the daft thing - and they chaps got this field punishment, tied to a tree with their hands tied behind 'em 'cos there were no field gun where we were. I thought to meself, well, thass a bit of all right, come all this way tuh be treated like that.

But our Commanding Officer was ever so good to we. Johnny Campbell. He were a main huntsman wi' the hounds. That's how he rallied the Coldstream over - wi' his tally-ho blowin'. He led them over like that. One time when we come out fer a break the news come through that he'd won the Victoria Cross. He were so pleased - went to a village and bought a heap of flour an' had a long jam roly-poly made fer us. That were suh hard you 'ad a job to get yer teeth in it. We had a laugh, though.

* * * * *

Major Sir Torquhil Matheson
3rd Battalion, The Coldstream Guards

John Campbell was awarded the VC for twice leading his men into action against withering enemy machine guns and rifle fire after his Battalion had been shelled to pieces - decimated. Between 1914 and 1918 the Regiment won seven Victoria Crosses, two by officers and five by other ranks - Oliver Brooks being one of them. During that same period 180 officers and 3,680 other ranks were killed in action.

Pte Sammy Taylor
3rd Battalion, The Coldstream Guards
15th September, 1916

I can always remember when our lot sent the tanks over for the first time, 'cos it were the same day as Johnny Campbell got his VC. We were in the front line when they started comin' up. There weren't very many but they were very light an' if they'd get in a big shell hole they couldn't get out of'n. We used to laugh 'cos our lot were poppin' away like the very devil when the Jerries were getting' up out of their trenches to bolt off. They couldn't make out what were comin'. There weren't much room in them tanks. Just enough fer two or dree blokes to drive'n an' work the machine guns. When we next come out of the trenches fer a bit of a rest I and my mate seed this little old tank what they'd knocked out of action. They'd took all the insides out, not fer Jerry to be able to copy it, I s'pose. Anyway, my mate and me got in there and had a good little snooge - there, that's a bit of old Somerset fer 'ee.

* * * * *

Somerset Guardian
13th October, 1916

Mr and Mrs Henry King, of Coleford, near Bath, have lost two of their sons in the present war. Both were well-built, fine men who were greatly respected and beloved by a wide circle of friends. A few years ago they had an ambition to join the Metropolitan Police Force but being slightly under the standard they enlisted in the Coldstream Guards in January 1913, hoping when they had served their time with the colours to be accepted by the metropolitan authorities. When war broke out they went on active service with their regiment. Charles King was killed in action at Soupir at the age of 21 and almost exactly two years later his brother, Sergeant Thomas King was wounded in action and died from his wounds the following day, aged 25.

9936 Pte. Charles Glazier King	9906 Sgt. Thomas George King
3rd Battalion, The Coldstream Guards	3rd Battalion, The Coldstream Guards
Killed in Action	Killed in Action
France and Flanders	France and Flanders
16th September, 1914	14th September, 1916
Aged 21	Aged 25

Pte. Alban Chivers
Royal Army Ordnance Corps
September, 1916

I'd really made up my mind that I were gonna go in the Derby Scheme an' I said to my brother, 'If I go, will you look after my boy?' - 'cos I'd got married in 1910. Well, no, he wouldn't, and me wife said that if I did go we were finished, so that were that. In the end, me brother Arthur volunteered and I never. He were in the Engineers. Got wounded. One day I got a note from him saying he was in hospital and fed up. Then he died. So I never saw Arth again. Only brother I had.

> 146286 Sapper A J Chivers
> 99th Field Coy. Royal Engineers
> Died of Wounds
> Salonika
> 19th December, 1918
> Aged 26

Anyway, when my papers came I had to report to Bath and from there to Taunton and from there to Portsmouth Guildhall. When I got there it was closed, and it was raining torrents - proper empt down. Well, I found a policemen and he didn't know what I should do so I told'n to stick me in the cells for a night - but he couldn't do that 'cos I hadn't done nothin' wrong.

Then he asked if I'd had anythin' to eat and I hadn't, not since breakfast, so he took me to a small rest'rant there and said, 'Give him as much bread and butter and tea as he wants'. And he told me to stay there till he came back, and he'd pay for it. I shall always remember that, there were good chaps in the force in them days, weren't there? Good Samaritan. When he came back he'd found a place for me, some houses with no doors or windows, but it was under cover. He'd got me some blankets, too. By morning there were about a dozen in there. All just joined up.

Well, from Portsmouth they sent me back to Taunton agen. Told 'em where I'd come from and they said, 'All the buggers do come back from there'. Eventually they sent me to Red Barracks, Woolwich, and when I'd almost got there I asked a man in the carriage to let me know where to get off. He said, 'What you goin' in as?' An' I said as a fitter. 'Listen,' he said. 'Tell 'em you know nothin' about fittin' or you'll be at the Front next week, sorting out guns what've jammed.' Bloody hell! I'd 'ave bin right in the middle of it. But as luck would have it, I wasn't.

Not knowing nothin' about the army, once I got to the Guard Room I thought I'd finished, but it seems I should've reported to the office. I ended up kipping in a corridor on a stone floor an' a Sergeant says: 'Anybody want a biscuit come along wi' me'. That were biscuits to sleep on - palliases. That's the only time any of us'd ever heard 'em called that. I remember one chap say he wasn't hungry. He slept on the floor.

Well, they gave me a towel and some soap and a knife, fork and spoon and fitted us up with uniforms and after a time I wound up in the office. 'Where've you bin?' they sez. 'Out in the corridor,' I zed. Seems like they'd been waitin' for me fer three days - so I were dropped right in it from the start. Then he said, 'Right. Sez here you're a fitter'. I zed, 'I don't know nothin' about fitting'. An' he said, 'Bloody army all over. Them buggers don't know what they'm doing'. I didn't bother to put him straight.

* * * * *

Somerset Guardian
29th September, 1916

On Sunday morning people will be called upon to put their clocks back an hour, in accordance with the provisions of the Summer Time Act, 1916. The immediate effect of the alteration will be that the mornings will open with daylight nearly an hour earlier and the evenings will be shorter or darkness will set in quite one hour earlier on Sunday evening than it did on Saturday. To comply with the restrictions all lights must be shaded or windows darkened one hour earlier on Sunday evening than they have been in the past few days. So far as I can gather the evening services at the great majority of the local churches and chapels are being held on Sunday next, but those responsible must see that within a few minutes of seven o'clock no light is allowed to escape which would constitute an offence to the law of the land.

I expect the majority of the places of worship will find that the attendance at the evening service, if it is continued at the usual hour, will be much smaller now that people will have to return home through streets which are in complete darkness. A number of people have also suggested that it would be a good thing if the local shops and places of business were to agree to close at an earlier hour in the coming winter months. I find that at Midsomer Norton some movement has been made in this direction, and all the principal places of business have agreed to close earlier, commencing on Monday next. Perhaps the Radstock people will follow?

* * * * *

Miss Shukar, headmistress of Clandown Church of England School, has received a postcard from Rifleman Harry Robbins, of Clandown, who is a prisoner of war in Germany, thanking her and the children of her school for sending him a parcel of cigarettes, tobacco and a pipe, and saying that their kindness he should never forget. He also stated that he had with him a photo postcard of Miss Taylor and her class with his own little boy in it, and he thought it very nice. One of the scholars of the school - Grace Milsom, of Clandown House - has received from Pte. Leslie Jenkins of the Queen's RWS Regiment, a letter thanking her for her wishes: 'Best of luck to Tommy or Jack' was written on an egg which he says he received at breakfast in hospital where he was owing to trench fever but would soon be with his regiment in the trenches again. He enclosed his address and wished the sender the very best of luck.

LOCAL APPEALS TRIBUNALS
29th September, 1916

Frank E Jones, 40, assistant superintendent for the Prudential Assurance Co., Paulton, appealed on the grounds of national interest and stated that he would be 41 in December. The Chairman pointed out that the company had not appealed for him. Captain Mawer: It is stated that all insurance agents are luxuries in war time and a nuisance at all times. (Laughter) Appeal dismissed.

13th October, 1916

Charles Fry, 32, single, Combers Grave, Midsomer Norton, appealed but his case was dismissed.

16th October, 1916

Jacob H Tucker, 32, passed for general service, of Paulton, an undertaker, appealed. Mr W F Long produced a petition signed by 600 residents of Paulton, on the ground that the appellant was the only undertaker at the place. Captain Mawer: We never knew 600 persons so anxious for the undertaker before. Mr Long said he had also had a letter from the Clerk.

The Chairman: Who is he?

Captain Mawer: The gentleman who says Amen.

The Chairman: I'm the one who says Amen here. Appeal dismissed.

* * * * *

Somerset Guardian
27th October, 1916

The new Lights on Vehicles Order, which came into force on Sunday last, is a very important matter to owners and drivers of motor cars, who will need to make themselves conversant with the regulations, especially as regards headlights. One very irksome condition is removed by the order. Cyclists who had no lights have hitherto been compelled to carry their machines. Now they are permitted to wheel them provided that the machines are wheeled as near as possible to the kerb. It is also provided that in future all vehicles except bicycles, tricycles and handcarts, must carry a front light on either side of the vehicle, and a rear light; but the operation of this clause is postponed until the New Year in order to give owners a chance to obtain the necessary additional lamps. Now a further regulation has been issued regarding the driving of cattle, sheep, pigs and other animals at night. The drover must carry at the rear a lantern visible back and front unless he is leading not more than four animals, when he may have the light at the front. In addition, when the flock is a large one - the number is specified - one lantern must be carried at the front and one at the rear. It is sometimes forgotten that it is an offence under the Defence of the Realm Act to ring or chime church bells, or to sound a bell that can be heard a certain distance during the period when lights have to be obscured under the lighting order.

Gwen Beauchamp
Schoolgirl
October, 1916

In October, 1916, I became a full time VAD nurse, even though my parents were against the idea. It wasn't done in those days for the likes of us. I had joined our local VAD in August, 1914, and Father's sister, who was Commandant of the VAD hospital at Mere, in Wiltshire, persuaded my parents to let me go to nurse there. Mere Hospital was in the village school, a very modern building for those days, with two enormous schoolrooms. One was turned into Kitchener Ward and the other French Ward, with four TB huts in the playground. I stayed with my aunt and her family and cycled to the hospital every day.

On my way there one day I skidded in an icy cart rut and fell off and cut my knee badly. Luckily the milkman came along and bundled me into his cart and took me to the hospital. After that they decided it was more sensible for me to be billeted in Mere and not have the long bike ride. Part of the time I was billeted in the local workhouse with the Workhouse Master. Dad paid for my digs as I had no pay - just a £20 a year uniform allowance. I had no pocket money at all.

* * * * *

Pte. Tommy Atkins
Army Service Corps
November, 1916

In February I'd had a bit of a nasty shock 'cause they asked us to send for our birth certificates and I was discharged. Under aged. Well, between then and November I got a job working in the gardens back at Ston Easton Park. Then I decided that I wanted to get into the Army Service Corps Motor Transport so I went to Shearn's garage in Midsomer Norton and got a job from November to March.

The car I learned on was a de Dion Bouton - two seater, all brass lamps, radiator and all that. Then, for a week before I re-joined the army I spent my time on an Oakhill Brewery lorry - a Seldon. I should have gone in the army anyway, because of the Conscription Act, but I thought if I go on my own I'll probably get into what I want to get in. I went for my medical and passed A1.

There was an ASC unit in Bath and the day I went in there I saw Lloyd George on the balcony of the Empire Hotel - his son was getting married in the Abbey there. Then I was sent to a Motor Transport depot in London, had my driving test and passed. I think that meant a couple of extra bob a week. I've still got the licence here now, says I'm licensed to drive a bicycle on government business!

Ivan Chard
Timber Haulier
October, 1916

When Charlie finally had to go he reported up to Caterham Barracks with **George Randall**, who were a farm-hand over at Farrington and hauled coal and stuff - like Charlie did. He and Charlie did always meet up at Farrington Market. Charlie reckoned there were several other lads he knew from round here when he got there.

First thing to do up at Caterham was to be fitted with equipment and all that, then, next morning t'were parade. Charlie reckoned there were about 50 young'uns on the parade ground and then this Sergeant-Major come along and pulled their hats down on their noses. 'Git yer heads back!'

When he come back next day Charlie were on the back line - about three along he useda tell we - and this Sergeant come along an' did the same to Charlie, pulled his cap down and that did make his nose tingle. Then he told Charlie tuh pull hisself together and called him a Somerset greenhorn and with that Charlie upped wi' his fist an' caught'n on the chin and knocked'n out. He reckoned he were in the greenhouse fer two weeks fer his trouble. I s'pose he meant the glasshouse, but he always called it the greenhouse.

Oh, the tales he did tell we! Uncle Charles were in Corporal Moore's squad for training - thass he, second in on the back row, afore they'd thinned'n down a bit.

Pte. Sammy Taylor
3rd Battalion, The Coldstream Guards

When Charlie were at Caterham he done all the London duties like all the rest of us while we were there - Buckingham Palace, the Tower, St James's Palace - but the Bank of England was the one I always liked best. We'd be at the Bank as soon as the staff did finish and stay till about seven next morning. That were a cushy guard - one hour on and three off, and the only job we ever got paid for. Privates got a shillin' and the corporal half a crown. I think the officer got a pound. They always reckoned the officer put his in the poor box, but I know our lads never. In them days you could get a nice supper for a shillin'.

* * * * *

DESCRIPTIVE REPORT ON ENLISTMENT
30th October, 1916

Name:	Fry, Charles James
Apparent age:	31 years 9 months
Height:	5 feet 11 inches
Chest measurement:	Fully expanded - 38"
	Range of expansion - 3"
Weight:	166 lbs - good
Distinctive marks:	Slight varicose veins

* * * * *

Somerset Guardian
8th December, 1916

There were large audiences at The Palladium, Midsomer Norton, on the first three evenings of this week, to witness the great War Office film, *The Battle of the Somme*. The whole film was exhibited in a beautifully clear manner, and was followed with great interest from start to finish. In addition to this film the second episode of *The Perils of Pauline* was also exhibited.

Pte. Alfred Flinn
1st Battalion, The Somerset Light Infantry
Diary entry, 15th December, 1916

Left England six days ago. Lovely six hour trip across Channel - bit sea-sick. Arrived Le Havre - dirtiest place ever seen - then Rouen. Hard to choose which is filthier. Nothing worth looking at bar the church. Left Rouen for line in cattle trucks - coal carts don't rattle half as much.

Somerset Guardian
15th December, 1916

Miss Waugh, of Midsomer Norton, and the members of her Bible Class, have sent a small parcel together with a photo of the class and Christmas Greetings to each of the 31 members of the class who are away serving their country - most of them on active service. These young men will, I am sure, appreciate the kind thoughts and tangible expression of the leader of the class and their fellow members who are left at home.

Pte. Alfred Flinn
1st Battalion, The Somerset Light Infantry
Diary entry, 20th December, 1916

First experience of shell fire today. Have headache. Have found the Battalion. Wish I hadn't.

1917

Pte. Sammy Taylor
3rd Battalion, The Coldstream Guards
4th January, 1917

In January we were pulled out of the trenches to near a place called Corbie, fer a late Christmas. I always had me squeeze box wi' me in the trenches an' when we come out I were carryin' me stretcher wi' this instrument under me arm, an' this nice young officer, name of **Lutyens** - couldn't wish fer a nicer officer - said, 'Come on, Sam. Play a few tunes fer us. I'll carry yer stretcher'. An' he chucked'n up over his shoulder while I played all the way back along the duckboards.

We did have to have the duckboards out there or we wouldn't 'ave bin able to walk at all. The ground were covered with massive great shell holes, wi' no more than a foot an' a half between 'em. Some were suh deep as a room, an' if you slipped off the duckboard you'd had it. You did get sucked down in them 'oles, all filled wi' slimy, reddy mud an' bloody body bits an' stuff, an' you did stay there till somebody pulled you out. The more you did struggle the more you did sink down in. Horses did drown in 'em.

Normally, when we were pulled out from the front we did spend our time jumpin' over trenches an' stickin' our bay'nets through sandbags. Trainin', you know. They'd find some little bit of square where we'd do some drillin', to keep us up to scratch, wi' all the local people watchin' us. An' we 'ad salutin' practice, 'cause they reckoned we were getting slack at it. One thing after another! They'd put us through the hoop fer a few hours.

Oh, the daft things they made us do when we come out of the trenches. We'd be out fer a couple of days an' 'ave to polish our buttons, an' then, when we went back in, we had tuh 'ave a bit of candle an' darken' 'em agen. That were daft, weren' it?

I used to get so lousy as a cuckoo out there. We had lice everywhere. Me name tags, on a piece o' string round me neck, were covered in the things. What we used to do when we come out were buy some candles an' cut it up in small bits, then we'd take off our shirts an' that, an' light the candle, an' run it up an' down the seams. They did go off like a machine gun then, all the lice eggs poppin'! Full of it, they were. They gid us some stuff they reckoned we should rub in, but that did make it a damn site worse, they did go fer that fer to eat it! Anyone'll tell thee the same, what were in the trenches, you couldn't avoid 'em. We did come back an' 'ave shower baths that they did give us. Caw, that were a game, I can tell 'ee. Shower baths! We were reckoned to be clean after, but we were still full o' lice even then. You just couldn' get 'em off!

Sometimes they did give us a change of clothin'. Some of it weren't half big enough - get socks that did come only 'alf way up yer voot. An' t'weredn't new clothin', t'were all what'd bin cleaned an' purified, they reckoned. But t'were not very often we got that, even. We 'ad to go back in in what we 'ad on. Might just get another shirt to wear, but gen'rally the clothes were caked with mud. Mud and blood.

[Lt. Douglas McMurtrie
7th Battalion, The Somerset Light Infantry

In the line we had a system that every day a pair of dry socks was brought up for each man and the worn ones taken away to be washed. We took great care over this. The shell holes were filled with water and all of our people wore thigh length gumboots. Every platoon officer saw to it that every NCO and man in his charge massaged his feet for 15 minutes every day and that their feet were inspected. I had to submit a certificate every day to the effect that this had been done. Trench foot was a nightmare but we very seldom had a case in the Battalion.]

A month later we were up at Sellencourt. T'were all quiet and we wondered what the quietness was all about. Then all at once Jerry opened up a great bombardment away to the left of us - shells the size of barrels - and worked the barrage all down through, right where we were. I an' me mate were up on top wi' the stretcher an' found a piece of galvanised an' got down flat wi' that over the top of us. Old Jerry blew those trenches to smithereens.

Well, when it had quieted down a bit we got up an' went into the trench an' a young chap come down wie' a gurt piece blowed out of his jaw, but when we went to help him he said, 'Sam,' he said. 'There's a chap hurt worse than me up there.' I went up to see him and that were a young chap from Devon - a nice chap, name of Gosling. He'd dug back under the bank and made a nice place to croop back in an' Jerry plonked a shell right in the middle, over the top of'n and that poor chap had his head blowed clean right off. I couldn' do nothin' for him but he must've had nerves left in his body fer a bit 'cos he crawled out of his hole, practically out into the trench, afore he passed out. Funny, weren't it? It's the honest truth, I saw it happen. I'd seen so much by then that it didn't turn me up a bit. All I felt were sorry, 'cos he were a nice young chap.

> 17963 Pte. William Gosling
> 3rd Battalion, Coldstream Guards
> Enlisted: Honiton
> Killed in Action
> France and Flanders
> 22nd February, 1917

* * * * *

L/Cpl. George Taylor
6th Battalion, The Somerset Light Infantry

Well I'll tell thee another 'orrible story! We had two brothers with us who'd never go nowhere ner do anythin' wi'out each other if they could help it. They were in my platoon, so stands to reason I knew 'em both almost as well as I know meself. And they loved one another - just like brothers should. They stuck together whatever they were doin'. Well, one day, when we were up the front, Jerry put this shell over and put the older one of 'em clean out - he were blown to smithereens - you had a job to find anything of him. Anything. Course, the other brother were all shook up - as you'd expect'n to be - and he ran away from it all. An' I don't blame'n.

About six weeks later I were more than surprised when who should be they be bringin' up but this young'un, what had runned away. He'd got as far as Boulogne and tried to get on one of the boats. They brought him right up past me an' I told him how I were sorry for him - but he weren't allowed to speak to me nor nothin'. Then he had to go in front the Court Martial. And next mornin' he had to be shot. And t'were the Cornwalls what done it - not the Somersets - but men from our own Brigade. They put he out the way. Wiped him out. Wiped him away. You won't find he in any regimental history. He ain't on no plaque nowhere. They made out like he never existed. I dunno, that do make thee think. Have you got brothers? Have you got sons? I have. I've got both.

19211 Pte. Arthur Thomas Jefferies	9970 Pte. Alfred Leonard Jefferies
6th Battalion, Somerset Light Infantry	6th Battalion, Somerset Light Infantry
Killed in Action	Shot at Dawn
France and Flanders	France and Flanders
16th September, 1916	1st November, 1916
Aged 33	Age not recorded

There were another poor devil in our Battalion what got executed like that, too. A Jewish lad. Come from the East End, up in London. Poor sod probably couldn't understand what we yokels were on about half the time. Anyway, when we first got out to France we had a hell of a time of it - took a hell of a battering. The first day the Battalion was ever in the trenches we had four killed, and about a week later Jerry started slingin' fire over and - guess what - it was us what copped it. Baptism of fire. Well, after about a month of this the London lad were lonely or shit scared - or both - and he runned away, just like Alfie Jefferies done. He were caught, too, and done for desertion. Court Martial reckoned he had good reason to be upset and that they should show'n mercy. But he didn't get none. They shot he, too. Had to set an example they reckoned. I dunno. Poor sod.

> Pte. Louis Phillips
> 6th Battalion, The Somerset Light Infantry
> Shot at Dawn
> France and Flanders
> 19th August, 1915
> Aged 23

* * * * *

Lt. Leslie Pollard
February, 1917
Indian Army

I was actually at Kut when it was finally re-taken in February but I didn't take any part in the attack. By that time I'd become a junior officer in the Signals, looking after signalling for the brigade of the 3rd Division to which I was seconded. My signalling then consisted of flags and heliograph, oil lamps and so on with some wireless thrown in. But when I started, flag waving was the main thing - semaphore and Morse - one flag for Morse and two for semaphore.

We left Basra, at the bottom of the Persian Gulf, and went up the Tigris as far as Kut. When we got there we lined up with the 3rd Lahore Division on one side of us and the 7th Meeruts on the other. As I was free from duties I was able to get my horse and rode out to a ridge where I sat and watched the troops moving about over the river. Watched the Turks disappearing from round the town and the Indian troops - Ghurkas I think they were - going in to re-occupy the place. A rather more satisfactory outcome to what happened when Arthur Coombs and his lot were there.

The brigade I was with then moved north and two weeks later we captured Baghdad. After that we moved on up to the Persian border where we joined up with a Russian Cavalry unit which proceeded to eat all our food.

Somerset Guardian
9th March, 1917

SOMERSET COLLIERY RECRUITING COURT - THE COMBING OUT PROCESS

The Somerset Colliery Recruiting Court sat at the Victoria Hall, Radstock, on Monday, Tuesday and Wednesday this week to deal with the cases of men of military age who had entered the coal mines of Somerset since August 15, 1915 . . . The men each went before a Medical Board, who examined them on the premises, their cases were then considered by the Colliery Recruiting Court . . .

George Peppard, 22, single, Bowden Hill, Chilcompton, started work at Moorwood on November 8, 1915, and previously worked at Norton Hill Colliery for two months. Previously he was employed in the Stone Quarries at Emborough for three years. - Mr. Maggs said he was a very good carting boy and he could ill afford to lose him. - As he was in category A he was ordered to join up in 14 days. A brother, **James Peppard**, 19, of the same address, started work at the colliery in August 1915. He formerly worked at the quarries but went into the pit for more money. - Passed in Class A, he was also ordered to join up in 14 days.

* * * * *

Jim Peppard
Carting Boy
March, 1917

Well, that were it! That were George an' me for the Army, along with dozens of other poor young 'uns what went down the Victoria Rooms. About a quarter of them what appeared got their orders tuh join. Then, a few days later, we got a big surprise through the letter box!

* * * * *

Somerset Guardian
16th March, 1917

Last week the Somerset Collieries Recruiting Court sat for four days in the Somerset coalfield - three days at Radstock and one at Pensford. All men and boys liable to military service who had entered the mines since August 1915 appeared before the court. All those who had been passed for general service by the medical Board were given 14 days' notice to join the colours unless the court exempted them from service. I understand that in the whole coal-face 42 men were ordered to join. These men were in most cases agreeably surprised on Monday morning when they received official notification from the Recruiting Officer, informing them that the notice to join up in 14 days had been cancelled. In many cases the managers of the mines were as pleased as the men themselves to find the notices had been withdrawn.

Pte. Jim Peppard
The Somerset Light Infantry
March, 1917

Well, come the time an' George an' me went in anyway. We both wen' in to Bath to the Drill Hall an' the Sergeant said to me, wi' a voice down in 'is boots somewhere, 'Whadayouwan?', an' I zed we'd decided to give the Army the benefit of our services - an' it happened as simple as that. Then we both had to go on home an' wait to hear from 'em.

Well, t'wasn't many days after that that George went to work an' were taken ill at the pit and brought home. He died two days later. T'were s'posed tuh be spotted fever. Mother had to burn all the bed clothes an' everythin'. Next thing we knew was my papers come, an' I ad tuh went on in by meself.

* * * * *

LOCAL APPEALS TRIBUNAL
30th March, 1917

Henry Mitcheler, 37, married, High Street, Midsomer Norton, hairdresser and tobacconist, who had had his conditional exemption withdrawn by the local tribunal appealed. In the course of his claim, he stated that he cut the hair of 200 boys at Downside Abbey. Captain Mawer: They must get their hair cut elsewhere or cut it themselves if it is necessary in these times. (Laughter) Appellant: I doubt if anyone could do that. Captain Mawer said the appellant would be able to do the hairdressing of a lot of people in the Army. Appellant: They don't want Army barbers. Captain Mawer: Then you must cut heads off if you can't cut hair, scalp them. (Laughter) Appeal dismissed.

Messrs. A Edwards and Son, Army and other boot contractors, Midsomer Norton, appealed in respect of Reuben Jones, 31, single, of High Street, Midsomer Norton, the only press man left, without whom, it was stated, the factory would cease work. He was passed B1 and had originally been given conditional exemption, but on military review the Local Tribunal withdrew the certificate. A representative of the firm said an 'understudy', aged between 17 and 18, had gone into the mines. - Mr Tanner: The same thing is being done all over the country. - The Chairman: It is disgraceful. - Mr Tanner: The mines are regular 'funk holes' in these cases. - Mr Swift: What is the man's name? - The representative: Carver. - Mr Tanner: What do you pay Carver? - £1 a week and we offered him 30s. - The Chairman: he ought to be 'combed out' of the mines and returned to the boot factory. - Mr Wills: You could if he were 18. The representative said he went into the mines three or four weeks ago. - The Tribunal gave conditional exemption. - Captain Mawer: I shall probably have the factory inspected so that I can bring this up again if necessary.

A NOBLE DEATH

The recent sad news of the death in action of Private Reginald Maggs, Northumberland Fusiliers, of High Littleton, *[see page 103]* has occasioned universal sympathy and regret among the inhabitants, not only of this village, but throughout the whole neighbourhood, where the deceased was well-known and held in the highest esteem. The deceased, who was the only son of Mr Gilbert Maggs and the late Mrs Maggs of High Littleton, was a carpenter and joiner by trade, but prior to his joining up was employed as a bread, etc., deliverer at the High Littleton branch of the Radstock Co-operative Society. Joining on August 9 last, the deceased served for some time in the Royal Engineers, but was subsequently transferred to the Northumberland Fusiliers. He proceeded on Active Service on December 28 and died on April 12 of wounds sustained in action on April 9, caused by the explosion of a bomb, of which the deceased received the full charge in his body.

The circumstances connected with the deceased's death is just another touching episode of the unexampled courage and gallantry displayed by our brave boys in the cause of justice, freedom and civilisation. The deed which cost Pte. Maggs his life is worthy of recording in the annals of history, for he undoubtedly made this great sacrifice and yielded his own life in order to prevent the loss of lives of probably several of his comrades. The deceased leaves a young widow and one child.

* * * * *

From the Chaplain
Northumberland Fusiliers
12th April, 1917

Dear Mr Maggs,

. . . Your son was terribly wounded when he was brought in here. He had lost both hands and both eyes, and he was wounded in other parts of the body. But he had a wonderful spirit. He really gave his life in order to save his comrades. A bomb (which was dropped by one of his chums) fell among a group of men. Your son saw the danger and immediately seized it to fling it away before it exploded. It burst in his hands, however, and he received the whole charge of it in his body. But he undoubtedly saved his comrades.

> 47172 Pte. Reginald Maggs
> 22nd (Tyneside Scottish) Bn., Northumberland Fusiliers
> Died
> 12th April, 1917
> Aged 22

Frances Craig
Women's Land Army
June, 1916

I'm a city girl, really, but I came down here to live when I joined the Land Army in 1916. I left my school in Dulwich and went to the recruiting office in Oxford Street. Said I would be 17 next month but I was only 15 at the time. They sent me down to Cox's farm at Chewton Mendip. In the care of the Vicar.

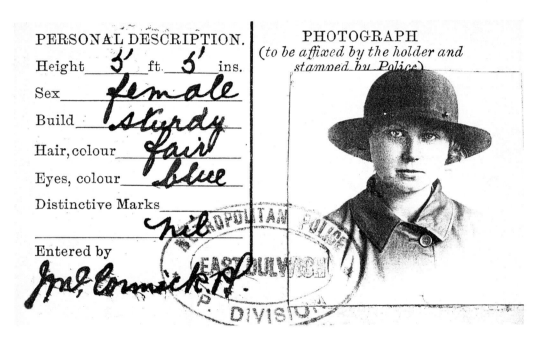

It was hard work, but I loved the life - especially the haymaking and working with the horses. The farmer used to breed shire horses and they found out that I'd have a go at anything if it meant being with them. Well, we had one big, dark chestnut and I went down one evening with a lantern and I could see that she was in trouble going to foal - she'd been sired by a big black stallion. The saying is that if you have to help a mare in foal she dies.

We had no phone in those days so I was sent to Ston Easton on horseback to phone the vet in Midsomer Norton. He had a car, of course, and came up at once but he couldn't save the mare, but the foal was born - a little black stallion. The vet said we wouldn't be able to feed it. I did. I used to milk another mare with a warm bottle and feed the foal. Then wrapped it up and slept with it. I went on doing that until it could feed itself. That foal grew into a beautiful stallion. Ebony. Sold for stud. Not bad for a city girl, eh?

Pte. Francis Oakley
4th Battalion, The Gloucestershire Regiment
17th April, 1917

In April I was on the move with the 4th Gloucesters again, on our way to join the 7th Gloucesters in Mesopotamia. On Easter Sunday we got to Marseilles where we had to wait till the Friday when we sailed on the *Cameronia*. Towards the evening of the 13th our two escort destroyers came in and tied up alongside us. There was lots of talk among the crew of it being the *Cameronia's* 13th voyage, on the 13th of the month, and having the 13th Hussars on board. The rats had left her. Oh yes, we were going down. They reckoned that the men on the destroyers were even running a sweep on us going down. They were quite sure that we were doomed.

On the Sunday after we sailed we went down through the Straits of Messina and as the sun was coming up we could see the glow of Stromboli in the sky behind us. Sometime during Monday we had a change of escort and two new destroyers, the *Nemesis* and the *Rifleman* came up from behind us, and the other two left. Then a party of us was detailed to clear out the armoury 'cause it was cluttered up with mailbags for Malta. We'd just had tea. I remember that it was five and twenty past five by my watch - and we were waiting for Corporal Leverton to come down and open the armoury door for us - when this great bump and explosion happened. It had happened. We'd been torpedoed.

The first thing that occurred was that I had a fight with another fellow who grabbed my life-belt - he hadn't brought his with him. I pushed him off and then went to the stairway that led up to the stern deck and as we were crowding up, other men were clamouring down to fetch their life-belts that they'd left on the mess deck. They were literally walking down over our shoulders, bruising us with their boots. It was absolute panic.

When we got up on deck we could see men rushing to the sides and jumping in the sea. You see, we had no officers of our own there. We were all different drafts from different regiments. It was not like a complete battalion going out together - and without our own officers there was no one to give us instructions. It was total confusion.

We were supposed to go to our stations and line up for the ship's captain's inspections but most people just made for the boats. I and another chap moved right across deck to one of the catwalks which led to the starboard poop deck. We weren't allowed on that deck once the voyage had started - there were boats there but we were held away from them by the Sergeant-Major and the Provost Sergeant from our draft. It was their deck and I suppose it was every man for himself. Those two and an officer and another Warrant Officer from another battalion held us off with their revolvers. I remember they were the last to jump into their lifeboats.

There weren't many of us left then, and those that were there turned back and went to the stern deck, hoping to find something there, but there was nothing. Then we tried the starboard boat deck. About halfway along there was an officer taking snapshots of the chaps in the water. Two of the lifeboats had smashed up when they were being lowered. They were overloaded and I suppose the ropes broke. They were there in the water, one of them waterlogged and the other overturned, with men clinging to it and a bit of blood about.

Eventually I went up to the upper deck where there were some lifeboats on the stocks. There were about a dozen men there with an officer sitting in the only boat which had the covers pulled back. They were all trying to heave it off the stocks but, of course, it was chained down and we hadn't been told how to release it. We found out later that if we'd put a match to a fuse there it would have bust the chain open - but we didn't know that then. I remember that the officer was getting panicky, waving his pistol about and shouting, 'If any man tries to get in, I'll shoot him'. He was very frightened - had a very white face.

All this time the ship's siren was making an awful noise and smoke and steam was billowing from the funnels and the smell of the explosion was pretty strong. Then, all of a sudden, she started to go down, with a tremendous sliding motion down in front, and then she pulled herself up, like a car being braked from speed. But her front was low in the water and I knew it was no good to stay on her any longer - I'd have to jump.

I left there and walked down the sloping deck to the front of the ship so I wouldn't have so far to jump into the water. When I got down close to the bridge I looked back and saw that all those chaps had got into the lifeboat. But it was still chained to the deck. Then I saw that the two destroyers were coming in close after circling round - some say they had been dropping depth charges. I climbed over the side of the ship to the deck rails of the boat deck below and then jumped into the arms of a sailor on the destroyer. That's how I got away. Didn't even get wet.

Some, of course, fell between the ships and got crushed but I could hear the noise of other chaps' boots as they landed on the destroyer. Then we circled round, helping, pulling other fellows up out of the water. I remember it was about five minutes past six by my watch at that time and when I looked at her she had her stern right up high in the water, about to dive down. They called us just then to haul on a rope to pull in a boat with some men in, and when I looked again she'd gone.

We went on getting fellows on. Where the ship had gone down the water was smooth, and we went in where the dead chaps were, floating heads down in their life-belts, going in little circles, taken by the eddies in the water. The destroyer pushed between them but there was no one we could save.

The other destroyer, the *Rifleman*, was stationary now and we circled around her while she pulled people aboard. Then, all of a sudden, the periscope of a submarine came up between us and the chaps on our ship fired and hit it right by the conning tower as it was submerging again. A lot of fellows with us thought the flash of our gun was another torpedo coming for us and they were ready to jump overboard again till the sailors stopped them.

We went on searching until about midnight and then went off towards Malta.

* * * * *

Somerset Guardian
20th April, 1917

On Saturday a party of German PoWs passed through Radstock, having halted for a short time at Bath. There were about 50 of them in number and they were making the journey south from a place in the Midlands, where they had been engaged on road and other constructional work for some time past. None of them were, therefore, captured at a recent date. They were accommodated in two corrugated carriages, at the windows of which were guards of the Royal Defence Corps. During the time the train was in Bath Station the Germans, who from the different uniforms they wore showed that they belonged to different army units, were not distracted by the gaze of curiosity of a number of people who gathered near the windows, from their quiet games of cards. All looked well cared for and contented, and most of them were smoking cigars or cigarettes. Some were fair haired Saxons but one, darker complexioned than the rest, reluctantly admitted to a questioner in broken English that he was a Prussian. Another, whom one could not help noticing, was of quite an outstanding German military type.

Pte. Stan Small
10th Battalion, The Devonshire Regiment
24th April, 1917

We been hangin' around about Salonika for well over a year - diggin' trenches and makin' roads, things like that. D'you know, they named us the Gardeners of Salonika - yes they did. That was because nearly every boat that were bringin' us food were being stopped by the Germans and we weren't gettin' no greens or vegetables of any kind. So they got the Artillery chaps to plough up acres and acres on the plains, 'cos they knew all about horses - a lot of 'em had worked on farms. These plains were irrigated by little streams like, and then we grew crops - potatoes, greens and the loveliest tomatoes. Oh yes, we were the Gardeners of Salonika.

The Germans and the Bulgarians were up north of us on a range of hills, in all the best positions, but they wouldn't come down. That were funny. If ever they had a'come down they'd have had us just like that - in the palm of their hand. At their mercy. They certainly would. But they didn't. Spot of good luck, weren' it? So we were sent up to meet them - had to probe where they was to - make a raid occasionally to find out where they were. And we lost a lot of men in the scuffles.

When we'd been there for quite a while I went sick with malaria and was taken to Malta. When we got there we were took off the boat and lined up on the quay in rows to wait for the ambulances to take us off to the hospitals. At one point there were 250 men from the Battalion in hospital with malaria or dysentery. But there were only 15 or 16 men in my ward when I got there.

They fed us delicacies there - fruit, custard and things an' I didn't want to leave that hospital, but after about three months they had orders to send every man that they could back to Salonika. The Battalion was very down in numbers what with men going sick and the attacks they had been making back there at Petit Couronné.

So after a week in a convalescence camp it was back to the Battalion. There was a machine gunner from

our regiment on the boat going back, a chap called Thompson. He was a reporter on a paper from Frome and I was on the same table as him and he was crying and he said to me, 'Stan. I'm gonna get killed this time'. And I said, 'What are you talkin' about? You ain't gonna get killed. Surely you ain't'.

Well, we got back to the Regiment and on April 24th we were moved into positions to attack the Bulgarians next morning - the big battle of Petit Couronné. The Scots Brigade had tried to take it but they couldn't do it. They couldn't do it. It was frightening and it was exciting, all at the same time. When the order came to go forward it was terrible, terrible. There were ravines going up each side full of barbed wire and machine guns perched on the top in concrete places. We used to call it the Devil's Eye, an' it were too.

As we were going up this ravine the Bulgarians started putting up them Very lights. Then they turned on their great searchlight things - and there we were, trapped with shells fallin' all round us and smashin' the sides of the ravine in on us. A lot of men were killed by the flying bits of rock. And hundreds of those who weren't killed were terribly wounded. We had orders to get back then as best we could. There were nearly 700 of us went up there but only 200 answered the roll call next morning.

Before we went on the attack I went up to see Bill Thompson in his bivouac. I said, 'How you gettin' on, Bill?' And he said again, 'Stan, I'm gonna get killed'. And I said, 'Get on with you. You aren't gonna get killed'. But he did. He got killed. And a lot more of them too, I'm sorry to say. But there t'is.

> 13857 Pte. John William Thompson
> 10th Battalion, The Devonshire Regiment.
> Enlisted Bath.
> Killed in Action
> 25th April, 1917
> Aged 32

* * * * *

LOCAL APPEALS TRIBUNAL
27th April, 1917

Harry W Kite, 27, married, Timsbury, baker, corn dealer, draper and grocer, passed for general service, said he was baking 15 sacks a week, with the assistance of a boy for delivering. - Capt. Mawer: We are told that a man cannot do more than eight sacks. - Appellant said his father had overworked himself getting the business together. - Capt. Mawer: You will, too, baking 15 sacks a week. We want to give you a little rest in the army. - Kite said his sister had got a husband and 17 pigs - (Laughter) The Chairman: which is the most trouble, the husband or the pigs? Appeal dismissed.

Somerset Guardian
27th April, 1917

A young Somerset officer, **Lieut. Wheeler**, Royal Flying Corps, of Midsomer Norton, has had a marvellous escape from serious injury in a flying accident in England. He had gone up in an aeroplane with a pilot to get some practice with a Lewis gun and when they were up about 1,200 feet a heavy snow storm came. They drifted into the height of the storm and the machine was greatly buffeted about. The pilot was strapped to the machine and was secure, but Lieut. Wheeler had to keep his place by holding on to the gun.

The pilot endeavoured to steer the plane to the earth and suddenly found himself within a few hundred yards of the ground. He endeavoured to rise again but the machine crashed to the ground and smashed. Both officers were picked up unconscious and taken to hospital. The pilot had both legs broken, fractured ribs and concussion of the brain, but Wheeler escaped with a very severe shaking and minor injuries. The pilot is still in hospital.

* * * * *

L/Cpl George Taylor

6th Battalion, The Somerset Light Infantry
Late April, 1917

Since the Battle of the Scarpe we'd been stuck in a composite battalion with the DCLI because we'd lost so many men - nearly 20 dead and more'n 100 wounded. Then a whole load of reinforcements come over from England. A lot of 'em were older ones, and who should be with 'em but thik Warrant Officer what'd stuck the daisy on the young'un he put in the glasshouse back in Plymouth - the one what'd promised to get his own back. Daisy Boy were already out there with us, and he said to me, 'Did you see who's just turned up?' Just like that. And I had.

About three weeks later we had to go over the top again. Well, as we were movin' up wi our platoon there were shells comin' over and one landed a couple of hundred yards from where this Warrant Officer were. But I also heard a rifle go, too. Just one crack. Quite clearly. I never took no notice of it, but when I went up there that Warrant Officer was laid out flat. Dead. He were the first one to go. Shot. And he wasn't killed by the Germans, neither! Later on Daisy Boy said, 'Did you see'n?' 'Ah,' I said. 'I seen him all right.' We never said another word about it.

> 5346 Regimental Sergeant Major C H Buss, DCM
> 6th Battalion, The Somerset Light Infantry
> Killed
> 3rd May, 1917

Somerset Guardian

27th April, 1917

It is felt by many that the wives and dependants of men who have been called up to serve their country may be at some great disadvantage in getting their gardens or allotments tilled and planted now that their male friends are away from home. Not only would it be wrong to allow these gardens to go out of cultivation at such a time, but the burden of house-keeping this would entail upon the soldier's wife in the coming months should be obviated. The National Service Committee formed at Midsomer Norton are hoping to obtain offers of part time service from men  within their district to undertake the work of cropping the gardens of the people who need such help. Anyone interested or those who are willing to offer their labour and those who desire the help of men to cultivate their gardens should apply to the secretaries to the Committee Messrs. L W Bottomley and C H Sunderland. Evening classes for instruction in gardening have been arranged to be held at Midsomer Norton on a plot of ground at Dymboro. The first of the meetings will take place on Tuesday evening next at 5:30 . . .

14th May, 1917

During the past fortnight a company of local women and girls have been busily engaged in painting the outside woodwork, level crossing gates and fences at the Radstock Somerset and Dorset Railway. Many people have remarked on the expeditious manner in which the work has been carried out. I doubt whether the Company have had the painting done as well and as cheaply as it has been done this year. The energy and spirit of this party of women war workers is to be commended. It is surprising to many people what women can do when they try.

28th May, 1917

The Government have decided that it is necessary to release more men from the coal mines for service with the colours. After consulting the Miners' Federation, it is proposed, in the first place, to recruit from among men employed at coal mines who are of military age and who entered the coal mining industry since August 4th, 1914, and were of military age at that date, except only men at present engaged as 1) winding enginemen, 2) pumpmen, 3) electricians, 4) fitters and mechanics (including blacksmiths, joiners and waggon and tub makers and repairers). Accordingly, the certificates of exemption of the men thus becoming available for service with the colours have been withdrawn by an Order dated May 12th and made by the Home Secretary. It is, however, only proposed at present to recruit men who may be medically classified A, while B and C men will be allowed to stay in the industry. Every man thus becoming available for service will have the right to appeal to the Colliery Recruiting Court on grounds of misdescription of his occupation, age or date of entry into the industry, and to the ordinary tribunal on private grounds within the normal time limits.

* * * * *

The History of the Somerset Light Infantry 1914-1918
13th June, 1917

BATTLES OF YPRES - HAVRINGCOURT WOOD

On 6th June the *[7th]* Somersets moved from the support trenches into the front line. On the 7th seven other ranks were killed, four by shell fire and three by snipers. The sniper's bullets came from an advanced enemy post and a raid was organized to deal with it. Patrols went out to reconnoitre the post on the nights of 8th, 9th and 10th, and . . . the raid was carried out on the night 12th/13th by a platoon of A Company, under the command of 2/Lieut. C J Lewin. A box barrage of 18 pdrs. was first placed on the enemy post and at 12 midnight the raiding party rushed the post with the bayonet, killing 18 Germans and capturing one man alive. Others were seen to run back from the post, but they were caught in the barrage and must have suffered further casualties. For conspicuous gallantry during this raid 2/Lieut. Lewin was awarded the MC.

* * * * *

Pte. Sammy Taylor
3rd Battalion, The Coldstream Guards
21st June, 1917

In the Spring they'd shifted us from the Somme 'cos they reckoned there was gonna be a big attack up at Ypres. We'd got on a lot better in France than we did in Belgium. We landed up at a place called Poperinge afore we went into the trenches. We had a great big armoured gun come up on the railway lines where they stopped us. That'd loose off so many rounds - huge great things, they must've gone fer miles - an' once they'd finished their bit the gun went back off down the railway line leavin' us to catch the shit that Jerry flung back.

While we were at Poperinge the Belgian people wouldn't let us have water from their wells - an' we never 'ad any of our own. So our officer went along wi' his revolver an' zed he'd have no arguin' but his chaps were gonna have water. Said we'd gone over tuh fight fer they lot an' threatened tuh shoot anyone who interfered. Frightened they, all right. We soon got the water.

While we were there we didn't know one week from the next, but I do know we were out one Thursday night and t'were pelting wi' rain. I remember we come across a little village and a house that were blowed down. An' all around were these lovely lily of the valley. Me an' my mate George picked some an' we were gonna take them back an' keep them - I 'ad mine in me 'aversack. Well, we were potterin' back up to the trenches in single file when Jerry slung up this high shrapnel shell a bit too close. It burst in the air an' sprayed the shrapnel down. I flopped to the ground as fast I could. I never found out if George caught one but I got hit, close to the spine, an' that put me out. When they operated on me down at Boulogne the doctor zed, 'You won't come over this side no more'. An' I zed, 'Thass the best bit of news I've heard!'

15461 Pte. George Slater, MM,
3rd Battalion, The Coldstream Guards
Killed in Action
No known grave
France and Flanders
13th April, 1918

* * * * *

LOCAL APPEALS TRIBUNAL
29th June, 1917

Charles Ashman, of The Crown, Nunney, represented by Mr Henry Hookway, Bath, who put in medical certificates to show that he had valvular disease of the heart, June 1912. As a result of an accident he was incapacitated from work and awarded 10/- a week for life. Captain Mawer said they were not so afraid of medical certificates. He knew a doctor who had valvular disease of the heart, who had a large practice, played golf and did a lot of other things. The appeal was dismissed.

* * * * *

Somerset Guardian
1st July, 1917

Lieut. L Wheeler, RFC, son of Mr. F W Wheeler of Midsomer Norton, paid visits to this neighbourhood on Monday evening and Tuesday morning. He flew over the district in an aeroplane but did not land. While over Midsomer Norton he was travelling at a low level and people had one of the best views yet afforded of an aeroplane in motion. I am glad to know that Lieut. H F Lane, of Radstock, who is in hospital as the result of an aeroplane accident, is not seriously injured. It appears that the accident was caused by another aeroplane crossing the course of the machine that Lieut. Lane was driving and he was forced to nose dive very steeply to avoid collision with the result that he came out of the machine.

Pte. Jim Peppard
1st/4th Battalion, The Somerset Light Infantry
June/July, 1917

One mornin' t'wards the end of our trainin', we was out doin' physical an' the RSM - great big fellow - told the Sergeant to fall us in at the double. Said he wanted four volunteers to make a draft up to go to Indial. Well, Maurice Baber, what'd been to school with me, were close to me an' there were two chaps from Exeter - Mudge an' Kilgannen - and I winked me eye tuh Maurice an' we four stepped out an' volunteered.

I come 'ome on special leave just afore I went to Indial. T'weren't many hours. Mother an' me went down to Mr White's in Norton an' had our photo taken together. I've got'n here - I always got'n on me. I'd like you tuh use 'n fer your book but t'is too damaged. You could buy anythin' in Norton then and she bought me a little Bible an' I 'ad tuh take that wi' me. I've got that'n 'ere too, an' there's a bit of shamrock in'n from Indial, see? 3/6d. Given to him on June 26th, 1917. God be with him till we meet again. Peace perfect peace.

I volunteered fer everythin' in the army, an' if I 'adn't 'ave volunteered fer Indial I shouldn' be here today, an' I'll tell you fer why. The rest of that company we'd bin in went to France, an' there were a boy along wi' 'em called Mark Holder - an' I watched 'em off. I can see Mark now, wavin' tuh me. When we was on the water, goin' to Indial, we heard that within a fortnight that lot was wiped out. Aye.

> 27626 Pte. Mark Holder
> 8th Battalion, The Somerset Light Infantry
> Killed in Action
> France and Flanders
> 31st July, 1917
> Aged 21

* * * * *

Lt. Douglas McMurtrie
7th Battalion, The Somerset Light Infantry

Mark Holder and his companions were sent to strengthen the Somersets' 8th Battalion. There were four Somerset Battalions on the Western Front during June and July and it was the 8th that suffered the worst casualties. On July 8th, one working party of 60 soldiers, had eight killed and 50 wounded, and on July 31st - the first day of the Battle of Passchendaele - they lost a further 57 with 90 wounded. Mark Holder was one of them. My own 7th Battalion was out of the line in July but we'd lost eight men early in June.

Pte. Herbert Caines
Royal Engineers
July, 1917

Once I'd finally been called up I was soon sent out to France with Number 22 Train Crew Company. There were about 250 of us in the unit and we were put on light railways - gauge about one foot eleven. We'd be dumped at a railhead and have to distribute all the stuff to the batteries and the trenches and bring back the wounded. The Canadians always laid the track for us - do miles in a very short time - but they didn't balance it, they'd go back and ballast the bad parts and we'd have to put up with the rest. They tried to arrange the track in a circle so the trains didn't have to meet one another - single track, see.

When I got out there they asked who knew anything about the control of trains, and I said I did. Well, bear in mind that I could work a signal box as a ten-year old - the telegraph and all. I don't suppose you've ever seen the needles on the old signal boxes but I could take trains through with the needles. Trains used to signal 'Train in Section' and you'd have to take that with four keys - four knocks of the bell. Then, 'Train in Line' - that was the next section, then 'Train Passed'. I could do all that when I was a youngster. So, I took the position of Controller over there.

The principle system we had was round Poperinge, then we operated round Kemmel, Ypres - Wipers as Tommy called it - and down to Arras. When a stunt was planned a detachment of us would go off to start a new system - set up a new railhead. One afternoon I found myself up in a place called Vlamertinge, near Poperinge, and I saw the infantry come through. I can see that now, as plain as anything. It was the Highlanders and they looked brilliant - all the kilts flying and the pipes blowing. They were going up to Passchendaele. Passchendaele was only a word then. We didn't know what it meant.

147

Major Sir Torquhil Matheson
Coldstream Guards
31st July, 1917

Passchendaele was an absolute hell-hole, if ever there was one. Before the battle began our artillery had lain down a phenomenal barrage of more than four million shells. That's four million in 15 days, mark you. And three or four days before that finished Charlie Fry was throwing bridges over the Yser Canal with the 4th Battalion, and losing several of his pals in the process.

The battlefield at Passchendaele was almost entirely polder land - been reclaimed from the sea - and irrigated by a myriad channels which our incredible bombardment proceeded to obliterate - smashed them to smithereens. Every shell hole filled with the water. Oozing, filthy mud and slime everywhere. It was an unimaginable, hellish bogland. And you can add to that the fact that the August rainfall that year was the heaviest for 40 years.

At 0440 hours on July 31st, the Guards advanced into this frightful quagmire, with Passchendaele lying just five miles ahead of them. Sgt. Carpenter - Chris Carpenter from Radstock - was at Pilkem Ridge, on the right, with the 1st Battalion. As was George Randall, Charlie Fry's pal. Randall was killed within minutes, one of 42 soldiers that the 1st lost that day. The 2nd Battalion, on the left, lost 45 - as a consequence of which Fry was drafted in with others from the 4th Battalion, to fill the gaps in the line.

> 19204 Pte. George Randall
> 1st Battalion, Coldstream Guards
> Killed in Action (Lost without Trace)
> France and Flanders
> 31st July, 1917
> Aged 28
> *[Randall's son, Douglas, was two months old]*

Passchendaele was the first battle in which the Germans used mustard gas and my father, who by then was Commanding the 20th Division, was one of the first casualties.

Anyway, the fighting continued through August and September, with the 2nd Battalion having another bloody time of it between October 1st and 16th, when they lost 58 more officers and men. The whole division was eventually pulled out to Eperlecques, on October 16th, for re-fitting and training. By that time Fry was suffering from trench foot and, from the sound of it, shell shock. Three days later he was posted home.

It took 99 days to take Passchendaele - at a cost of half a million British and German casualties. Five months later it was re-taken by the Germans.

From the Trench Diary

7th Battalion, The Somerset Light Infantry
16th August, 1917

LANGEMARCK

Battn attacked LANGEMARCK at dawn as follows. All Coys were in position by 3.30am across the STEENBECK. Capt. Ledsham having been wounded, 2/Lt. Lewin MC took command of A Coy. All Coys dug in, few casualties occurring during this operation although the enemy were close by and continually sending in lights. At 4.45am the creeping barrage came down and the leading Coys moved forward to the attack. A Coy were checked almost at once by flanking machine gun fire and 2nd Lt. Lewin was wounded and Lt. Kinsey was killed leaving A Coy. without any officers. Casualties estimated at 4 officers killed 8 officers wounded. OR 35 killed 18 missing and 121 wounded.

* * * * *

𝔖𝔬𝔪𝔢𝔯𝔰𝔢𝔱 𝔊𝔲𝔞𝔯𝔡𝔦𝔞𝔫
WOUNDED IN ACTION

2nd Lieut. Claude Lewin, MC, The Somerset Light Infantry

Second Lieutenant Claude John Lewin, of the Somerset LI, fourth son of Mr C J Lewin of Radstock, has been severely wounded in the recent advance. It was only last week that it was officially announced that he had received the Military Cross for conspicuous gallantry and devotion to duty. When in command of a raid upon an enemy trench he led his men with the greatest dash and determination, successfully turning the enemy out with the bayonet, in spite of all the wire being uncut in front of the trench. He afterwards showed great coolness in collecting his men and bringing them back to our lines. The official telegram which came to hand on Monday stated that 2nd Lieut. Lewin was in hospital in France, wounded, upper right arm, severe.

Lt. Douglas McMurtrie
7th Battalion, The Somerset Light Infantry
August, 1917

Claude Lewin was the last officer of his Company to fall and I suppose, in a sense, I took his place with the 7th Battalion. Almost half the Battalion was killed or wounded. It was Claude's 19th birthday and the end of his war - his injuries were far too serious for him to fight again. For my part, I'd have had no thoughts whatsoever of joining the army if there'd been no war. I had always intended to become a mining engineer and to take over from my father who was managing the Waldegrave Collieries in Radstock - but as there was a war, going to Sandhurst was the quickest way of going into action. I went straight there from Clifton in 1916. The day before I went over to France we heard that Uncle Jack, from Radstock, had been killed.

> Major John McMurtrie
> 151st Field Company, Royal Engineers
> Died
> 26th July, 1917
> Aged 32

That same evening Norman Thatcher, from Midsomer Norton, and I stayed at the Wilton Hotel. Next morning we had a fairly good breakfast before crossing the road and reporting to the transport officer at Victoria Station. We then slept soundly in the corridor of a Pullman car all the way to Folkestone. We left there at three o'clock on a very hot, lovely day - a very pleasant crossing.

We spent our first night in France under canvas in a rest camp, and reported back at the station at mid-day. After a light lunch, we bought some beef and sandwiches and then got a second class carriage to ourselves for the long and tedious journey to Rouen. When we arrived there, Norman and I went into town and had a breakfast of boiled eggs and French bread and butter at the Hotel d'Angleterre. After breakfast, we learnt that Thatcher was going to join the 6th Battalion of the SLI, and I the 7th.

I stayed at Rouen for two weeks on the Central Training School course which included gas, bombing, physical training, bayonet fighting and trench warfare. This was very boring but compulsory. It was held on the Bull-Ring - a huge piece of sandy ground about two miles long and one across, where both Napoleon and Caesar were said to have trained their armies for the invasion of England. I went into Rouen several times while I was there - visited the Cathedral and went to the Café de la Foste for tea several times and to the Brasserie de L'Hotel de l'Opera for dinner once. The food was very good and the prices fairly moderate.

On Monday, August 20th, I was issued with a revolver, ammunition and iron rations and given orders to proceed to the Front. The next day I paraded at 6 pm and took over a draft of 100 men to take with me to the 7th Battalion. We then formed up with other drafts and marched off in one large body about 700 strong, with bands playing. It was all the fun of the fair. On the march a man named Eales had to drop out. He seemed pretty old to me. How a Medical Officer could pass a man like that as fit for active service was beyond me but by the time I joined the Regiment the number of unfit men in the ranks was awful. Frightful. Generally speaking, all the young people had been killed off. God! What generalship.

At the station a man came up to me and asked if I would have him as my servant. I was rather glad and of course said yes. I then got all the men into cattle trucks, had their rations put on the train, put an NCO in charge of each van and then found a place for myself in a 2nd class carriage. Before leaving I got some buns and a mug of lovely hot cocoa at the YMCA and got into the train. There were three other officers in the carriage and we set to and had a good supper and then all went to sleep.

We arrived at Arneke at about four pm next day and, after a long wait, we got into buses and were taken to the Depot Battalion at Bollezele. Here, for the first time, I saw the flashes of guns in the Ypres salient and at times could also hear their report. I was very excited. Everything seemed new and I was enjoying life very much. The next day we were taken to a camp outside Proven. I was posted to C Company, under Captain Jenks. Then, two days later, Jenks went on leave and so I had to take command and was responsible for leading them in some extensive training - the platoon, company and battalion in the attack.

* * * * *

L/Cpl. George Taylor
6th Battalion, The Somerset Light Infantry
22nd August, 1917

We went into Inverness Copse and held it, but we paid for it. That were bloody. After we'd been in there a while we were damn near surrounded and things were looking pretty desperate. I was a Battalion Runner by that time and the CO told me to go back and bring up all the Somersets I could find. Well, I went down and found 28 and took 'em the five mile back to the front line - marched 'em all the way up and never lost one - not one weredn't hurted. When I got 'em back I told 'em where they were to stay. Joe Evans, what'd joined up wi' us, was there an' while we were talking I said, 'Joe' - I shan't never forget it - I said, 'Joe, I've bin and sid a German up behind thik tree'. And that weren't 30 yards from where we were to. 'Now watch theeself.' Oh, he would. Well I body-crawled away but I hadn't gone a dozen yards when I heard a bullet go. And that were Joe. Killed.

> 18855 Pte. Joseph Henry Evans
> 6th Battalion, The Somerset Light Infantry
> Killed in Action
> France and Flanders
> 22nd August, 1917
> Aged 20

Philip Gibbs
The Daily Telegraph
24th August, 1917

We are well beyond Langemarck, and I went among the men who got there first, fighting their way past machine gun blockhouses, which is the new system of German defence, past the deadly machine gun fire that came out of them, and through to the village and its surrounding swamps. These young officers, who have lost many of their comrades, and these men of theirs belonging to light infantry battalions, were sleeping and resting in their tents behind the fighting lines, and cleaning themselves up after days in wet mud and the filth of the battlefield.

They were men who had escaped death by prodigious chance, and officers and men greeted each other joyfully and with a splendid spirit of comradeship as brothers-in-arms who were glad to see each other alive and remembered how they had stuck it together in the worst hours. They belonged to the Somerset LI, and they came from old towns and villages which seem a million miles from such scenes of war.

One young officer of the Somersets knew most of what had happened, and his own adventures that day would fill a book if told in detail. He took me into his tent and showed me how his kit had been pierced by a bullet and torn by the blast of shell fire, and he marvelled that he had no more than a hurt hand cut against the teeth of a German sniper and a body bruised all over, but with a whole skin. 'A bit of luck', he said.

On the way up to Langemarck, to the left of that solid blockhouse called Au Bon Gite, where the enemy held out behind iron doors while our troops went passed them swept by machine gun fire, there were many German snipers lying about in shell holes. They were very brave men, put out into these holes to check our advance, and knowing that they were bound to die, because that is the almost certain fate of snipers on such ground. They lay doggo, pretending to be corpses when any of our men were near enough to see, but using their rifles with deadly aim when they had any elbow room. I heard that one man killed four of our officers, and another killed 14 men and wounded 11 before he was shot through the head.

One of these men well behind our advancing waves lay very still, close to the young officer of the Somersets of whom I spoke, and who saw the fellow move and raise his rifle. He pounced on him and struck him across the face with his bare fist and tore his hand open against the man's teeth. They were bad teeth, and the hand is now festering.

Another sniper gave himself away, and the young officer shot him through the head with a revolver which was very busy all that day. I have already told how these light infantry men had to struggle through bogs around Langemarck, how they fell into shell holes full of water, and how under great fire, they made their way into the place where Langemarck village had once been and attacked the dug-outs and blockhouses there.

Some of the strangest episodes happened between the village and a point called the Streiboom. There were two more blockhouses on the Langemarck road girdled by machine gun fire. The first one was rushed by 20 men led by this young officer I have been telling about, and bombed until 30 Germans tumbled out and surrendered. But beyond was the other blockhouse, and upon this the officer of the Somersets advanced with only six men. A machine gun was firing from the right of it, and it was a strong place of concrete with no open door.

The seven Somersets went straight for it and the officer flung two bombs through the loop holes, but they did not seem to take effect. Then he hurled two more bombs which were his last, at the iron door, but they did not burst. With his bare fists he beat at the door and shouted out, 'Come out, you blighters, come out'. Presently, to his surprise, they came out, not two or three, nor six or seven, but 42 stout and hefty men. Among them was an English soldier, badly wounded, who had been taken prisoner three days before. He was a Yorkshireman, who had lain among the enemy, well treated, but dying. The Germans could not send him behind their lines because of our bombardment, which had cut off their supplies, so that they were four days' hungry when they surrendered.

All told this little group of men took 100 prisoners that day, and their officer himself is said to have killed 16 Germans, and to have wounded many more. After the blockhouse affair he chased a number of the enemy running down the Langemarck road and, using his revolver in the cowboy fashion, dropping his wrist from the shoulder, he plugged them as he ran. After that he went on and held an exposed advance post with a mixed lot of Somersets and King's Own Yorkshire Light Infantry and Rifle Brigade men.

They had next to no ammunition but they held on all night, hoping for the best, but not sure of it. And this young officer, who was their leader, told me that he enjoyed himself, and was fearfully bucked with his day's work. The excitement of it all was in his eyes as he told me in much more detail than I have given the story of 36 hours. He was only one of many who were equally brave and wonderful.

It is indeed an astounding chapter of courage, all this attack on Langemarck by men who before the attack had been bombarded with gas and other shells, and who then floundered in deep bogs where they got stuck up to the waist but worked in small parties up and on, fighting all the way, against an enemy who put up a gallant and stubborn resistance, and sold every hundred yards of ground as dearly as he could. The runners who went back again and again through that slough of despond under damnable fire were real heroes.

* * * * *

The History of the Somerset Light Infantry 1914-1919

The Brigade moved back on the 25th . . . the 6th Somersets had 6 officers killed, 9 wounded and 2 missing. In other ranks the Battalion lost 44 killed, 213 wounded and 74 missing.

Lt. Douglas McMurtrie

7th Battalion, The Somerset Light Infantry

9th/10th September, 1917

My first experience of the Front Line was at Passchendaele. I was in high spirits and looked forward to the experience. On September 9th, the Battalion left camp and we were taken by train to Elverdinghet from where we marched to the Yser Canal. On the way, I saw ruined houses for the first time and all around there was nothing else to be seen but shell-holes, barbed wire, unexploded shells and dead horses.

That night there was a continuous rumble of guns and I found it very hard to sleep because our guns were firing just behind the canal and the rats in the dug-out were far too near to be pleasant. Oh, and the Yser Canal had stagnant water in it - and stank abominably.

As it was getting dusk we left the Yser Canal and moved towards Pilkem Ridge. No sooner had we arrived than the Germans opened up and hit an ammunition dump quite close to us. Shells exploded everywhere and several of our men were hit. We moved on forward and got them into shell holes - half full of water and stinking of the dead.

Later on we made our way downhill into Langemarck - which the Battalion had taken just before I joined the regiment. The village was now totally ruined and we saw quite a few dead soldiers there. We finally got into our positions on the road to Polecapell, where we relieved a Welsh Battalion. Both front lines were on a plain between the Pilkem Ridge and the Passchendaele Ridge, which was where the German guns were.

Mid-way through the night the Germans began shelling our lines but fortunately they did no serious damage other than costing me my Sergeant who was taken away with shell-shock. We spent two days and nights in the trenches before we were relieved by the KOYLIs on September 12th and then, on the 14th, we returned to our positions at the Front. German planes were now continually coming over us, dropping their bombs and killing men and horses. Wherever we looked there was one vast, bleak panorama of shell holes, barbed wire, wasted material of all description and dead and bloated horses. And rats.

At one point I led a party of 100 men up the line, in the dark, each of them carrying a 60lb gas shell. It was no easy matter at the best of times carrying these heavy things but moving along slimy duck-boarding that had already been damaged by shelling was abominable - it was the worst party I was ever on. The men were very tired and several of them tried to dump their shells. That wasn't remarkable at all. Time after time I'd finish going from A to B with two or three rifles round my neck because the poor devils couldn't carry them. At their age they were worn out.

Just before we got to our destination the Germans began to shell our duck-boards heavily. Then men came running back telling of large numbers being killed at the front. I went forward with two volunteers and found one soldier terribly mangled by a shell. He died in my arms. Then I went further up and found another man badly wounded in the leg. We got him back to the rest but I could find no trace of others who had been hit. The enemy continued with its shelling but we had no more casualties. Very late the next day we were relieved by the Ox and Bucks.

* * * * *

Somerset Guardian

Sergt. Christopher T Carpenter, Coldstream Guards, son of Mr and Mrs Henry Carpenter, of Radstock, has been decorated with the Distinguished Conduct Medal for bravery and distinguished work during the great offensive on September 9th and 10th. He was called before the General commanding the Coldstream Guards at the front and decorated with the honour. The award was made for work done when in charge of a platoon.

Sergt Carpenter succeeded in capturing 38 Germans and two officers, besides killing some 28 others of the enemy and wounding 15. The General warmly congratulated Sergt. Carpenter on the achievement which he described as splendid. He is the youngest Sergeant in the Battalion to get the coveted decoration.

* * * * *

Major Sir Torquhil Matheson
3rd Battalion, The Coldstream Guards

Lieutenant Cyril Lutyens died at Passchendaele. It was he who'd carried Sammy Taylor's stretcher so he could play his squeeze box on the Somme. On the day he was killed he was commanding a Company and I can show you the letter his adjutant wrote to his mother:

I shall never forget Cyril coming into the Battalion HQ (a shell hole) to ask for orders about his left flank. He came up and saluted in the middle of very heavy shelling, as if he were on parade, and cheered us all up by joking about a cut he had got on his hand. That was the last I saw of him.

> Lt. Cyril A G Lutyens
> 3rd Battalion, The Coldstream Guards
> Killed in Action
> 9th October, 1917
> Aged 20

Somerset Guardian

12th October, 1917

On Tuesday evening Mr and Mrs F W Wheeler of Midsomer Norton received news of their only son, Lieut. L Wheeler of the Royal Flying Corps, to the effect that he was a prisoner of war in the hands of the Germans but was unwounded. The suspense and anxiety of Lieut. Wheeler's friends has been very real since he was officially reported missing on September 16th. Little information has been obtained since as to what happened to him. It was known that he formed one of a patrol of planes that went over the enemy's lines and that of the patrol two failed to return from a heavy engagement they fought with enemy machines. One of the two missing machines was seen to land well under control, but no-one could say what became of the other. Everyone in the district was delighted that Lieut. Wheeler was alive and un-injured, for the gallant and plucky young officer had made many friends locally since he joined the Royal Flying Corps. Lieut. Wheelers's exhibitions of flying over the district always attracted considerable attention. He had often taken the local detachment of the Somerset Volunteer Regiment at drill and his smartness and efficiency was always admired by the men in the detachments.

19th October, 1917

On Friday morning Mr and Mrs F W Wheeler, of Midsomer Norton, received news stating that a German airman had dropped a message in the British lines, stating that their only son, Lieut. L Wheeler, RFC, was a prisoner of war and wounded. The first intimation concerning Lieut. Wheeler, since he was officially reported as missing, came from the War Office, who reported him as a prisoner of war and unwounded. It now transpires that the German airman's message said 'wounded'. Everyone will hope that more reassuring news will soon come to hand and that Lieut. Wheeler will make a speedy recovery to full health.

* * * * *

Pte. Jim Peppard
1st/4th Battalion, The Somerset Light Infantry

I were stuck out in Cape Town for several weeks that autumn. We'd gone out on the *Huntspill* with 14 ships an' four destroyers looking out to us. I remember one Sunday night it was so calm I were sat on deck and watched the sun gradually go down until it disappeared. You know, you wouldn' think the boat was movin. We had the piana up on deck an' 'ad a service, singin' 'ymns. An' I thought how nice it was. One day, before we got to Cape Town, all the bells went an' we 'ad to put our life belts on an' go up on deck. The escorts an' all the ships looked lovely out on the water, an' then we saw this submarine come up. A long distance away. We carried on fer a couple of hours an' it come up agen an' then one of the escort let go with its guns an' put up such a wave. We never saw the submarine agen. While we were in Cape Town the folk at home must've thought we were lost but it seems someone found us 'cos eventually we changed ships to the *Empress of Britain* and went on to Indial.

STATEMENT of the SERVICES of No. *19914* Name *Charles J. Dry*

Corps	Battn. or Depot	Promotions, Reductions, Casualties, &c.	Army Rank	Dates	Service not allowed to reckon for fixing the rate of Pension (years / days)	Signature of Officers certifying correctness of Entries
General Service		Attested	Pte	10.12.15		
General Service		To Army Reserve	Pte	10.12.15		
	5	Mobilized	Pte	30.10.16		
		Posted		30-10-16		
		CATERHAM.		31-10-16		*Adjutant Guards' Depot*
				FRANCE		
4(?)		POSTED.	Pte	26.6.17		
2		POSTED.	Pte	12-8-1917		
5		POSTED.	Pte	20.10.17		
6(?)		POSTED	Pte	14.3.18		
5		Posted	Pte	7.6.18		
		Transferred to Class "Z" Army Reserve on Demobilization. Date........ Signature........ Officer i/c Records Place....GRENADIAM GUARDS Home address........				

Ivan Chard

Timber Haulier

20th October, 1917

When Uncle Charles were sent home from the war he wasn't the Uncle Charles who had gone away. Not my Uncle Charles. Not as he were before. He come home to Welton Station an' we fetched'n wi' the pony an' cart while we were out deliverin' milk. Took'n up home caked with mud. Filthy. His clothes were stiff wi' all the muck from the trenches, an' he were suh lousy as a cuckoo. Lousy as a cuckoo. His sisters took everything off him and boiled the lot.

I were real excited that he were home but I hardly saw'n. He slept most the time an' we young 'uns weren't allowed in with 'em in the evenin' - we had tuh stay out the way in the back room. Then, in the daytime, I had to go to work. We were on government work then, making duck-boards and things for the trenches, working from five in the morning till all hours at night, so I never saw'n when I got back neither. He hardly went out or done nothin' except sleep - course he was s'tired as a dog 'cause they never got no sleep in the trenches - always on the look-out for bangers, Charlie reckoned.

Charlie reckoned he'd been buried in a shell hole with five of his mates what went over there with him. He was the only one to scrabble out alive. One day while he were home, an' felt up to it, he took the time to walk over to Farrington Gurney to see George Randall's missus and her little baby. But she were out when he got there - taken tea up the road for German prisoners fellin' trees up there.

Charlie weren't home long enough. Seemed like it were just time for 'em to get his clothes clean an' he had to go. I weredn't told when he was going. That hurt me. I come home one evenin' an' said, 'Gran, where's me Uncle Charles?' She were an invalid then an' sat in her chair an' didn't make no reply fer a bit, so I asked again. 'Where's Uncle Charles to, Gran?' An' then she said, 'He's had to go away, me son'. That's all she said. Well, that weren't a very satisfactory answer for me, I reckon. 'Cos I loved my Uncle Charles.

* * * * *

Ralph Mattick
Farmer

That's Uncle Ralph - Grenadier Guardsman - Long John's boy - Charlie Fry's cousin. We were often told as kids how when he was walking out of the trenches to come home he passed Charlie marching in.

When Charlie came home from France he was posted to the 5th Battalion and I know that for a while he worked on a farm in Scotland, at a place called Glencorse. Ralph and Charlie had another cousin, Alexander Mattick, who was working up there in a Military Hospital in Glasgow, and that's where Charlie went for them to calm his nerves down. Alexander used to write to tell Charlie's family how he was doing. But the real damage had been done.

The last time Ralph came home it was straight from the trenches with a week's mud and filth on him. Never even washed or anything. He walked up here from the station and got in the bath. He was hardly home before he went back to the trenches and was killed. We never saw him again.

23898 Pte. Ralph Mattick
2nd Battalion, The Grenadier Guards
Killed in Action
France and Flanders
3rd December, 1917
Aged 26

* * * * *

Ivan Chard
Timber Haulier

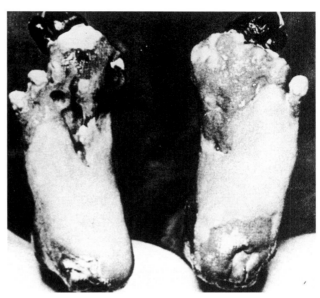

Charlie's feet did play him up fer the rest of his life. You know what yer fingers go like if you'm in the bath a bit too long. Well, you can imagine fer yourself what his feet were like after fighting waist deep in water for days on end. The skin did come away in chunks an' you could see the bone inside his leg - like you can see the inside of a tree where the bark curls away because of canker. He'd to come round our place every day fer Mother to help'n. 'Artie, will you wash out these socks?' He used to have two pairs some days. 'Artie, let's have another pair of socks.' She'd wash his feet and bathe em an' wrap 'em up in cheese-cloths. And then he'd always put his puttees back on to keep his legs comfortable. We weren't put on this earth to do what they did in France, you know.

* * * * *

Somerset Guardian
26th October, 1917

While the Red Cross collection was being made in the streets and Market Place on Saturday afternoon, a Red Cross train passed through the Somerset and Dorset station on its way to Bath. The convoy contained a far larger number of serious cases than any previous convoy that had passed through Radstock and it was noticed by many who happened to be in the neighbourhood that very few of the patients were at the carriage windows. Some of the men could be seen laid on stretchers by people who were close to the crossing gates or on the platform.

26th October, 1917

The Major General commanding the 41st Division has sent Lance Corporal Walwyn Oram *[see 109]*, Hampshire Regiment, a card on which he says: 'I wish to place on record my appreciation of your gallantry on September 21st, 1917, during the enemy's counter-attack, when you remained in an advanced post in charge of seven men, five of whom became casualties. Your utter disregard for personal danger set a fine example to all.' For this incident L/Cpl W Oram has been awarded the Military Medal. On Friday last he came home expecting to enjoy 10 days' leave, but on Monday he received a telegram ordering him to rejoin his regiment immediately.

* * * * *

Pte. Alban Chivers
Royal Army Ordnance Corps
October, 1917

I went to work in the docks in Le Havre first, working in a supply depot, cleaning all the equipment of them what had got killed. Entrenching tools and helves. Stuff all mired with mud and God knows what. I'd sort 'em out and scrape 'em and make 'em fit for issue again. Caw, that were strict there! We slept in a sort of hanger with bunks all up the side - three bunks then some steps up and there'd be three more and so on. The doors were kept open at both ends and that were enough to freeze thee in there - real brass monkeys - and they wouldn't let 'ee put anything up to stop it.

That were a bad winter that year - the wust we had. Later on we were in a marquee wi' no sides an' to keep us warm they'd get us up in the night an' take us fer a route march and then send us back to bed. I did hear that a whole tent full froze to death at a place near us called Harfleur. Chap next to me said we should make our beds together once, so's we'd have double the blankets. What I didn't know was he had sweaty feet. Cor, never got no sleep that night. Said we should do the same again next night but I said, 'No George. Thank you but I've had enough of that'.

On top of the cold we had the rats, big ones, all over the place. They did run over you while you slept. You'd cover your head when you went to sleep but you couldn't stay like that. My wife used to send me parcels, sometimes, wi' a cake in. I used to keep it in a little tin box. One night I could hear the lid moving about and I got up and watched and that were a rat what'd got inside after the cake - lifted the lid. Well, I got me boot and I gave that box an almighty thump. Chap next to me sat bolt upright. 'Bomb! That was a bloody bomb!'

Sunday evenings we used to go down into town, just to make a change, and I remember once, soon after we got to France, we went around to the station and saw all these young French chaps going away. We knew there was something on 'cos their wives and sweethearts and that were all there crying. Next time I were down there the women were all there in widows weeds - heads all covered in black. Their men had gone to Verdun. That was such a slaughter.

160

One day I stopped work to go to the toilet and I bumped into Joe Cottle, from Radstock. He were a proper card. 'Hello you young bugger,' he said. 'How long you bin out here? Don't stop they'll 'ave you fer malingering.' He'd started out with the Coldstreams but he was a mason by trade so he'd got attached to the Engineers. Later on I went up to Joe's camp at Cinder City. Had our photo taken in somebody's back garden - Joe knew where to go - even got a seat for me, look! Then we went and had a cup of tea. Best place for a cup of tea was the Sally Army - better value than the YMCA. Back down in Le Havre there were both of them and the Church Army, too.

Course, there were other places where you could get your money's worth down there. Where the ladies were. Where the women were out on the doorstep inviting you to come in, 'cos t'was competition, their place against another. I an' a Scotsman went in once, just for a drink, 'cause they did sell beer as well. You'd go in an' have a drink an' there were all these girls - course, you could take your fancy. They'd come and sit on your lap an' make a fuss of you, that sort of thing. And that were just for starters, mind.

They were licensed places an' the girls were all inspected by French doctors. There was ever so much VD about, but I don't think it came from those places.

* * * * *

Somerset Guardian
26th October, 1917

VENEREAL DISEASES

Despite the very unfavourable weather which prevailed on Wednesday evening there was a very satisfactory attendance of male adults at the Victoria Hall, when Sir Francis Champneys, Bart, MD, addressed the gathering upon the subject of venereal diseases. The Chairman of the Radstock Urban Council, Mr G E J McMurtrie, JP, in introducing the lecturer, said Sir Francis Champneys was about to address them upon a subject which was practically unknown to many people. They were very fortunate in having with them Sir Francis Champneys, who was one of the leading, if not the leading authority on the disease which they were met to consider. (Applause)

Sir Francis Champneys, in opening his address, thought the subject should be more ventilated than it had been in the past. The subject had been kept too much in the cupboard. The Royal Commission on venereal diseases gave it out, after hearing evidence, that in large cities 10 percent of the population was affected by one branch of the disease, and by another branch about 15 percent of the population were affected. Smaller centres had it less and in rural districts the disease was less common still. Their men would soon be coming home from the front. Some were in hospital now suffering from those diseases or its effect. Ought they to look down upon them? Certainly not. (Applause) They should treat them with sympathy and try to make it better for them to lead straight lives in the future. (Applause) It was the experience after every war that the disease was more rife after the war than during the war. Their men might be coming home any day, and the first thing to do was they must be prepared.

Mr G A Goodwin, of the National Council for the Prevention of Venereal Diseases, briefly dealt with many of the recommendations of the Royal Commission. He pointed out that some people, who lived in country districts, might think that the matter did not concern them, but if their young men went into the cities they were at once up against that terrible temptation and those young men, thinking no one knew them, were soon pushed off their feet. One of the great authorities upon the subject stated that the nation that succeeded in first reducing venereal diseases would score heavily upon its competitors. Had their boys laid down their lives for an England of brothels and drinking hells?

A short discussion took place upon the subject of endeavouring to promote further attractions for the young people of Radstock.

* * * * *

Gwen Beauchamp
VAD Nurse

One day, when I'd just finished a very complicated dressing the Doctor came on his rounds and wanted it removed so he could see how his patient was progressing. Well, he was pleased by what he found and sorry that I had to re-dress it. He then asked Sister if she'd let me to do a similar dressing for him, every day in his other ward. And I duly did. In each case a very large area of thigh had been blown away.

The next day Sister told Staff Nurse to speak to me. 'Do you know what VD is?' Well, no, I didn't. 'The doctor asked if you knew because both patients whose dressings you are doing have it, and he's anxious that you should be very careful because of infection.' I was then told all I should know about VD and so on. I really was innocent in those days. When we started treating mustard gas burns we had a whole section of a ward devoted to men with mustard burns to their private parts and Sister showed me how to do the dressings, removing the old ones and swabbing the part before binding the damaged part with strips of bandages and ointment. After doing this for about a week I went to treat a young corporal and found he was terribly swollen. I told him I'd call the Sister to look at it but he insisted it would be all right if I simply dressed it as usual. I really didn't understand what had happened. It seems extraordinary in restrospect just how innocent I was. I'd already been nursing for two years!

Later on, I remember one case we had, took four of us to hold him down. Turned his brain. You'd be surprised how many soldiers died of it. I read the other day that in one year alone 170,000 soldiers used the brothels in one street in Le Havre. Just one of the streets! I ask you. One soldier in 20 was treated for VD, which was no more than there had been in Britain before the war, but the public was horrified.

* * * * *

Somerset Guardian
2nd November, 1917

Mr & Mrs F W Wheeler have now heard from their only son, Lieut. L Wheeler, Royal Flying Corps, who fell prisoner in the hands of the Germans after a short but exciting and useful career on the Western Front. A postcard was received from him on Thursday week, dated October 5th. Lieut. Wheeler informs his parents that he is in hospital in Stettin, has had his big toe amputated, but is going on well and is well looked after.

He also says that he was over German lines and up at a distance of 12,000 ft, when his aeroplane was damaged and he received a bullet wound in his right foot. He fought his way down to an altitude of 3,000 feet and was shot through both legs. His machine fell quickly but the fall was broken before reaching earth by the machine striking the German telegraph wires. In the crash he damaged his face and was picked up and taken to a hospital behind the German lines. From there he was removed to Stettin, which is some hundreds of miles from the front.

CAPTAIN LEWIN

The statement appeared this week in a Bristol paper that a Captain Lewin, who has been recently killed in action, is the son of Mr C J Lewin of Radstock. This is incorrect. The deceased officer belongs, it is believed, to a branch of Mr Lewin's family but the relationship is remote. *[Captain Francis Lewin M C., Queen's Own (Royal West Kent Regiment), Died on 12th October, 1917, Aged 22.]* Of Mr Lewin's two officer sons one is at the front, the other is still in hospital at Newcastle-on-Tyne.

Lt. Douglas McMurtrie
7th Battalion, The Somerset Light Infantry
11th November, 1917

In November we took part in the Battle of Cambrai. On the 11th we were marched to a small valley where there were dozens of tanks on the move. There was a tremendous amount of traffic on the road - big guns being taken up by traction-engines, ammunition going up in lorries - there was movement everywhere. No one had any doubt that this was going to be a serious affair. Very obvious that the stunt was going to be a pretty big one, and that tanks were to play a major part. Field Marshall Sir Douglas Haig was expected to make an appearance that day but he didn't turn up.

The next day we rehearsed an attack with the tanks and we all got a ride back on them once it was over. Some of us were lucky enough to get inside but most of the men sat on the outside and we rode them for about a mile. They were extraordinary machines. They moved at walking speed and as they weighed 35 tons anything that got in their way was simply crushed.

* * * * *

Gunner Sid Hawkins
Sixth Tank Battalion

We had over 400 tanks at Cambrai - more tanks than anyone had ever seen before. The one I drove was called *Ferocious*. I wasn't with the Tanks to begin with. I'd started off in the Machine Gun Corps - had my own motorbike, so I was sent to join them - but then they went overseas and I wasn't old enough to go with them. The CO was sorry but was there any particular regiment I'd like to go to? Well, I knew there was a draft going to Bovington and I wanted to drive so he worked me in with them. So that's how I came to drive a tank at Cambrai - the world's first big tank battle.

* * * * *

Lt. Douglas McMurtrie
7th Battalion, The Somerset Light Infantry

The road and rail traffic continued to be enormous - with everything moving in one long continuous stream. It was fascinating and exciting to see all the preparations. Scores of bivouacs were being put up and all sorts of dumps were being formed. There was a unit of Indian Cavalry quite close to us and Staff Officers everywhere.

164

Over the next five days we spent a great deal of time practising attacks with tanks - by platoons, by companies and by battalion. Our Battalion was supposed to be taking somewhere called La Vacquerie and the Royal Engineers had rigged up a place to represent the village. They'd constructed a model of the ground we were going to advance over - it was about 50 yards wide and 30 yards long and very well made. All the roads, canals, railways, tracks, trenches and hills were there - everything modelled accurately - and the German trenches were marked with tape. There was an elevated wooden platform, about two feet wide, going the whole length of the model so that everyone could see it properly. We practised attacking La Vacquerie over and over again. By that time we all fully understood that this attack was a very big affair. But the Somersets were going to suffer appalling losses.

On the Sunday before the battle we all went to the Church Army service where **Major Berry** preached about the forthcoming attack and the next day, which was November 19th, we left camp at about 2:30pm. Every man was in fighting order, with his water bottle filled. He had 170 rounds of ammunition as well as wire-cutters and wire-breakers. They also had SOS rockets with them. I was nineteen years old, and within three months of leaving England, I was in charge of the Company.

That evening, when we were in position, a party was sent out to cut the wire in front of us, to make a clear path for the infantry next morning. There were lights flickering all along a line about 200 yards behind the front line. This was the gunners training their guns for next morning. It was the first attack for which they hadn't laid on a sustained bombardment for a week before it started. They hadn't been able to fire any sighting shots, so they had to make sure they didn't hit the advancing infantry - us, that is - when the attack began.

There were dim shapes moving about all over the place, lights here and there. Officers and men going backwards and forwards. Everybody was busy. Success or failure of the attack depended on secrecy and surprise. At about one in the morning we heard the tanks moving into their positions and at four we went to our own assembly positions and I got the men into shell holes for protection in case the enemy began shelling us. The tanks were already there, shunting about a little and making what seemed like an awful noise. Behind us were row upon row of guns of all types - almost wheel to wheel.

It was a cold misty morning and at about ten minutes before Zero Hour the tanks moved forward and we advanced in artillery formation. As we reached the wire each section and platoon ran through the gaps we'd made the night before and reformed on the other side. We'd practised doing this many times and we soon got beyond our own front line and every-thing seemed to be going well.

Then suddenly, there was an appalling noise as our guns opened up and a huge red curtain of flame came down on the Germans' front line. All along the line crimson flame was spurting out in all directions. It was an astounding sight.

Gunner Sid Hawkins
Sixth Tank Battalion

The sky was all a sheet of flames as far as you could see, either way. They old gunners must've wore out them guns with their barrage. As I drove forwards I could see the enemy - some of those ex-Prussian guardsmen - they'd turned 'em into machine gunners to try and hold up the advance at selected places. They'd stop there in their shell holes till we was practically on top of them, then they'd try to get their guns back into another ditch further back - they were good soldiers.

They used to try to hit our front sprockets out to stop the tank and that were easy meat fer 'em then - that's what they did aim for. And they were good gunners. Anyway, we got through it all OK. We got to the Hindenburg Line in about an hour - took 30 prisoners and handed 'em over to the 9th Royal Fusiliers. I was never frightened - excited I think, more than anything.

* * * * *

Lt. Douglas McMurtrie
7th Battalion, The Somerset Light Infantry

We had extraordinary luck that day but the fire was pretty hot and a few men were hit - one lance-corporal who was in a funk was shot through his stomach while I was talking to him. Bullets were whistling over our heads so we were pleased when we reached a sunken road which led to La Vacquerie where we stayed until four o'clock. Soon after this, I saw several columns of our Field Artillery come galloping around the hill over the other side of the valley and watched them un-limber and immediately opened fire. It was absolutely tremendous to see the horses racing along with the guns. Then all afternoon we watched as the cavalry rode over the brow of the hill in their hundreds and thousands.

In the evening, we went forward again. It was raining heavily, and we got soaked to the skin. On top of that it was pitch dark and there was barbed wire everywhere. Everything was slippery and we rolled and slid more than we marched. We crossed the main La Vacquerie road and then struck up over a slope and came to the Hindenburg Line. On our way we'd come across two tanks embedded in the mud; a lone Indian cavalryman; little groups of wounded and prisoners;

ration mules, and a lone Royal Engineer Officer laying telephone wires. We seemed to have seen every branch of the army and everyone was tired out. We'd also met the cavalry on their way back - having done absolutely no good. And we'd seen several tanks on fire.

* * * * *

Gunner Sid Hawkins
Sixth Tank Battalion

Fire was always the greatest danger to us. If we took a hit the tank'd usually catch fire, and if it did then the heat would lock the doors and the crew couldn't get out. Everything that could burn did burn; all the wooden handles, the aluminium bits of the Lewis gun, everything. A tank weren't that easy to stop but if it was hit, the petrol what we had with us - inside and out - was almost bound to go up and the inside of the tank got like a great furnace, pretty well instantly. The fire extinguishers we had were a waste of space. There were never much more left than the burnt up bodies of them what were in it. I lost more'n enough mates like that. It were a hor-rible death.

* * * * *

Lt. Douglas McMurtrie
7th Battalion, The Somerset Light Infantry

In the morning we attacked again and captured a place called Masnières - about five miles beyond La Vacquerie. By then we were overlooking a canal lock which the enemy was trying to shell in order to flood the surrounding ground. The situation we were in was about as nasty as it could be, and we expected a counter-attack at any moment. We were already being shelled from the front, the right and the rear - and nothing is more unpleasant than being shelled from the rear. Then two dud shells dropped right by my platoon and so I moved them just before several more shells fell and exploded where we had been. We were lucky not to lose a lot of men.

In the afternoon, we watched the 6th Division attack along our side of the canal. It was extraordinary watching the tanks go forward followed by the infantry. Several of the tanks were knocked out and the infantry was unable to get very far. The enemy shelled them heavily and we saw men falling everywhere.

That evening I had orders to find a decent suitably-sized building with a roomy cellar where I could house the whole company. Next day there was nothing for us to do unless the Germans attacked so we went into Masnières. There were signs of a hasty retreat all over the place. We found dug-outs, machine gun pits and snipers' posts of all description. At one point I found a German, face down in a pool of blood, just below a hole in a wall through which he'd been sniping at our men as they advanced. In another place there was an observation post hidden in a tall tree with steps up to a platform. Half way up there was a dead German who'd had all of his mouth and half his face shattered by machine-gun fire.

There was still a good deal of mysterious sniping in Masnières but we couldn't find where it came from until a soldier rushed in and said there was a man - most likely a German - dressed in British uniform and firing down the street. I went out and saw a man in khaki kneeling in the middle of the street as he reloaded a rifle. Immediately a bullet went whizzing past us and he sent two more bullets after me before we finally surrounded him and disarmed him. He was carrying several bandoliers of ammunition and he looked awful. Later on we found out that he was a Company Sergeant Major from one of the Battalions in the front line. He'd gone insane from the effects of incessant shelling.

On November 25th I was told to go out to the Hindenburg Line to new company positions. The Hindenburg Line was a very strong line with three wide belts of barbed wire in front. There were dug-outs and very comfortable shelters dotted everywhere and the trenches were deep and broad, with unusually wide fire steps. Machine gun posts had been made all along the line so that it was a very strong fortification indeed. The company was in a covered trench and our HQ was a very cosy little room with a table, chairs and bunks and a stove. The Germans had lined the walls with wood. From where we were we could see the spires and towers of Cambrai appearing above the hill on which Masnières stood.

Early on the morning of November 30th, I was eating some cake and Devonshire cream from home, when the Germans started another very heavy bombardment. After about 15 minutes of intense shelling, we saw them advancing. We opened fire and our Lewis guns began killing them in huge numbers and almost immediately they began working round our right flank. At the same time, their planes were flying over us, machine gunning us from about 60 feet. Men were falling left and right and I saw the Company Sergeant Major go down, shot through the head. It would have been a worthless waste of life to remain there so I gave the signal to withdraw.

* * * * *

From the Trench Diary
7th Battalion, The Somerset Light Infantry
7 a.m.
30th November

Enemy put a heavy TM barrage on old outpost line. Between 7 and 7.30am enemy attacked in strength and apparently broke through line on right. Bn. HQ immediately stood to and lined high ground near Bn. HQ. Many hostile aeroplanes were now overhead flying at about 50-100ft high firing at Infantry. Number of aeroplanes estimated at about 45. Enemy now found to be attacking Bn at rear and Bn on right retiring. At the same time enemy seen to be advancing in mass from high ground . . . and many waves advanced on outpost line from western side of canal bank. Lewis guns were immediately brought into action and fired until all magazines empty. Enemy continued advance from front and right.

P E Chappell, Capt.

Lt. Douglas MacMurtrie
7th Battalion, The Somerset light Infantry

By this time, many men had begun to panic, and were trying to get away from the front line. At Sandhurst we'd been told that if this happened we should threaten to kill them, and if that didn't work we should actually shoot some of them. Well, it was that sort of situation. We were in a good place to make a stand so I cocked my revolver and began threatening them with it. And it worked. Immediately they turned around and began firing away at the enemy.

Shells were still bursting everywhere. While we were there I saw one of our observation balloons go down in flames and the observer come down in a parachute. Almost at the same time one of our aeroplanes was shot down and crashed to the ground. Across the valley we could still see Germans advancing in vast numbers. Again we had to withdraw under very heavy machine gun fire. We got back several hundred yards to a sunken road where, at last, we brought the enemy to a standstill. But by this time I had lost all of my own company. We went into Cambrai with 20 officers and about 560 other ranks. We came out with two officers and 90 men.

* * * * *

The History of the Somerset Light Infantry 1914-1918
1st/2nd December, 1917

Throughout the 1st December the attack *[had]* continued, the 61st Brigade holding the rear element of the Hindenburg Line . . . against repeated attempts by the enemy to break through . . . but these efforts broke down before the splendid defence put up by the British troops. CSM Bulson had put up a splendid fight, covering the withdrawal of the remnants of his Company with Lewis-gun fire: he was afterwards awarded the DCM. Captain L Wild (commanding C Company) and Lieut. R L Tawney (commanding D Company) were both killed fighting, revolvers in hand, to the very last. Capt. Andrews (A Company) fell at the head of his men as he was leading them forward to make a local counter-attack with the bayonet: he was captured by the enemy. The Battalion Signal Officer - Lieut. Paul - who had taken a hand in the fighting, was severely wounded rifle in hand, he also was taken prisoner. Early in the morning Major Preston-Whyte, who with Battalion Headquarters was making a stand, was also wounded, as was Captain Jenks, the acting second-in-command: both were got away. The Battalion's Non-Conformist Padre - Reverend Hines, the Battalion MO - Captain Pickup, RAMC, and the Bombing Officer - 2/Lieut. Stoker, all with Battalion Headquarters, were wounded. Besides Captain Wild and Lieut. Tawney, 2/Lieuts. Pearcey and Caulfield were killed; 2/Lieut. Cox was wounded and died of his wounds on 8th December. During the night . . . the 7th Somersets marched back . . . The 7th Somersets had been practically wiped out.

Somerset Guardian
7th December, 1917

Some people are uncertain as to what should be done this year with regard to children's and other Christmas parties and entertainments. For their guidance it should be pointed out that answering an inquiry addressed to him, Lord Rhondda writes that while there is no Order preventing such a gathering, such entertainments which lead to an undue consumption of food, and particularly breadstuffs, should be discouraged. Such entertainments fall naturally into two classes - those in which amusement is the main consideration and refreshments are merely incidental, and those in which a good meal for the poor is the main objective. In the first case refreshments should as far as possible be entirely dispensed with; and in the second the food provided should consist as far as possible of non-essential foodstuffs and care should be taken to avoid those articles of which there is a temporary shortage, such as tea.

For Xmas 1917

To my dear Mother and Dad

from Bert

1918

Pte. Jim Peppard
1st/4th Battalion, The Somerset Light Infantry
Spring 1918

When we got out to Indial we were just doin' ordinary work - guard duties, lookin' out to magazines an' the like. I were a young chap an' full o' life, but I'll tell you this - an' you can tell who you like - I were a dunce. Not too bad mind 'cos I could read an' count, but I knew out there that I 'ad to do somethin', an' I did. I learnt more in the army than ever I did goin' tuh school. There were a lad out there along wi' me from Radstock, Jack he were called, an' he were called to the office one day 'cos there was an enquiry from home from his people who were worried about him - they never heard from him 'cos he couldn't read nor write. He should 'ave said. I used to write home fer a couple of 'em, Harry Hughes, the gypsy, an' another chap.

I got on all right out there an' I used to like to treat everybody else right, don't matter if they were black or white or yellow, but some of our boys used to really lay into those Indian fellows tuh make 'em clean their kit. That used tuh make I wild. Thass not the way tuh treat anybody. I always got on very well wi' 'em, they'd do anythin fer me. All's I had tuh do was take my equipment off - boots or anythin' - an' put it down, an' there was one of them would come to see if I wanted it done. He'd clean my drill, blanco, do all me buttons - I never had tuh do anythin'. An' d'you know how much I did give'n a week? Four annas - fourpence a week.

Mind you, none of us had much to spend out there. I certainly didn't. When my sister's 'usband were killed up at Emborough quarry she were left wi' a little girl an' no compensation - nothin' whatsoever - an' when I wen' in the army I allowed half my money to her - that were three an' sixpence each week, an' I had the rest to play with. She 'ad that all the time I were away. It were a close family we 'ad.

There you are, thass us, G Company out in Wellington Barracks, in Indial. We'm a smart lot, ain't we! See Mr Coombs? The officer sitting there by Captain Strachey - on the left. This other photo is yours truly, 203853 Private Peppard, J 1st/4th SLI. Old Jim out in Indial. Yeah. I borrowed the uniform fer tuh have me photo took - that were the Somersets' Regulars' peace time suit - an' I had those two pictures of Father an' Mother put in those hearts up in the corners. Don't you think my Agnes picked a nice boy?

Somerset Guardian

1st March, 1918

Friends will be pleased to hear of the promotion of Mr Hedley Stephens from the rank of Lieutenant to Captain. Mr Stephens was formerly at the Church of England School, Radstock and was mobilised at the outbreak of war with the local territorials, at the time in camp on Salisbury Plain. Later in the year he left with the Somersets for India from which place he proceeded to England being granted a Commission as a 2nd Lieutenant in the Somersets.

8th March, 1918

STATION MASTER OF BAGHDAD

A Wellow porter, Sgt. Albert Pritchard, Somerset Light Infantry, mentioned in General Sir Stanley Maude's Mesopotamia Despatch, is Station Master of Baghdad. He was a porter on the Somerset and Dorset Railway at Wellow station and went to India with the 1st/4th Somersets.

A large number of people assembled in the vicinity of the railway station at Radstock on Tuesday evening when it was expected that a party of 30 German prisoners would be passing from one railway to the other on their way to Hallatrow, where they were to be housed and engaged in agricultural work in the district. The arrangements however, which had been made, were cancelled and the men did not arrive until last evening at 5:45 and crossed from the Somerset and Dorset Railway station to the Great Western en route to their destination. A large crowd watched their departure.

There has been some talk of people being averse to their introduction locally but I would remind people who hold this view that there is a great shortage of labour on the land and that unless the labour is found the land will not produce the food that is necessary. Many of the prisoners are skilled farm-workers and they have to be kept fed and clothed and they should also be made to do some really useful work. The best and most patriotic way to treat the prisoners, should they arrive, is to let them get about their work unhindered and unnoticed and thus allow them to materially help the country they were once fighting against.

* * * * *

Annie Cleeves

Oh, come on. The PoWs were all right. I knew the ones over at Hallatrow. They used to work all over the place. We had one working for us on the farm. The only thing we were ever told not to do was to feed them, 'cause food was rationed, but Father said the amount they were being given a day wasn't enough for a man to work on, so every day I used to go up

with a basket of dinner for the man. He always knew when it was time. He had a little stick pushed into the earth on the hill and he could tell by the sun when it was time to eat and time to stop work and so on. They used to come and go on their own, no-one ever fetched them or took them back. There were never any problems. Sometimes Sergeant Tucker used to bring them up to Paulton for a drink. That big fellow on the right there, with the moustache, used to work over at the Paulton smithy - he always moved about quite freely. They were no trouble.

* * * * *

Pte. Tommy Atkins
7th Battalion, The Royal Fusiliers
March, 1918

I was always on the move. Having started off with the Engineers and then re-enlisting with the Service Corps I was then transferred to the Royal Fusiliers who were encamped at Newmarket racing stables. We marched out of there on March 12th, 1918. The band headed us down the High Street and we were on top of the world. But we didn't know what we were going into.

We went by train into London and from there down to Folkestone where we slept in empty houses on the sea front. Next morning we sailed to Boulogne. It was a lovely morning and we sailed with a destroyer on each side of us in case of U-boat attacks. When we got to France we climbed into trucks and were taken to Etaples. Usually at Etaples they put people through the Bull Ring - intensive training - but they scrapped that for us. All's I can think is that they'd lost so many men they were desperate for reinforcements up the line. That's what I think, 'cause they didn't put us through it.

Well, from there they shunted us around to different places - and those French trains didn't go very fast, mind you. Matter of fact we'd sometimes get out of the trucks to pick flowers and then run and catch the train as it was going along. All day we could hear the rumble of guns in the distance. Eventually we arrived at a railhead and disembarked. Then we had to march in pouring rain to a place called Ytres, about 15 mile from Cambrai. Two days later, in the evening, we went up the line.

* * * * *

The History of the Somerset Light Infantry - 1914-1919

The Battle of St Quentin
March, 1918

Towards the middle of February it had become evident that the enemy's preparation for his offensive were well forward. He had already transferred some 38 divisions, all practically fresh and rested troops to the Western Front. His artillery had also been considerably increased, his rail and road communications had been greatly improved and the formation of large dumps of ammunition had been observed along the whole front . . . On 18th March the 6th Somersets were holding front-line trenches in the neighbourhood of La Folie, having relieved the 7th KRR, and it was in this sub-sector that the Battalion was practically wiped out.

* * * * *

Captain Douglas McMurtrie
7th Battalion, The Somerset Light Infantry
20th March, 1918

I'd just finished arranging a rugger match against the Ox and Bucks when Major Berry, the Adjutant, turned up with a wire in his hand to tell me we had to stand to, to be ready to move at an hour's notice. The enemy was expected to attack within a day or two. In the middle of that night the Germans started a huge bombardment and all morning the gunfire was terrific. It was the start of their Ludendorff Offensive and they poured tons and tons of shells into our lines - it was the heaviest bombardment there had ever been anywhere. Germany and her allies were at their last gasp and this was their last big attempt to break through.

Pte. Edward Hurd
1st/4th Battalion, The Gloucester Regiment
21st March, 1918

At that time we were on the extreme right of the British line, adjoining the French at a place called Noyen, where there were a lot of woods. Mind you, where Noyen was, I couldn't tell you, everything was so desolate, no houses, nothing living - no life except the rats. We'd been expecting the Germans to do something. They'd prepared for a big push, to separate the British from the French - the tale was it was their last big effort to get to Paris. There were a million men lined up against one another, and we were outnumbered by two to one.

Early on that miserable morning I was just starting to have a bite from a parcel my wife had sent when, all of a sudden, the massive bombardment started - they'd opened up the start of their big advance. We had to get up and go back quickly. Men had to dump heaps of stuff. I had to leave my haversack and that behind, but I did manage to hang on to my greatcoat - and I'm very pleased that I did, some men nearly froze to death later on.

* * * * *

The Trench Diary
6th Battalion, The Somerset Light Infantry
21st March, 1917

At 4.30am the enemy opened an intense bombardment with all calibre shells, using a new kind of gas shell, the smell of which was not unpleasant, but had the effect of sleeping gas.

At 8.30am he finished gas shelling but continued with other shells. It was very foggy and extra sentries were posted at all points. All Signal Commn. was cut by 4.40am.

At 10.20am the news was recd. by runner the enemy was in the front line. Support Coys. Bn. HQ moved into strong points Egypt where fighting immediately commenced. 2 pigeons were despatched and papers all burnt, the enemy at 10.30am were streaming down the ST. QUENTIN Road from both flanks and poured into LA FOLIE QUARRY.

At 10.35am he was reported to be pushing towards BENAY and CERIZY. 1 officer, 6 runners & 3 signallers commenced to fight their way to Bde. H.Q. with the news & to warn strong points. 1 officer reached Bde. 11.10am. 2 runners arrived 10 minutes after, 1 signaller also got over successfully.

Estimated 20 officers 540 other ranks actually in the front line at the time of attack.

H Frampton
Capt. & Adjt.

Captain Douglas McMurtrie

7th Battalion, The Somerset Light Infantry
22nd March, 1918

Orders came for us to move at about three pm on the 21st and sometime later we arrived at the bridge over the St Quentin road into St Simon. On the way we'd passed frightened peasants clearing out their homes as best they could and leaving with whatever they could carry. It was a pitiful sight, seeing old men and women and young children with such terror in their eyes. They were pretty tearful times. When we got there the enemy was already shelling with black shrapnel just over our heads and the CO took us Company Commanders forward to see the ground. He showed me my front, said the position was very precarious, and told me to get the men digging in immediately.

* * * * *

Pte. Tommy Atkins

7th Battalion, The Royal Fusiliers,
22nd March, 1918

The last part of our journey was through a communications trench and as we were going in, troops were coming out from the front and we were asking them questions, curious to know about this, that and the other but we couldn't understand what they were saying 'cause they were all making funny gasping sort of noises in their throats. Gassed.

Anyway, we got to the front line and straight off I had to do two hours on the firing step. It was dark and I wasn't taking any precautions - had my head stuck up over the parapet trying to see what I could make out. The lance-corporal with me had a go at me 'cause during the day the Germans would take sightings at different spots along the parapet and have a machine gun clamped in position to take pot-shots at night.

When I'd done my stint I went down the bottom of the dugout. It was the Hindenburg Line, the Siegfried Line - German dugouts, German positions. Our people had captured them earlier. Oh, they were lovely but all the exits and entrances were facing the wrong way for us and our people had to alter them so that they had firing steps towards the Germans. Those trenches were 30 feet deep and underground they had wire netting bunks strung between uprights, one man up, one down. Great, but by the time I got down there they were all full up and I had to sleep on the floor. I can still remember what I had to eat that night. Bread, cheese and a Spanish onion.

I fell asleep and the next thing I remember was half hearing a lot of bumping, but I didn't wake up till the Lance Corporal came down and shouted, 'Come on! Get up top! We haven't had anything like this all winter. Jerry's coming over the top'. Well, my knees started knocking together but I got up there fast. The German bombardment had started before five and went on until nineish. We couldn't put our heads up, it would've been suicide. Couldn't see anything, couldn't do anything. Even when the sun come up we couldn't move more than a yard with all the fog and smoke.

At one time the Adjutant was stood behind us with another officer who had a dog under one arm and a pistol in the other hand, threatening to shoot anyone who didn't look to the front. Well, a shell dropped behind us and knocked the Adjutant out and the other one was nowhere to be seen - blown to pieces. I asked my mate if he'd been hit and he hadn't but when I'd sorted myself out I found I had a piece of shrapnel in the back of me tin hat, a piece in the butt of me rifle and another piece in me bayonet scabbard.

Not long afterward the fog lifted and we saw some Germans coming over the ridge - at a rough guess about twenty of them. Silhouetted against the skyline they looked like giants but all the rifles and machine guns along our line opened up and they were all cut down. Every one of 'em.

* * * * *

Captain Douglas McMurtrie
7th Battalion, The Somerset Light Infantry
22nd March, 1918

The following morning the enemy broke through and our Battalion's right flank was seriously threatened. I got my men out and back just as the enemy opened up with their heavy machine guns. We were soon able to see men coming towards us on the horizon but the machine gun fire was pretty hot and it was impossible to make out if they were ours or Germans. They turned out to be men from the 60th King's Royal Rifles who had been forced out of their positions.

I was on my way to give the CO this information when the enemy started shelling us very heavily. Their machine gun and rifle fire increased and I turned to see what was left of my company, headed by an officer, running as fast as they could over the marshy ground - in terror - with men dropping in all directions. My company was being broken up - killed or wounded - nothing left except the dead, dying, wounded and maimed.

It was impossible to form up in the swamp so I led the men to Battalion HQ where I found that the enemy had started advancing and was trying to encircle us. The Huns attacked for about an hour and we continued to fire back, just managing to keep them at bay. At this point the CO was shot through the neck and Berry, who was next to me, got up to look over the bank. He got a bullet right through the head and was killed instantly. He fell on top of me with a groan. It was awful. He was one of the best and kindest men I have ever met. I was terribly upset to see him killed.

> Major Samuel George Berry
> 7th Battalion, The Somerset Light Infantry
> Killed in Action
> France and Flanders
> 22nd March, 1918
> Aged 42

Cliff Carpenter

[Pte. Arthur Carpenter
3rd Battalion, The Worcestershire Regiment]

Arthur was my fourth brother to go. Went into the Warwicks to start with and then transferred to the Worcesters. When he came home on embarkation leave he had an 'LG' and a wreath of laurels on his arm. 'What's that then?' I asked him. 'Oh,' he said. 'That's an extra shilling a day.' And I said, 'Well, I hope that's all it means, Arth. What does it really mean, then'. And he said, 'It's up to us to get out there with the Lewis guns and bang the enemy back when they're trying to advance'. And that's what he did, but he only did it once. He'd only been in the trenches six hours when he died. Only six hours.

At first we just had 'reported missing'. Frances, Countess Waldegrave - she was President of the Red Cross - she got in touch with Arth's officer who was there when he was killed. Later on she brought back his reply down to Mother. It said that the order was given for the Lewis gunners to run out between the lines to force the enemy back. The officer went out with them but soon realised they were doing no good and ordered our fellows back. He said, 'Carpenter was running ahead of me when he fell. I rolled him over and could see he was shot somewhere in the kidneys. If he wasn't trampled to death then he was certainly bayoneted by the oncoming Germans'. Later that day there was a message for him to say our brother Chris had got him a transfer to be with him in the Coldstream Guards.

> 41853 Pte. Arthur Carpenter
> 3rd Battalion, The Worcestershire Regiment
> Killed in Action
> France and Flanders
> 22nd March, 1918
> Aged 19

* * * * *

The History of the Somerset Light Infantry 1914-1919

At dawn on 23rd the two Companies on the canal bank reported the presence of German patrols in St. Simon, and that hostile cavalry were advancing on the canal. The charges beneath the bridges were then fired and they went up with a roar. As soon as the sun rose the fog became worse and now it was possible to see only just across the canal. Charges beneath the bridge at Jussy had failed to explode and the Germans were across. The only Company of the Battalion then in touch with Battalion Headquarters was A (Captain McMurtrie), which was ordered to form a defensive flank from Headquarters to the three Companies along the canal bank. But the marshy ground effectively prevented this order being carried out, though A Company managed to keep in touch with Headquarters. The end came quickly. Rifle and machine-gun fire had suddenly become intense and casualties were heavy. Captain McMurtrie took command of Battalion Headquarters as well as the survivors of his own Company. The three Companies on the canal bank were completely cut off and surrounded and, fighting all the way, Captain McMurtrie and his party fell back.

* * * * *

Captain Douglas McMurtrie
7th Battalion, The Somerset Light Infantry

I now had to take command of Battalion HQ. A great many men had already been killed or wounded and I had no alternative but to withdraw still further. We fell back in fairly good order until we found a Colonel who was holding a small hill. He had a mixture of all sorts of regiments and I was given about 50 men and told to hold the left flank. We were unable to fall further back as we were almost completely surrounded. We all expected that by nightfall we'd either be killed, wounded or prisoners.

Dawn next day - the 24th - was very cold and thick with fog and as soon as it lifted the enemy started machine-gunning us very heavily from the high ground on our right, and shells began exploding everywhere. We stuck this until our own ammunition and bombs began to run out and then I got the order to withdraw.

* * * * *

The History of the Somerset Light Infantry 1914-1919

Captain McMurtrie's party was ordered to form part of the rearguard and hang on as long as possible to the position. So well did these gallant fellows carry out their orders that when the time came for them to fall back they found themselves completely surrounded and cut off.

* * * * *

Captain Douglas McMurtrie
7th Battalion, The Somerset Light Infantry

The enemy was now lining the ridge and pouring deadly fire into us. Shells and shrapnel were exploding all over the place and enemy planes again flying over us and firing into our midst. Men were dropping everywhere, some were horribly wounded, groaning in their pain or shrieking for help. Many were silently dying, others already dead. It was a ghastly situation.

The end was very near and soon we ran bang into a huge number of Germans and were captured. An officer on a horse came up and signalled he wanted my revolver. He took it and fired one round into the ground. I was convinced he was trying it out before killing me. I waited, but nothing happened. The Germans could not believe that a 19 year-old could be a Captain. I then began my journey into Germany where I joined Norman Thatcher in four months of starvation.

* * * * *

L/Cpl George Taylor
6th Battalion, The Somerset Light Infantry

By now Jerry had come over and taken the whole of the Somersets. In fact he come straight through an' took the best part of Gough's army. I'd got back to the Battalion HQ and told them how he'd broke through, but they weren't gonna do nothin. They were gonna stop there. I thought to meself, well you can do what you like, but I'm off and I turned around and started to make a bolt fer it.

* * * * *

The History of the Somerset Light Infantry 1914-1919

At about 10:20am a runner had arrived, breathless almost, with the news that the enemy was in the Battalion's front line. The Support Company and Battalion Headquarters then moved into a strong point, prepared to sell their lives dearly. By 10:30am the enemy's troops in great number were streaming down the St. Quentin road from both flanks. It is probable that by this time the 6th Somersets, as a Battalion, had almost ceased to exist . . .

* * * * *

Pte. Edward Hurd
1st/4th Battalion, The Gloucester Regiment
23rd March, 1918

Once we got the order to move we went back so far and then ran down a sloping field stopping at the bottom 'cause officers were shouting orders at us. Then shrapnel started coming over and men were getting hit and we kept down there till bullets began to come. You'd always know if they were level with your head 'cause they'd go 'houiss, houiss', but these were popping over the top of us, but they were still too close so off we went again. I looked back and saw the Germans coming over the fields towards us in waves and, course, I fired at them, but God knows if I hit one or not. That is the beauty about it all - you don't have the bad conscience that you've hit anybody. You might have, but you don't know it. They just kept on coming anyway, so back I went.

Well, that retreating went on for two or three days - no food, mind - with the Germans sending over shrapnel. Caw, didn't that bark when it went off! Eventually we came to a place with a bridge over a canal, with a towpath running along the other side. We crossed the bridge and lined the canal. Out came our entrenching tools and we dug little holes and stuck the earth up in front of us. Then we could look over the top for the Germans, with first the towpath, and then the canal in front of us. The French forces on our right didn't cross the canal but they dug in on the opposite side. Lying as we were, in single file, the messages were sent along from one to the next, and eventually word came to keep that position at all cost. That meant we had to fix our bayonets.

After we'd been there a few hours, not seeing nobody and not shooting nobody, the shrapnel started again and I looked to my right and saw the French running away. Whether they hadn't had the message to hold on at all costs I couldn't say, but they were off, shoutin' and runnin' down to another bridge. Then, all of a sudden, a face come up over the parapet in front of me and disappeared again - the Germans had got over the canal, further along, and trickled along the towpath beneath us. I looked up and there were a German officer by the side of me, waggling his revolver. His men were behind him and one of the damn fools threw a stick grenade and pieces hit me in my leg. Well, that was it. Down goes my rifle and my accoutrements and there I was - captured.

* * * * *

Pte. Herbert Caines
Number 22 Train Crew Company
Royal Engineers
March, 1918

Well, we moved back - about eight or ten of us - and then got broken away from the main unit. We were told to work our way round the back of Amiens, to keep out of the way of the Germans and to head for the coast, looking for our company. We'd been moved down the line to set up a new railhead, and we'd set the place up lovely with the last word in switchboards. I was Controller and we were due to kick off at midnight. Then, before we could get started, Jerry started dropping shells and the order came we had to move. Headquarters had orders to dump everything in the river and clear out.

We marched in the daytime and slept rough at night - no rations so we had to scrounge food as best we could. We sat in fields and pulled up swedes and cut 'em up to eat with the few biscuits that we did have. We pooled everything and bought a few eggs - the French wouldn't give 'em away. To be honest, I was about the only one who had any money. We cooked our eggs in the same tins we had our tea in.

Eventually, after six or seven days, we got to some place on the road to Abbeyville and I suddenly saw our Captain. The Sergeant who was with us hailed him, 'Sir, we'm lookin' for you!' 'And I'm damn well looking for you, too!' It was pouring with rain and there were no billets for us so we were put in horse lines - gadding about where the horses had been. And there was nothing to sleep on. I ended up sleeping on a piece of corrugated iron. I sloped it so the rain would run off.

* * * * *

Pte. Tommy Atkins
7th Battalion, The Royal Fusiliers
March, 1918

I don't know what day it was but I s'pose it was about 12 o'clock when we'd got the word to move out and back. We heard the German planes going over, 'Mmmuh. Mmmuh. Mmmuh'. Gothas, they were. Once we got moving we lost count of time and distance. We were on the move most of the time but eventually we got to a place called Rocquigny.

At one point when we were moving back I remember passing a bunch of men, sat on a bank by the roadside. I thought they were badly wounded, shouting and carrying on as they were. Afterwards I supposed they were drunk 'cause the troops had got hold of a lot of whisky and stuff from the YMCAs and canteens that were abandoned. And what our troops didn't get I gather the Germans did. That's reckoned to be one of the big things that slowed down their advance - they'd captured so much of our whisky and just got drunk.

When t'was getting dark a corporal came up to me and said they had a shell shock case in the lorry, and would I take him up to the casualty station. Well, I got him up there and there was a hell of a queue and there I was, holding on to this little chap. He wasn't very big - 'bout five foot - round cheeks. Not fit to be a soldier, but a lot of us weren't I suppose. I gradually worked us up to the Medical Officer, an American doctor. He told me to put this lad on a chair by the side of the hut and that's the last I saw of him. I went off to find somewhere to eat and somewhere to sleep.

Next morning I was at a loose end, with no idea where my Battalion was. Then some old soldier came up to me and asked which outfit I was with. I told him I couldn't find them. He said, 'Take my tip. You attach yourself to somebody or another and get the officer to give you a chit or they'll have you for a deserter'. Course I said I would and the first officer I saw were sat down on the bank with a red band round his hat, red around his neck and red epaulettes and I thought, 'Well, that's an officer all right'. So I went up to him and saluted and said, 'Excuse me, Sir. Could you tell me where I can find the 7th Battalion, The Royal Fusiliers?' And he looked at me and said, 'My good man, I am a Divisional General and I don't know where my Division is!' All right - so that didn't really happen, but that's how it felt that day. No-one seemed to know where the hell anyone or anything was. Everything was in a turmoil.

Anyway, I looked around and saw a convoy coming up the road and I thought, 'This looks good. It's going back the right way. I'll tag on the back of them'. I went up and explained my position to an officer and was told to fall in behind. So, fall in behind I did and I thought things were beginning to look up a bit. T'was a horse-drawn convoy of limbers and I didn't know what they had on board till we had gone a few miles and then stopped to unload. That was six Vickers water-cooled guns. I thought, 'Uho, that's torn it!'

So they set these guns up along the side the road overlooking a place called Delville Wood - a steeply sloping wood. My job was to carry the things of ammunition. There was an Irish Gunner and a Scottish Corporal on my gun - good combination, weren't it! The Corporal had a pair of binoculars and was looking through them and said, 'I can see the bastards, Paddy. Have a look through these'. 'Ah, b'Jasus! I can see the bastards, too.'

Well, they opened up with this Vickers gun and the Scots Corporal shouted, 'I can see the buggers goin' down, Paddy. I can see 'em goin' down!' I don't know how many belts we fired but right afterwards the Germans sent over just one shrapnel shell and a fellow right behind us was killed. They weren't long picking up our range, were they?

We went all over the place across country from there, sleeping when it was safe to sleep. I can remember at one point seeing a skull looking up out of the ground and I thought, I don't know, he's probably thinking, 'After we captured this ground, you're running away from it'. But we ended up in a place called Warlow Baillon where they sorted us out and sent me back to the Fusiliers and my mate, Chivers.

* * * * *

L/Cpl George Taylor
6th Battalion, The Somerset Light Infantry

After I left the Battalion HQ I saw Jerry come down and go into the officers' place - looting I suppose. I crawled on fer about two miles and seed all their soldiers bringing up the Germans' guns and food and stuff. I were led out by then, dead like. When I thought t'were safe I walked on till I got to the river Jussy where I saw the Germans stop. They'd come up and go back and come up and go back. Well, about twelve o'clock I thought I'd risk it and I got into the river to swim over. Jerry must've heard the water go 'cos they come up and looked but they never saw me.

When I did get the other side I met up with some unit and told them what was happening over the river and then I found somewhere to get some sleep. When I woke up next morning everyone else had gone but I could see that Jerry was on the move again so I went off for about three miles an' come across a YMCA up on a hill. I went in and there were everything you could want - fags, whisky, everything. I don't mind telling 'ee, I had a bottle of whisky and a few fags.

As I was leaving the YMCA I found a machine gun left there - ammunition and all. Well, I could see the Germans comin' over by then so I stuck a pan on the gun and fired - and I know I got some. Then I smashed the pan on the gun and went off so fast as I could. I went fer miles till I bumped into some French unit - in a wood. They fed me and looked after me a treat. Next morning Jerry come on to us again - but the French stopped them. They had guns wheel to wheel in them woods and that's as far as Jerry got. No further.

Eventually I got back to Etaples and after about a fortnight I was posted to the 8th Battalion. I wasn't with them that long 'cause in April, on the Somme, they lost nearly 400, killed and wounded and I were one of 'em. Jerry put over a shell and caught I on the leg. Put me out. That were me finished. I ended up in a hospital in Cardiff an' a doctor come through and put a mark on me leg, above the knee. I said, 'You b'aint cuttin' he off. He's got me this far - you ain't havin'n now'. It were too easy to cut arms and legs off in those days. Simpler.

* * * * *

Captain Douglas McMurtrie
7th Battalion, The Somerset Light Infantry
Prisoner of War
24th March, 1918

The idea of my becoming a prisoner had never entered my head. I'd expected to be wounded, perhaps maimed for life - but somehow I never thought I would be killed. Now I couldn't get over the feeling that for me the war was over. Soon after we were captured we were halted at a former English casualty clearing station, where German doctors were working very hard to attend to crowds of English and German wounded. There were dead and dying every-where. Others were waiting patiently to be tended.

We then began a tiring march to St. Quentin, passing a huge line of German infantry, gunners, transport and reserves of all kinds. It was like a procession of farmers and farm wagons, not the soldiers of a great army. Everything was in a terrible state. There were poor, bony, starving-looking horses, with ribs sticking out, and awful old carts that could fall to pieces at any moment. Another thing that struck me was the mixture of young boys and old men who seemed to make up their reserves. There was no discipline, no smartness, no decent uniform - they looked like civilians in patched-up clothes, tramping along, seemingly bored to tears.

There were no medical arrangements for them. If a man was severely wounded, he was left to die. The walking wounded were bandaged up and then left to make their own way to the nearest aid post, and then get back to Germany as best they could. There were no stretcher bearers, no ambulances, no ambulance trains. It was simply fend for yourselves. We passed many dead, both ours and the enemy's, and they had all had been stripped of their boots, and often their clothes. Germany was in desperate need of clothing and leather.

After 25 kilometres marching we reached St Quentin. The next day, as we marched through a fairly large town, an old French woman came up to give us food, but a passing German officer saw it and began shouting at the top of his voice, hitting the poor woman over the head with his whip. Then they arrested her and carted her off. We had a brief wait there for some French Officers to join us and then set off again at about mid-day for the worst march I've ever been on. It was a dusty road and we were absolutely starving - weak from lack of food. All that we had were some raw turnips and carrots that we got from a field that we passed.

The day after, they halted us in a place called Leval. It was Good Friday and all the villagers came out with coffee, biscuits, bread and eggs. Later on, we arrived at a small camp. We were given barley that evening and next morning coffee and a slice of bread, then soup at mid-day and again at six pm, but that was all. Then I had my first shave for about nine days - and it hurt!

On the following morning we were put on a train and all that day we travelled through beautiful country. Two days later we finally arrived at Rastatt Camp - and it was a pretty forlorn place. We were starving - we'd been on the train for almost three days and during that time had only had three meals. Rastatt was the biggest hell I have ever been in. We had a straw pillow and terribly hard straw mattresses and barely enough blankets on our beds to keep us warm during the colder days - and we were still famished. The sanitary conditions were awful and officers were everlastingly coming round to inspect the camp. And from the news we could get the Allies seemed to be almost certain to be beaten.

* * * * *

Pte. Edward Hurd
1st/4th Battalion, The Gloucester Regiment
Prisoner of War
March, 1918

Although I'd been captured, I don't think I ever felt they were gonna win. It was just a case of hoping you would live, and being a prisoner meant you had a better chance. I suppose we ought to have had a different fighting spirit but you had a feeling that you were safe - you'd finished with it. You'd see it through. I've no idea where we went once I'd been captured but there were German soldiers there to keep us in order and I had to hobble along as best I could with the shrapnel in my leg. After quite a while we were entrained - stuffed into the trucks like animals - couldn't move.

Eventually we stopped at a railway station where they had food for us and we were allowed to get out, so many at a time. The locals must have known there was a trainload of prisoners coming 'cause while we were waiting for our food the German women were standing round us shouting, 'Englander - schweinerei', and spitting at us. I suppose it's only what they'd been told. We was always swines.

Well, they gave us soup from big cauldrons, 'cept you couldn't call it soup. No meat or anything, not soup as we would know soup - just watered down sour kroot stuff, nothing' with any strength to it. And that's what made a lot of men ill, including myself. While we were packed tight in these trucks some men needed to urinate - or do the other - and we had no option but do it there, where we stood. And the stench and smell - well! Eventually we got where we were going and were put into a disused brewery, with a big yard and buildings with bunks in.

By then my leg was swelling up badly, and I were put to bed. A French doctor came on the scene then and had me moved out on a stretcher. I think what happened next was laughable. As these two Germans were carrying me across the open yard, with a big red cross in the middle, they heard one of our planes coming. These Germans were terrified - just dropped me out there in the open and ran like hell. And there I was - left out there till it was all over.

Another time I got out of bed and crept and hobbled out towards the barbed wire where there was a German sentry. There were a Frenchman by me and I distinctly heard him say, 'Hangley no bong, hangley no bong, hangley no kamrad'. You know what that meant? English no good. He was begging for food. You can't blame him though - the French were just as hungry as we were, and we might have done exactly the same - though I was pretty hungry, I don't mind tellin' 'ee. While we were still there we saw a party of German soldiers halt by their field kitchen. And do you know what they had to eat? A load of boiled stinging nettles! Yes, only stinging nettles. Could you see a British soldier fighting on stinging nettles?

* * * * *

Somerset Guardian

29th March, 1918

Potatoes

Last year the County of Somerset

Produced 24,800 Tons of Potatoes

Consumed 41,800 Tons of Potatoes

Deficit 17,000 Tons

Lord Rhondda and Mr Prothero
appeal to every man who has a farm,
a garden or an allotment to plant
more Potatoes to make the County

SELF-SUPPORTING

Frances Craig
Women's Land Army
March, 1918

During the war they couldn't get potatoes in London and there was no rationing so I went up from the farm by train, armed with a whole load of the stuff - a huge hamper and a great sack - for friends in Sheppey. When the train arrived I had to get from Paddington Station to Victoria and I wondered how the dickens I was going to get across London. Hadn't the money for a taxi so I stopped one of the buses and said I'd give the driver half a pound of butter if he'd take me to Victoria. And he did! When I got there I gave another man some potatoes to take me up Tulse Hill. Priceless!

When I got to Sheppey it was full of troops. My friends there had a horse and I used to ride it down to the aerodrome to watch, and one of the pilots came out while I was on this pony in Land Girl uniform and said, 'Would you like to go up with me?'. Would I! He said I should come back at a certain time and he'd do it. Course, he shouldn't have. It was against all the rules. He was flying one of those fighters they had in those days. He gave me goggles and a muffler thing and up we went. Flew all over the Medway and Sheerness with me feeling all queer and queasy. He broke every rule ever made. Then he asked if I'd like to go to Queensborough for a meal, but as I was staying with friends I couldn't. Then I rode back to the farm.

* * * * *

Somerset Guardian
29th March, 1918

In connection with the calling up of young single coal miners, a Medical Board commenced duty at Radstock Victoria Hall on Monday. A certain number of men are being called up for examination each day and it is expected that the work will take three weeks to complete. The government have decided to recruit 50,000 coal miners from the British mines and the proportion allotted to the Somerset coalfield is 311, all young men between the ages of 18 years and 8 months and 25 years. A certain number will be from each colliery and that number will be calculated in proportion to the number of men employed in each pit in December 1917. Only single young men and widowers without children are being called up, and only those who are passed as fit by the National Service Medical Board will receive their papers to join the Army. Men will be called up for service in the order in which they are drawn until the number required has passed into the Army. If any man should refuse to present himself for medical examination at the time required he will be medically classified as Grade 1, which means fit for general service.

Pte. Tommy Atkins
7th Battalion, The Royal Fusiliers
April, 1918

After the Vickers Gun business we had a rough time at Auvelais Wood for nearly two months. We were up against an outfit called the Jaeger Rifles - huntsmen. We made one attack that was supposed to capture the wood. Went in about 600 strong and came out after two days with 127 men and a Second Lieutenant. Then they sent in a Battalion of the Marine Light Infantry and they did something I'd never seen before. They mounted their guns along a ridge behind the attacking troops and fired over their heads as they advanced. I can remember seeing the tops come off the trees as they went forward. The Marines re-captured the wood.

One day Chivers and I got up into the front line and found some rations abandoned by the Artists Rifles. Oh, they used to amuse our lads no end! Normally, when we relieved another outfit at night, we'd call out, 'What mob are you?' And they'd answer, 'The Lancs' or 'The Dubs' or whatever, but with this lot we'd call out 'What mob are you?' and they'd answer, 'We ah not a mob, we ah The Ahtists Rifles'. Always the same: 'We ah not a mob, we ah the Ahtists Rifles'. Our lads used to fall about! Anyway, so we found these rations what they'd left; bread and cheese and so on. And a half a gallon of rum. We took the cans back to the dugout and the Corporal said he'd take care of the rum - thought he might. He gave us a drop each and then sat down in a corner with a pint enamel mug and the can. T'wasn't very long before he was asleep an' then we had our turn.

One day we were taking rations up the line, struggling through the mud and slime, and Chivers reckoned he'd rather be dead. And next day he was. Where we were was on a bit of a slope with an Artillery battery behind us - 4·5 pounders I think they were - that used to fire over our lines. We came under attack at eleven and he went straight down. He didn't appear to be in any immediate danger but I asked an officer if I could go back and get a stretcher. But I was told there was no point. He was dead. Later on that day, when we'd come out the line, I went to the bivouacs for a kip - just canvas stretched over poles - and Martin, who I'd just shared a parcel with in the line, was already there, asleep. Well, like always, even when I dropped off I could still hear these shells firing and bursting and the next thing I know the Provost Sergeant is pulling at my blankets. 'Where's Martin's tunic?' 'I don't know. Ask him.' 'I can't. He's dead' 'He was asleep just now.' 'Well. he's dead now - you'd best look sharp if you want to see him. They're taking him away.' Seems the poor devil had woken up and gone out for a stretch and a German shell come and blew him to bits.

Pte. Albert Chivers
7th Battalion, The Royal Fusiliers
Died
5th April, 1918

Pte. James Martin
13th Battalion, The Royal Fusiliers
Died
5th April, 1918

[Forty six men with the surname Martin died whilst serving with the Royal Fusiliers in the Great War. 2,755 more Martins from the UK and its former colonies also died whilst serving with other units.]

189

𝔖𝔬𝔪𝔢𝔯𝔰𝔢𝔱 𝔊𝔲𝔞𝔯𝔡𝔦𝔞𝔫

26th April, 1918

News was received in Radstock on Friday morning of the death of 2nd Lieut. Leslie Foster, Somerset LI, elder son of Mr and Mrs Thomas Foster, of Elmdale, Radstock. 2nd Lt. Foster was a very bright and cheerful young man who identified himself closely with the activities of the Wesleyan Church, Radstock.

Victor Foster
Schoolboy

Leslie was my eldest brother. The Post Office were very sensible about it, they'd had the telegram overnight but didn't send it up until the morning. A girl brought it up with the normal mail at eight o'clock. I was the only one here, and I did not know what to do with myself. The whole world collapsed. I couldn't go to school.

My brother was seven years older than me and when he left school he had helped father with his building concern, then he started going to evening classes and took drawing exams and building instruction and decided to go into teaching. He'd just got his first job, at the Manual Training Centre in Twerton, Bath, you know.

Then in January 1916, he joined the army, exactly a year after my cousin Cecil was killed with the Coldstream Guards. Leslie went into the Somersets at first but then he got a commission and transferred into the King's Liverpool Regiment, which was what one of the Lewin boys had been in, I believe. I learnt afterwards that Leslie had taken over command of his company shortly before he was killed. There were a whole lot of my brother's classmates who were killed, you know, a whole stack of them.

In the end I did take a train in to school - just had to do something, and the Head saw me. Said, 'Well, we didn't expect to see you today, Foster'. It was just the way he said it - I could have chucked something at him.

> 2nd Lt. Leslie C Foster.
> King's Liverpool Regiment.
> Killed in Action
> France and Flanders
> 13th April, 1918
> Aged 25

𝕾𝔬𝔪𝔢𝔯𝔰𝔢𝔱 𝔊𝔲𝔞𝔯𝔡𝔦𝔞𝔫

12th April, 1918

THE CALLING UP OF YOUNG MINERS - THE RESULT OF THE DRAWS

The medical examination of unmarried miners and those who were widowers without dependent children has been proceeding this week at the Victoria Hall, Radstock. The draws have been made by the Rector of Radstock, the Revd. A N Bax, as a person having no direct interest in colleries or miners. The first draw took place on Friday afternoon.

* * * * *

Joe Ruddock
Coal Miner

Oh ah! I were down there at the last goin' off - down the billiard room at the Vicky Hall. At one time, see, the miners couldn't be taken, but they got so short of men they changed the rules. What they done was have the vicar - Reverend Bax - draw so many as had tuh go out of a hat. Over 300 of them. They had chaps from 23 pits down there and that took nearly two weeks to sort 'em all out. Here, this's me with a bunch of 'em what went - the 'andsome one at the back, with the specs. I were born in 1900 - I waddn' old enough to be illegible.

Some of 'em reckoned they'd skip the draw and go straight in the Navy - but they couldn't, 'cos they were told the Navy was full, thank you very much. An' if this goes in your book spell me name right. I'm a Dock not a Dick.

Pte. Tommy Atkins
7th Battalion, The Royal Fusiliers
April, 1918

We were in the outpost one night at Auvelais Wood and an officer came round to ask if there was anything to report. He was only a youngster - their life expectancy wasn't very long - three months or so. They used to get picked off if they were in front and in the end they dressed them up in ordinary uniforms - not like officers. Anyway, I said I thought I'd seen someone moving about in the German lines. Well, he couldn't see anything so he went on his way to the next outpost on our right. He hadn't been gone long when I heard Crash! Bang! Wallop! from the outpost on my left. They'd been firing a Lewis gun at the German lines all night and Jerry must have got fed up with it because they'd sent over a raiding party and stopped 'em, using their stick grenades - potato mashers. They were longer than ours but lighter and you could throw them farther. Two of our chaps were wounded and ran away but the third one they'd caught and taken back with them. Just in case they put him through the mincer and shelled where we used to sleep, we slept out in our fox-holes after that.

Another time we were trench mortaring them and it seemed that they were dropping short so I said I'd go and tell them. As I was making my way back along a lane they started firing back - just to show there was no hard feeling - and I dropped down into a ditch away out the way of whatever it was - gun, mortar, manure, anything. I could see the flashes and hear the cracks of the bullets over our heads like someone slashing a large whip in your ears. While I was in the ditch I could smell a horrible smell and I found this corpse of an officer who'd been dead for weeks if not months. His skin had gone black as coal and bloated, with his uniform all blown up. I noticed that he had long finger nails and long curly hair. It'd gone on growing.

About Easter time, Padre came round trying to get people to go to Holy Communion, because most people are a bit shy about going. He persuaded two of us to go - the only time I've ever been in all my life. I'm C of E. I don't think it made much difference to my future.

* * * * *

Captain Douglas McMurtrie
7th Battalion, The Somerset Light Infantry
Prisoner of War
1st June, 1918

On June 1st we were moved from Rastatt to Graudenz with guards who had orders to shoot if we tried to escape. One officer did get away but was later caught and got eight days cells. (At Rastatt an officer who tried to cross the wire was shot through the head and killed. Later on three others did manage escape but were eventually caught and thrown into the cells for their trouble.)

After we'd been at Graudenz a while, 16 officers made an attempt to escape. They'd got into the cellars and then bored through a yard of concrete with only a pen-knife and made a tunnel, 34 feet long, shoring it up it with bed-boards. When they had about two hours work still to do we were asked to make a row to attract the attention of the sentries. We shouted and sang and whizzed tins down the stone corridors and created absolute pandemonium. Bosch sentries immediately appeared but there wasn't an English officer in sight. As soon as they had gone we started the row again and the same thing happened.

In the meantime the escaping officers had finished their tunnel and got clear of the camp armed with maps and haversacks with food. The first two ran into a sentry but the other 14 escaped. They were all caught in time, but one party got as far as Danzig and were free for over two weeks.

Another officer - Captain Clinton - did escape in an almost impossible fashion. There were about half a dozen insulated wires running from the second floor of our block to a wooden telegraph pole. Clinton climbed along these wires under the eyes of a sentry with a loaded rifle who was too astonished or slow to open fire. He got clean away - on his sixth attempt.

* * * * *

Pte. Edward Hurd
1st/4th Battalion, The Gloucester Regiment
June, 1918

After I was captured I was shunted around to various places and then I was taken to a place called Stendahl, in the Province of Saxony. I was put in a field hospital - all tents - and this is a strange thing, I seemed to be all on my own. I was quite a novelty. They'd come round and look at me and say, 'London kaput, Paree kaput, London kaput'. I remember one German there, and he was human - he gave me a little muslin bag with tiny biscuits in - 'Here Tommy, good'. There was proper doctors there, too, and they cut open me leg and got out the shrapnel, but they never put me to sleep - naw. You had to be hard - hah!

There were some wicked incidents happen out there but there were some laughable ones, too. I remember once a group of us went out for a walk with an armed guard and then we all stopped in a field for a rest. This guard stuck a bottle up on a post and fired at it and missed. Well, one of our fellows who'd been out there for some time could speak pidgin German and borrowed the rifle and had a go and hit the bottle. Borrowed a loaded rifle!

One day a British doctor turned up from somewhere and took a look at me, 'cause I still had this dysentery thing. How he got it I don't know, but he gave me some Scott's Emulsion - that's a very white liquid that tastes and smells like fish. That got me on my feet and ultimately I became as sound as a bell.

Lance Corporal George Henry Taylor, Signallers, has been awarded the Military Medal for service in France during the 'push' of March last. He has been in the American Hospital in France with a wound in his left arm, and has since been transferred from his old Battalion to another. His old Commanding Officer has written congratulating him on the fine spirit he has shown. He is only 19 years of age, although he has been serving nearly three years and has been wounded twice. After his first wound he left hospital and came home on leave, and his parents did not know he had been wounded till he had been home for several days. They have not yet heard anything about his award.

* * * * *

Pte. Sid Hawkins
6th Tank Battalion
8th August, 1918

Our Whippets were meant for Cavalry support but it never really worked out properly. Early in August we found ourselves lined up in the edge of a wood near Amiens, with the Cavalry - the elite horsemen - behind us in the trees. The Dragoon Guards were there and the Hussars - several of the well-known regiments. Everyone was waiting fer 6 o'clock or daybreak, whatever it was. Then the whistles did go and off we went and, oh, that was a wonderful sight, that was, as they all came galloping through and streaming out of the woods. I don't know what happened to them after that - we didn't see them any more.

1st/2nd September

Colonel West - he with the stick in the picture - were only in charge of the Battalion for ten days. He knew no fear. I remember one day he touched me on the shoulder and said, 'Hawkins. Come on, I want you to come along with me'. And he and me and another soldier went up near the German lines. Then he told us to get in a shallow - well, we did that quick enough, while he were stood up there with all the Germans shooting at him. Bullets were whistling by'n but he took no notice. We always were issued with pistols - revolvers, Colts or Smith and Wessons, I had me Colt and me Marksman's Certificate - but it would have been suicide to shoot back, but there he were, just stood up looking through his glasses at the ground where we should get at 'em next morning. God knows how they missed him.

Next day we were attacking at a place called Lagnicourt and it were a bit rough. Colonel West rode out in front of us, on a white horse - a white horse, mark you! - shouting to us to give them what for. 'For God's sake put up a good fight,' he was shouting. Daft article. There was incredible machine gun fire that day. He was bound to get killed. And he was. I saw him go down. He got the VC for that.

* * * * *

Somerset Guardian
August, 1918

CHIEF PETTY OFFICER GEORGE PROWSE'S MAGNIFICENT RECORD

Although employed as a coal miner **Chief Petty Officer Prowse** volunteered for service and enlisted on Feb. 27th, 1915, with Able Seaman William Sherborne, another Camerton man. CPO Prowse sailed for the Dardenelles on September 5th, 1915, but came back to France in August 1916. He was wounded *[in the shoulder and thigh]* in the Battle of the Somme on November 13th, 1916, and also at the Battle of Arras *[a three inch wound below the heart]* on April 23rd, 1917. His gallant conduct when in action has been brought to the attention of his superior officers on more than one occasion.

THE LONDON GAZETTE

August, 1918
Distinguished Conduct Medal

Chief Petty Officer George Prowse

Led his men with great gallantry against a machine gun post holding up the flank of his company. On a subsequent occasion he held a position against repeated counter-attacks which were supported by an intense bombardment for twenty four hours. His courage, leadership and cheerful disposition had an invaluable effect on his men.

Somerset Guardian

September, 1918

. . . Chief Petty Officer Prowse's invalid father quite recently received a most interesting account of his son's devotion to duty during the great advance on September 2 and 4 last. A recommendation, signed by 23 officers and non-commissioned officers and men of his Battalion, was forwarded to the Commanding Officer stating that 'his almost super-human courage and devotion has commanded the deepest respect and admiration of his Company, who all trust that the highest award possible will be made to a brave soldier'.

This recommendation related that on September 2nd a portion of Chief Petty Officer Prowse's Company was disorganised by heavy machine gun fire from an enemy strong point. He collected all the men around him and organised and led them with the greatest coolness and bravery against this strong point, which, after very stubborn resistance on the part of the enemy, he succeeded in capturing with 23 prisoners and five machine guns. Solely through his gallant assault on the enemy position, many casualties to the company advancing to the right were avoided. After reaching the objective, he, on his own initiative, took a patrol forward in the face of much opposition. After lying isolated in open ground, swept by machine gun fire until darkness set in three hours later, he established a machine gun post on the high ground east of *[name of place omitted]*. By this daring action he succeeded in cutting off all enemy communications to and from the village and caused important captures of men and transport.

Several furious actions took place during the night. On one occasion he rushed 50 yards in front of the position to an ammunition limber that was endeavouring to escape, engaged three Germans in personal combat, shooting them and capturing the limber. He was the inspiration of the successful coup de main effected by the company on that night. He was among the first to enter the village on Sept. 4th and took a Lewis gun section to the outskirts of the village to cover the advance of the remainder of the Battalion on the right. Accompanied by only two men he rushed forward with complete disregard of personal danger, and with bomb, bayonet and revolver attacked the nest, killing six Germans and capturing 13 with two machine guns. CPO Prowse was the sole survivor of his heroic little band, and by his gallant action he enabled the Battalion on his right to push forward without more loss by machine guns from the village.

A heavy artillery barrage on the village, prevented the arrival of support, and to a determined counter-attack with bombs and machine guns, the forward positions were compelled to fight a rear-guard action through the village to the main English position. In the withdrawal, Chief Petty Officer Prowse's gallantry in picking up, under heavy rifle fire, wounded men who would otherwise have been abandoned, was quite noticeable. He placed a wire barricade across the main street, barring the enemy's advance and remained alone to effect this purpose. Throughout the whole operation his magnificent example and leadership were an inspiration to all, and his courage was superb.

* * * * *

Sub-Lieut. John Mullooly
Drake Battalion
Royal Naval Division
30th September, 1918

Dear Mr Prowse,

I am very sorry to have to inform you that your son was killed on September 27th during an attack on a hostile enemy machine gun nest, which attack he led and owing to his example and determination, was succesful in wiping out the enemy's machine guns and crews. Unfortunately your son was struck by a bullet and died instantly. The Naval Division have been engaged for such a length of time in constant attack that there are very few of the old battalion here who personally knew your son to drop you a letter. For his work, example and courage he was awarded the Distinguished Conduct Medal and his honour was a well-merited one. I speak as a newcomer but words cannot express the praise your son has had from anyone who had come in contact with him.

With my deepest sympathy

I remain yours sincerely,

John Mullooly

Sub-Lieut. Tom Simmonds
Drake Battalion
Royal Naval Division
31st October, 1918

Dear Mr Prowse,

I am unable to give you any information regarding your son's death as I was hit previously. We were together at the time when I was hit. George was quite all right when they carried me away and it was not until I arrived here that I actually learned of his death which I can assure you I have deeply felt. No one realises the value of such a man except those

197

who are closely connected with him. I can assure you that his loss is greatly felt. It is one of those losses that we cannot replace very easily nowadays and in losing your son this Company, and also his Battalion, has suffered. A more upright, honest and quieter man I have never met and his whole conduct in action and among his men won the admiration and respect of all connected with the Battalion.

He was loved and respected from his Commanding Officer downwards and his name will always live in the history of the Battalion. It was gratifying to me that he was awarded the DCM and also that the further recommendation for the Victoria Cross is still under consideration, the result of which we should hear any day now. No man ever earned distinction more than your son and when I recommended him for the VC he fully and justly deserved it and I can assure you that every man in the Battalion was delighted when they knew and it is my sincere wish that the award is granted.

I am more than sorry that he will never wear his well-earned distinction but I sincerely hope that you will cherish the award granted him and always look on him as a brave and true soldier and - above all - a true gentleman. If I wrote all day I would not be able to express my feelings towards him and no-one knows how deeply I feel his loss. I am extremely sorry that I am unable to give you any information about his sad death but I must ask you to please accept and convey to all concerned my deepest sympathy towards you in your sad bereavement in the loss of such a gallant son.

Just as I am finishing this letter I have received this morning's Times and am delighted to see that your son has been awarded the VC so please accept my heartiest congratulations, and if you should have the opportunity to visit me here I should be delighted to see you.

Yours most sincerely,

Thomas Simmonds

Z/424 Chief Petty Officer George Prowse
Drake Battalion, Royal Naval Division
Killed in Action
France and Flanders
27th September, 1918
No Known Grave
Aged 32

Pte. Stan Small
10th Battalion, The Devonshire Regiment
18th September, 1918

After the battle for Petit Couronné when we had so many men killed and wounded we had to lie low and get re-organised - get men out from England to make up our numbers. We had some come from the Lothian and Border Horse - nice chaps. Then, in September, we attacked again, went back up with Greek forces on the right and us on the left - and this time we broke through. After a bit we were pulled back from the front and riding on top of my mule I could see absolutely tremendous explosions going off in the enemy's lines. Well, we got back to our camp at round about two in the morning and hadn't bin there more than half an hour when the Sergeant said, 'Harness up'. We were goin' straight back up where we'd just come from.

Well, we got back into the ravine, waitin' to attack. They were puttin' up these Very lights from the Bulgarian lines and they did come down from the sky and show everythin' up on the wrong hand. They were doin' that till just before daylight. Then the order came. Advance! Oho! I shall never forget it! The Devons were in the lead - the first of all the Division. We went up to the enemy lines and found these deep trenches and then had to run around to see what we could find to fill 'em in to get the wagons over.

That day we kept goin' forward without too much trouble but the next day the Derby Yeomanry lined up in front of we because the Bulgars were occupying a village the other side of a bit of a plain. They drawed their swords and CHARGE! They went off all across this plain, full belt, wi' us behind 'em. Pigs, ducks, fowls and all sorts scattered all over the place - that were so funny.

The Germans and the Bulgarians had gone by the time we got there, leaving their dead horses and heaps of other things. I found a wooden box and levered it open and found it was full of German helmets - lovely helmets with the spikes on - but I had nowhere to put one to take with me.

Well, we went on for another few days until we come to a place where they were making some resistance and I took my half-limber back to fetch 20 or 30 more boxes of ammunition. I loaded up the stuff we needed and as I was going back up this track I could see them coming towards me in regimental order. Then the officer in front put his hand up to me and said, 'We don't need that stuff now. The Bulgarians have surrendered. The war is over'. Well! I just couldn't believe it. For me the war was over!

Then, 'By the way, Small', the officer said. 'My horse had his head chopped off wi' a piece of shrapnel back there. I've left my saddle and a bottle of whisky. Would you go up and fetch the saddle and the bridle and the whisky?' Course, I went up and found the horse with his head chopped off and took the saddle off and had a drink of his whisky. Fancy that. The war over.

Somerset Guardian

4th October, 1918

Many of my readers will be interested in the news of Mr C J Lewin and his family which has reached me this week. I find that Mr Lewin's work at present is at Burnham-on-Sea where he has fitted up a temporary office. He resides at Weston-super-Mare and after the war a permanent County Library will be erected for him there. Captain Cecil Lewin, MC, has taken part in the recent fighting and up to the present is safe and well. Lieutenant Claude Lewin, MC, is at Reading University taking the Agriculture course. His shattered right arm is progressing slowly but satisfactorily. Mr W Roy Lewin, who finished up his school career by obtaining first class honours in the Oxford Senior Examination, has joined the Royal Air Force.

[November, 1918]

Mr and Mrs William Carter, of the Batch, Paulton, had four sons who served in the army during the Great War. To them fell the sad distinction of being the parents of the first and last Paulton men to be killed in the war. Corporal Vincent Carter, 1st Somerset Light Infantry, the oldest of the four brothers, was a miner when war was declared. He volunteered for service and was killed in action in France on May 9th, 1915. Private Herbert Carter, Royal Welsh Fusiliers, was called up in the first group of young miners. He was only in France a short time when he was killed in action at the Battle of Cambrai by machine gun fire. He was the last Paulton man as far as is known to be killed.

> 93551 Pte. Herbert Carter
> 17th Battalion, Royal Welsh Fusiliers
> Killed in Action
> France and Flanders
> 8th October, 1918

* * * * *

Pte. Alfred Flinn
1st Battalion, The Somerset Light Infantry
Diary entry, 4th October, 1918

Over the top. Talking & laughing with pals, when our barrage dropped at 6 pm. Went straight over, and ran into barrage. Looked back - saw three runners - supposed to be with me. Waited for them, then ran forward again into barrage. Saw one runner drop. Bit further on other two runners dropped - shell wounds in BACK. Went forward again alone. Met ser-geant - told me to come back, as was moving into the barrage. Came back little way, then forward again - moving towards Hun lines - felt shock in left arm - thought I had stopped bullet. Went forward again. Felt arm was wet. Asked pal if was bleeding, he said yes. Didn't believe him, as couldn't see it. Went forward again 'til pain too bad, looked round for way to dressing station, saw none. Sat down in entrance to Hun Tambour. Tried to move away when Fritz opened fire with MG - missed me by few inches. Remained under cover. Several times attempted exit with like result. Eventually crawled out - managed to fall into shell hole, when machine gun had another pot at us. Shells bursting all round. Din like nothing else on earth. Never expected to get out alive.

* * * * *

Pte. Jim Peppard
1st/4th Battalion, The Somerset Light Infantry
October, 1918

I stayed out in Indial on general duties. Poonah, it were. Then I got taken ill. I led out on the sand an' thought I were gonna die. They said t'were a touch o' cholera, or sim'lar the same - an' they sent me up in the hills to Wellington, for convalescence. We did go up the mountain in an engine on cogs - ever so steep, an' when we got to the top we could look down an' see the cattle an' that, ever so small, down on the plain. That were beautiful. I must have stayed there two or three months an' I got back to the depot the same afternoon as our lads left in the morning fer Russia - what fer I could never find out. But I found out that Maurice Baber had been transferred to the Hampshires then were taken ill an' died. That's he, standin' alongside me in the picture there. He were always so healthy.

> 0811 Pte. Maurice Baber
> 1st/9th Hampshire Regiment
> Died
> Poonah, India
> 21st October, 1918

* * * * *

𝔖𝔬𝔪𝔢𝔯𝔰𝔢𝔱 𝔊𝔲𝔞𝔯𝔡𝔦𝔞𝔫
October 25th, 1918

Influenza of a very severe, virulent and fatal type is at present epidemic in the district, although its effect has not been so pronounced so far in Radstock as in Clandown, Midsomer Norton and some surrounding places. Several deaths have already been recorded. The greatest precautions are being taken to deal with the infection. All the schools have been closed and . . . Dr Bulleid, as Medical Officer of Health, advised the closing of all places of worship.

THE BATTLE OF VALENCIENNES

. . . it was here that the 1st Somerset Light Infantry ended its glorious record of fighting in the Great War . . . At 5:30am a heavy 18-pounder barrage fell on the German positions and the attack began, the troops moving quickly behind the screen of fire. The Seaforths swept on through the village, leaving the latter to the Somersets, who then began to mop up the place. This was no easy task. Large numbers of German snipers were still active in the village and nearly all the cellars contained Germans who readily surrendered when called upon to do so. The snipers were more difficult to deal with and caused considerable casualties before they were finally mopped up . . .

* * * * *

Somerset Guardian

Captain Cecil Lewin, MC, who fell while gallantly leading his men during the very last engagement in which his regiment took part, was the eldest son of Mr C J Lewin, formerly of Radstock. The deceased officer joined as a private soldier in the King's Liverpool Regiment, immediately after the outbreak of the war. He soon became Sergeant, and went out to France. Not long after, on account of special qualifications, he was made Company Sergeant Major on the field. In the battle for Trones Wood his commanding officer having become a casualty CSM Lewin took control of the men and carried on even after he had received two severe wounds.

The third bullet, which knocked him out, was not extracted until eleven months afterwards. For his conspicuous bravery he was awarded the Military Cross. Upon his recovery, after a prolonged illness, Sergt Major Lewin took a commission in the Somerset LI. He returned to France, and after some time was promoted to the rank of Captain. He came unscathed through much severe fighting, but was killed in the advance on November 2. Two of this officer's brothers had already made the supreme sacrifice, Captain Rex Lewin being killed in September, 1915, and Lieut. Kenneth Lewin in March, 1918. A younger brother, Lieut. Claude Lewin won the Military Cross last year and was badly wounded. The youngest of Mr Lewin's sons is at present a cadet in the RAF.

> Captain Cecil Lewin.
> 1st Battalion, The Somerset Light Infantry.
> Killed in Action.
> France and Flanders.
> November 2nd, 1918

𝔖𝔬𝔪𝔢𝔯𝔰𝔢𝔱 𝔊𝔲𝔞𝔯𝔡𝔦𝔞𝔫

Sergeant Christopher T Carpenter, 1st Batt. Coldstream Guards, son of Mr and Mrs Henry Carpenter, Radstock, who a year ago was decorated with the Distinguished Conduct Medal, has just been awarded the Military Medal. The award is made for valuable services rendered on November 3 and 4 last. He led an attack upon a German machine gun post at Villers Poll, outside Mauheuge, on November 3, and wiped out the crew of the post for the loss of one man killed and three wounded. On the following day his Company was held up until he led his platoon along a sunken road and the result of his work caused the Germans to retire and permitted his company to continue their advance.

* * * * *

THE LONDON GAZETTE

13073 Sgt. C T Carpenter, C. Gds. (Radstock)

For conspicuous gallantry and devotion to duty. When an enemy strongpoint, with a garrison of fifty men, was holding up the advance, he led his platoon with great gallantry and initiative round the flank under heavy fire and enfiladed the position. Owing to his prompt action the enemy was kept engaged and the position was captured. He has invariably set a magnificent example of courage and devotion to duty.

* * * * *

Captain Douglas McMurtrie
7th Battalion, The Somerset Light Infantry
Prisoner of War
10th November, 1918

At about mid-day on the Sunday, a German photographer came into the camp and took our photographs for nine marks a dozen. He told us a revolution was going to take place that day in Graudenz. We didn't believe him but an hour later, we saw all the Bosch officers and soldiers straggle out and into bunches with the officers remaining together. They had several shows of hands and then they all went away. Afterwards, we learnt that the men had told the officers that their powers were suspended and that the men had elected their own representatives.

By then we could get any German paper we wanted, and we also saw a few English newspapers which were smuggled into the camp in parcels, so we always knew more or less how things were going. As soon as the push had begun, we'd bought a large map and hung it on the wall with Union Jacks showing the line in a pretty obvious fashion - for the Bosch's pleasure. That night the officers came in to take the roll-call in caps and without their usual shoulder badges. Every officer and man had taken down his cockades (representing the German and Prussian empires) and every officer had taken off their badges of rank - and any who objected had been helped. That night everyone, English and German, prisoners and guards were very happy.

Armistice
November 11th

𝔖𝔬𝔪𝔢𝔯𝔰𝔢𝔱 𝔊𝔲𝔞𝔯𝔡𝔦𝔞𝔫

The declaration of the signing of the Armistice between the Allies and Germany and the cessation of hostilities was received with great joy throughout the whole district on Monday morning. There were many more people about that morning than is usual on a Monday morning when all the collieries and works are in full swing. It is evident that nearly everyone expected the news and had been waiting for some authoritative announcement for two or three days.

Although everybody seemed highly pleased that hostilities had ended so soon after the signing of the Armistice yet there seemed to be no desire to go mafficking. I well remember the scenes in Radstock and district which followed the declaration of peace after the South African War and everything that was done was perhaps not creditable to the people who did it. But a very different state of things prevailed on Monday. People have learned a lot since the days of the South African War.

The war just ended has touched almost every home to a greater or lesser degree and it was anticipated that the joy that accompanied the declaration of peace would be of a sober and quiet nature, but none the less real and sincere. The news spread very rapidly throughout the district and soon the flags were seen floating from the church towers and flag poles in the neighbourhood and displayed at public buildings and private residences. There was apparently no organised attempt at decoration or illuminating in the evening, many people being afraid to attempt the latter in view of the lighting restrictions.

As the trains at eleven o'clock ran into the stations the explosions of detonators on the railway could be heard and the passengers on most of the four trains that came into Radstock at about that hour were thus first made aware of the great news on arrival at Radstock. The local collieries and works also let off some explosives and at some the steam whistles were sounded at full blast. The faces of the miners as they came from the pits at one or two o'clock clearly indicated their pleasure at hearing the news.

Children from the two elementary schools in Radstock assembled in Victoria Square and sang the National Anthem which was followed by ringing cheers. The scholars were given a half-holiday, and the youngsters seemed as highly pleased as the adults. No general holiday was proclaimed at the collieries or local works, but many of the men took one or two days on their own. Some of the pits were unable to start on Tuesday morning owing to the insufficient number of men and boys presenting themselves.

* * * * *

Gwen Beauchamp
VAD Nurse
11th November, 1918

I was on duty on November 11th. As usual, night duty was a six weeks' stint and for the first week I couldn't sleep much in the day time. I was so tired I had gone to bed at 10 in the morning. When we got to the hospital that night we heard that a large convoy was expected and it started arriving as soon as we got on the wards. However, the stretcher bearers had celebrated rather too much to be able to negotiate the duck-boards and therefore most of our patients were deposited in the flower beds. That night, as every night at 10pm, Corporal Jones played the *Last Post* at the hospital gates. It always varied according to how long he had been at the pub, but on Armistice Night no one was going to complain!

Pte. Tommy Atkins
7th Battalion, The Royal Fusiliers
11th November, 1918

Me? I was in a field in Belgium. At 11 o'clock there were two gunshots fired and somebody told me it was the Armistice. You knew things were going wrong on the German side but we didn't know the war was anything like near its end. We didn't celebrate in any way other than having a great feeling of relief - and there wasn't anything to celebrate with.

Course, men went on being killed after the Armistice was signed. The Germans had left booby traps for us - you'd perhaps go into an estaminet and play a piano and when you got to a certain note up went the building and everyone who was in it. We were told not to touch anything until the Engineers had inspected it.

Captain Douglas McMurtrie
7th Battalion, The Somerset Light Infantry

About 11am we heard that the Armistice had been signed and that evening we saw the terms in the papers. Then the Commandant appeared - in mufti - almost in tears. How are the mighty fallen! From then on we all started collecting souvenirs - cockades, eagles off the pith helmets, daggers and so on. On the 20th, 200 officers were told to be ready to leave on the 23rd but Saturday came and went. On Monday, 25th, everybody was allowed down town without a guard. We all went, going into hotels and restaurants. Bosch waiters would rush up and take your gloves, and cap and coat. The hotel we went to was full of English officers and not a Bosch in sight. It was very hard to get used to it. The situation was absolutely unique.

On Tuesday afternoon, we were ordered to parade at 8:15pm. We packed our suitcases - which we had bought at the canteen and which were made out of the paper et cetera from our parcels and cost 38 marks - and marched out of the camp for the last time, down to the station and left Graudenz very happily at about 10:30pm. It was the start of our long journey back to England. Rastatt and Graudenz soon faded away. War and blood vanished and we were left with no war, no Ypres salient, no Flanders mud, no soaking cold nights in filthy trenches, no marching up duck-board tracks with shells and machine gun bullets. I then began two month's leave with all the hopes of a twenty year-old.

Pte. Alban Chivers
Royal Army Ordnance Corp

I were on leave at the time and I never believed it - you couldn't believe it - you'd heard it so many times before. And when I come through on the Friday they were still fighting proper. There were no celebrations round here that I knew - if there were I never heard of them, I don't remember any. So I went back. The next lot to go on leave never came back - then an order went out that every man had to go back to his unit before he could be demobbed. And then there was trouble, 'cause a lot refused to return.

Pte. Edward Hurd
1st Battalion, The Gloucester Regiment
November, 1918

After the Armistice we had a uniform come. That was a navy blue peaked cap with a yellow band and a glazed peak, and a very dark blue tunic with a yellow collar and a wide yellow stripe down. We could go out and move around the town on our own if we were sensible, but later on the place was cleared out and we were marched to Schweidnitz station and entrained. I spent Christmas Day in Berlin Station. From there we went to Swinemunde and embarked on a Danish ship to Copenhagen, in Denmark. After a week there we left for Hull. Once there, we handed in our blue clothes and got issued with khaki. I said goodbye to Billy Aldin on Hull Station. I'd spent most of my imprisonment with Billy; we'd shared parcels from home and seen it all through together, but I don't think we even exchanged addresses. I never heard a sound of'n since. I come on home and that was that. When I got back I couldn't get no work. I didn't know what to do. I was gettin' browned off an' bitter to think what I'd come back to. I'd been offered jobs if I'd stayed in Germany and here I was, getting 29 shilling a week unemployment. And I had to hand in my greatcoat or pay 25 bob for'n. I handed'n in.

Pte. Francis Oakley
4th Battalion, The Gloucestershire Regiment

Those of us who survived the sinking of the *Cameronia* were taken to Malta. Our two Gloucester drafts got there without loss of a single man but other drafts were not so fortunate. Of the 3,000 or so on board, 145 were lost. Ten days later we were taken to a transit camp in Alexandria in Egypt, where we were kitted out again and after that we went to India, to the 7th Gloucesters' Indian depot in the Mahratta Hills, below Poonah. My wounded face - my teeth had not yet been replaced - kept me in India until the ending of the war. The surgery I needed was finally seen to there but before it happened I got leave to visit my brother Charles - able to go over to see him at Barrackpore. Of the ten days leave I was granted, seven were taken up with travelling across India and back. But it was worth it.

Pte. Stan Small
10th Battalion, The Devonshire Regiment
26th November, 1918

After the Bulgarians surrendered we had the order come to march 50 miles up to Bucharest to represent the British when they put the old king back on the throne again. It was a forced march and we had to cross the Danube to get in to Romania. We had four days to do it and we got there a day early. A day early! And what a greeting we had! In the coronation procession we marched eight abreast, right behind the royal carriage. We were the first British soldiers they'd seen in Bucharest but there were Union Jacks all over the place! Oh yes, we had quite a welcome.

Well, when we'd put he back on the throne we come back down to Gurgivoo *[Giugiu]* and then on big barges to Russia. When we got there that was beautiful. I don't know the name of the town *[Batumi, Georgia]* but it put me in mind of a fishing village. We were put in some cavalry barracks there to wait while some men from the Rifle Brigade joined us. I was only there about a week when the Sergeant-Major said, 'Small, you've never been home. Look, hand your mules over to your Sergeant, get your kit together and get on the next boat. And don't miss it'. And I didn't.

Pte. Sammy Taylor
3rd Battalion, The Coldstream Guards

I stayed in hospital for nearly a twelve-month. I were really hardened to the things I saw over there but me nerves caught up with me after the war and I were afraid to go anywhere on me own, even in the village. Funny, weren't it. While I were in hospital I used to correspond with my mate George *[p.146]* from Newcastle for a bit and I asked what had happened to my squeeze-box. He wrote and said the lads had given it to young Jack Britten who used to play with Oliver and we in Welton. Well, I were glad of that cause Jack could knock out a tune or two. But then I heard that he'd been killed. I were very sorry - he were a nice young chap. Oh, I were glad to get out of that place. It were a real hell-hole. But I were proud to be in the Coldstream - I never begrudge the day I joined em.

> 15202 Pte. William Britten
> 3rd Battalion, The Coldstream Guards
> Killed in Action
> France and Flanders
> 12th April, 1918
> Aged 22

Pte. Jim Peppard
1st/4th Battalion, The Somerset Light Infantry

When we got demobbed we come back through Salonikal way - all by trucks. We come up through France and got a boat and ended up at Devonport. Then I come up here on the Pines Express. As we come through Chilcompton, Howard Veale were by the track and he seen me and we waved. Well, the train didn' stop in Chilcompton, nor at Norton Hill, so I had to wait until Radstock and then walk back up to Chilcompton. I were never so excited as when I walked up there that day. I walked in through and opened the inside door. I can see Mother now, sat in the chair. Aw, she didn' half look at me. An' I zed, 'Well, Mother, do seem good to catch hold of the old door-knob once more'.

1919

Captain Arthur Coombs
1st/4th Battalion, The Somerset Light Infantry
1919

In Mesopotamia we didn't know when we were going to get home and the rules came that the men would be returned as they were needed. The coal miners went off first, then various other people - students and things like that - and I, being nothing, stayed to the last with about 50 others. I found myself in charge of the cadre coming home on the troopship. There was a fog in the Channel so we were two hours late getting into Bath Station - at eight in the evening instead of six.

There were absolute crowds there to greet us and all of the people who had been out in India with us had paraded to meet us. I think the whole of Bath must have turned out to line the streets. I've never seen such masses. The police made a passage for us to get through the crowds and I gave the order to march, but then I turned round and there was only a young Lieutenant and the CSM behind me - nobody else. The crowd had scuppered them. Well, the police formed a rugby scrum and we got the men up to the YMCA where they were taken care of. We were then taken to the Fernley Hotel. It was eleven at night by then, and the first thing I did was to order a whisky. 'Very sorry, Sir. This is a teetotal hotel.' I have never found out who was responsible for that.

From *The Coldstream Guards 1914 - 1918*

Following the precedent of the Crimean War, His Majesty the King ordered his Guards to pass him in review and to march through London. This ceremony, as far as the Household Troops were concerned, was their final act of the Great War . . . The Royal Review took place on the 22nd March, l919. The procession formed up in Buckingham Palace Road; it was headed by the three Regiments of Household Cavalry, and then came the Guards Division led by their first Commander; General Earl of Cavan, with whom was HRH the Prince of Wales, and by Major General T G Matheson, CB, CMG, General Officer Commanding the Guards Division.

* * * * *

Casualties

Somerset Light Infantry

Battalions	Killed*
1st (Other Ranks)	1,315
1st/4th (ORs)	118
6th (ORs)	849
7th (ORs)	663
All Btns (ORs)	4,487
Officers (All Btns)	269
Total for all Btns	4,756

Coldstream Guards

All Battalions	Other Ranks	Officers	Totals
Killed*	3,680	180	3,860
Wounded	9,183	325	9,508
Prisoners	753	16	769
Totals	13,616	521	14,137

* numbers shown include those killed in action or died from wounds or other causes

The Thankful Villages

Somerset's eight Thankful Villages were Aisholt, Chantry, Chelwood, Rodney Stoke, Stanton Prior, Stocklinch, Tellisford and Woolley. The smallest of these was Aisholt, with a population of 48. Chelwood, which was home to 164 villagers, was the largest. Woolley, with 13 families, sent 13 men.

Acknowledgements
and Epilogue

To thank the men and women whose stories are included in these pages would be superfluous; this book is intended to honour them.

Sir Torquhil Matheson (right), more than anyone, gave me the confidence to go ahead with my book and the support that he gave me was superb. I first met him about two years after I began compiling it, and a few months after I had 'found' Sammy Taylor. The fact that Torquhil lived a mere twelve miles from my home was a huge bonus for me and, for him, the discovery of Sammy was bliss. I now re-listen to the tapes I made then and find them peppered with Torquhil's, 'Oh, this is wonderful. Just wonderful. These men were heroes, absolute heroes. What joy to learn these things'. Torquhil was an outstanding man, with a huge zest for life and an impish sense of humour. He and his brother, Sir Fergus, were two of the 32 members of the Queen's Honourable Corps of Gentlemen at Arms; her ceremonial bodyguard. On one occasion Torquhil realised that I planned to include the picture of Oliver  Brooks receiving his VC from King George. 'You know that is Crown Copyright, don't you? It's the Queen's. Never fear, I'm seeing her on Tuesday. I'll mention it!'

Torquhil's devotion to the Coldstream Guards, and in particular his beloved 3rd Battalion, was all embracing. What particularly impressed me about him was his knowledge of the details of so many private soldiers. He knew not only their names and their service records he also knew their pre-war - and often post-war - family situations. They meant the world to him. I am extremely grateful to Sir Fergus for agreeing to write the foreword for his brother.

Even before I met Torquhil, the Coldstream Guards had been very helpful and I am indebted to Warrant Officer Clive Candlin to whom I first wrote about Charlie Fry in 1980. One of the first things I learned was that Charlie had never been in the glasshouse - or a greenhouse *[page 128]* - it was an old soldier's tale. I thank the Oxford University Press for permission to quote from *The Coldstream Guards 1914-1918* by Lieutenant Colonel Sir John Ross-of-Bladensburg, KCB, KCVO, and similarly the Somerset Light Infantry Museum in Taunton for the help they gave me in allowing me access to trench diaries and their own regimental history, *The Somerset Light Infantry, 1914-1919,* by Everard Wyrall.

I am grateful to The Imperial War Museum for permission to use the pictures on pages 63, 81, 138 and 147, and to others for the use of their treasured photographs. Staff at The Commonwealth War Graves Commission were consistently helpful and their website (www.cwgc.org) has been of great value. I made considerable use of the Somerset Guardian and I am grateful to that newspaper as well as to the Frome Library and the admirable Midsomer Norton and Radstock District Museum, for allowing me access to the relevant issues.

In 1999 the Museum Society invited me to speak at their AGM. The date for my talk was the 60th anniversary of the start of WWII and it was suggested that I should take that as my subject. However, as my knowledge of the Second World War is no greater than the next man's, I offered WWI, and re-opened my shoe-boxes. My thanks to the Museum Society!

My family have been long suffering in their patience with me, especially Birgitta, who proof-read, and provided coffee, encouragement and the reassurance that I *had* to put it all into print. Many other people have helped and encouraged me in ways they probably don't realise but I am indebted to my American friend Bill Crichton, who was the first to read the text. With little knowledge of the war from the British perspective, Bill's suggestions were both astute and welcomed.

Others have lent pictures, advised, proof-read and made introductions or suggestions. They include: Shirley Appleton, Trevor Bailey, Bob and Lis Bates, Edward Boucher, Sheila Bishop, Maurice Chivers, Susan Darling, Janet Flagg, Mike Gorman, Francis Hillier (of the Somerset FA), John Howell, Paul Huber, Rachel Humphries, Richard Jeffrey, Geraldine Langley, David MacMurtrie, Nell Matheson, Andrew Moon, De Pickford, Tony Pickford, Paul Ring, Jeremy Robertson, John and Jane Sanders, Mike and Dave Selway, Joan Stevens, Nick Stock, Veronica Stokes, David Taylor, Gemma Taylor (and Quincy Greene), Ian Telfer, Geoff and Marie Urch, Ian Wallen and Jonathan Wood.

I am especially pleased that three of my former pupils were involved with the latter stages of the book: Robbie Polley for his excellent artwork; Nigel Carter, the Commercial Director of Butler and Tanner, who was invariably generous with his friendship and expertise and insistence that the book should be published, and Paul Norris, the Systems Manager at Radstock Reproductions - whose patience was exemplary.

I am, of course, extremely grateful to the many families who allowed me into their homes whilst I was recording material and, more recently, enabled me to prepare a few final lines about their parents and grandparents. I am, of course, especially indebted to Margaret Clare who introduced me to her father; SAMMY TAYLOR. 'When Dad got better after the war he went to work for Bristol Stone and Concrete - walked four miles there and four miles back every day - and stayed with them all his working life. He went on living up the road, by himself, until a couple of months before he died. And he was still singing his First World War songs right up until the end.'

Sammy died in 1991. A Coldstream Guardsman sounded the *Last Post* at his funeral and I never heard it played more sweetly. The notes are in my head as I am drafting the paragraphs that follow.

TOMMY ATKINS

'When the war ended, Dad went on into Germany for a while, until they'd got things sorted out. He learned to speak the language and said time, and time again how much he liked the German people - people who'd been trying to kill him! Preferred them to the English, he said. When he came back he spent all his working life as a driver; lorries, charabancs, cars - the lot. Went on working until he was 70. One thing he loved to do then was to study the stars. He was fascinated by Halley's Comet - he saw it when he was eleven and couldn't wait to see it again. But he didn't, he missed it by just a few weeks.' (Janet Flagg)

GWEN BEAUCHAMP

Gwen played tennis for Somerset, was Commandant of the local Red Cross Detachment, and in 1924 married Keith Malcolm and moved to Wimbledon where she lived for most of her life. She overcame her youthful innocence. When she was 86, she told me that a police inspector had just called to warn her that a man had been exposing himself on the Common. 'Oh,' she said. 'If he tries that with me I shall tell him: Young man, put it away and don't be so silly! I was a VAD nurse in the Great War. I've seen *heaps* better than that.'

GEOFFREY BISHOP

'Like his father who was a doctor - and in the 4th Somerests before the war - Geoffrey decided that he would become one too, so he went off to Bristol University and the Bristol Royal Infirmary to qualify. He then became a country doctor and practiced in Shepton Mallet for the whole of his career with the exception of World War Two. He always stayed with the Somersets and was commanding them when war broke out. He spent the first year of the war with them in England up until the call came for him to stop playing soldiers and join the RAMC.

He served with them in forward Casualty Clearing Stations in North Africa and Italy, and was eventually made up to full Colonel with a staff job in the Area High Command, near Salerno - which is where I was serving as a Red Cross Welfare Officer, and where I met him. We moved here to Bath when he retired in 1964. Geoffrey died in 1987.' (Sheila Bishop)

OLIVER BROOKS

Oliver Brooks first served in the Coldstream Guards between 1906 and 1913. He was recalled at the outbreak of the war and went immediately to France with the BEF. He left the army in 1919 and worked until his retirement as doorman at the White Hart Hotel, in Windsor. He died in 1940. In 1967 Mrs Brooks, and their grandson, Coldstream Guardsman Brian Lucas-Carter, presented Oliver's VC to his old regiment.

HERBERT CAINES

'Dad loved his railways and, apart from when he was on the run from the Germans, he really rather enjoyed his war. He stayed on for a year when it ended, helping to clear everything up, with German prisoners to do all the work. When he did come back he returned to the railways for a while but then went into mining and became secretary of New Rock Colliery. He was just a few days short of his 102nd birthday when he died.' (Irene Sheppard)

CHRIS CARPENTER

'When he was demobbed Chris was going back in the mines but his Captain gave him a gold cigarette case and arranged for his father, who was in charge of the Metropolitan Police, to get Chris in with them. Easy as that. Everything was set up and he was due to go up to London to be fitted for his uniform but then his wife said she was going to have a baby and he decided against going - but if she was, she waited three years to have it. So he went back down the mines. He always told us how he'd been created a King's Sergeant on the field, by King George himself, and when he was dying with the miners' illness in 1961 he told me he wanted a black headstone with the Coldstream badge and the words King's Sergeant of the Coldstream Guards on it. But the man who cut the stone just put Sergeant. That upset me.' (Cliff Carpenter)

ALBAN CHIVERS

'They kept us out there clearing up the mess until the end of 1919. It was first out there, first back. The regular soldiers went back to England first, then Kitchener's Army then the Derby lot and then - least and last - us. I started back at the brewery in January, 1920, but t'was never the same. After the war the trade had gone. It was never the same.'

'I suppose if it is possible to have such a thing as a good war then Grandad did. Apart from losing his brother it never seemed to have had any great effect on him. Did he ever tell you about the time he sold his sentry-box to a Frenchman for firewood?' (Maurice Chivers)

ARTHUR COOMBS

'In 1920 I went out to the tea and rubber plantations in Ceylon. Stayed for 32 years. At one point I was running a tea plantation and someone commented that I was far too young to be in charge. I was 38! It was pointed out that I'd been a major in the last war - which I was for a while, standing in for someone for a couple of months. When I retired I came to Bath to live and I now lunch every Wednesday and Friday with Geoffrey Bishop. Once a year those of us who are left from the 1st/4th get together for our Braemar Association dinner. We had a good crowd once: Cox and Nifton and Openshaw - the doctor's son from Cheddar - Clutterbuck, Willie Moger, Humphrey Tanner who was Frome - Butler and Tanner, you know - he was wounded out there, as was Sir Charles Miles. Lewis, whose father ran the paper in Bath - he was also wounded. Worger from Radstock always came. Charey died last year. Stourman - he's dead. Not everyone made it back of course: Baker, of Weston super Mare, and Lillington from Shepton Mallet, and the other Lewis were all killed out there. And the others. Only a few of us left now. Only a few.'

* * * * *

More than 900,000 British soldiers died in the First World War. Seventy-two of them came from Midsomer Norton and fifty-eight from Radstock. There were countless thousands of other casualties. Reg Jones, who missed conscription by a matter of weeks, said that, 'Towards the end of the war you'd get a tap come on your door and there'd be a man with one arm or one leg, sellin' matches or bootlaces. You did see these blokes everywhere, everywhere. Fingers gone, legs gone, arms gone. Mind gone. I used to wonder what it were all about. What *were* it all about? That didn't impress me a lot. This were going to be a land fit for heroes'.

* * * * *

CHARLIE FRY

Charlie was a casualty, though he will not be found in statistical returns. He was not immediately discharged on his release from hospital because there were still jobs for him to do - as Torquhil Matheson put it - 'In the regimental cookhouses and shitehouses at home'. Charlie came home in March, 1919, with rotted feet and a confused mind.

It was largely because of Charlie that this book was written. His farm, such as it was, lay on one side of Underhill Lane, in Midsomer Norton and I was born in one of the three houses on the other. In 1944, had he a mind to, he might

have seen this five year-old attempting to march along the lane behind the Coldstream Guards who were then stationed in Midsomer Norton. But I doubt he was interested. Charlie fell from his cart in 1955 and died. He was still wearing his puttees.

SID HAWKINS

Sid was 100 when I met him, and the last old soldier to contribute to the book. 'He worked in a bike shop for a few years when he came home and then spent the rest of his working life as an engine driver on the Great Western Railway.' (Veronica Stokes)

EDWARD HURD

'Grandad was a policeman for 30 years after the war - had five children in five different police houses all over Somerset. It was only after your talks with him that he began opening up to us about his war - told us about when he was a prisoner of war and swapped a loaf of Red Cross bread for an Iron Cross he kept in a drawer in his bedroom.' (Paul Ring)

CLIFFORD JEFFREY

'Once he'd come back, Dad stayed on the farm all his life until he retired in 1956. Forty years. If he'd not come out when he did, who knows what might have happened. He'd already been to Gallipoli and back. Albie David came back, too. They were the lucky ones.' (Richard Jeffrey)

CHARLES LEWIN
[From the Minutes of
The Somerset FA's AGM, 28th June, 1919]

'Mr Lewin said it was strange to say that it was five years to the very day that they had last held their annual meeting. Five tremendous years, fraught with changes for the whole country, affecting almost every individual, had passed. He could not trust himself to say very much about that, but on looking back at the minutes of their last meeting he found that he had then expressed his belief that footballers would not play an ignoble part in the great upheaval . . .'   Charles Lewin was on the National Football Association Council in 1904; first represented Radstock on the Somerset Football Association in 1896, and was the Association's permanent Chairman from 1903 until his resignation in July 1945. He died three months later. Youngsters in Somerset still compete for The Lewin Youth Cup.

CLAUDE LEWIN

'I spent quite a lot of time with Claude out in Africa. He was a pretty clever bloke, you know. When he was invalided out of the army, because of his mangled arm, he went to Reading University, and eventually went to Nigeria where he produced a special strain of cotton which went down very well. Then he had a most appalling show when his only two daughters went ski-ing in Switzerland, and were both killed by an avalanche. The Lewins were a pretty gutsome lot, you know.' (Douglas McMurtrie)

217

Douglas MacMurtrie

'After the war I became a regular officer with the Somerset's 1st Battalion for six years. Then I got tired of regimental life and went to Africa with the Royal West African Frontier Force. Which was when I met Claude Lewin again for the first time since before the war.'

(David McMurtrie) 'Father was actually in Africa on three different occasions. After that first stint he returned to England in about 1930, when he got married, and then he went back two years later and remained out there until the Second World War when he rejoined the Somersets' 1st Battalion and went to France. He stayed with them for a couple of years but then, as he was an expert on Africa, they sent him back out in late 1941 to create a Training Depot and the 11th Nigerian Battalion.

He left Africa in 1944 as a Lt. Colonel and then raised the 16th Holding Battalion in Clacton, for men returning from Europe. He stayed there until 1946 when, being also a Courts Martial expert he was posted to Palestine. He sailed first to Egypt and was making his way by rail to Palestine when his train was blown up by Israeli terrorists. He eventually settled for a peaceful retirement in the New Forest!'

Jim Peppard

'My nerves went after the war - absolutely gone. An' that wen' on fer two year. I got so low. I just wanted to be on me own - didn't want to see nobody. Go in the garden. Hide. Once I'd got over that I learnt the mason's trade. I told you how I volunteered fer everything during the first war, well I done the same in the second. First thing I done was build a hostel for land workers on Bodmin, then I went in to Bath to clean up fer the blitz, same in Bristol and then t'were London - I were up there when the first two rockets come over, in Forest Hill and the building I were in copped it. You never seen such a mess. But I've always been the lucky one. It's bin a good life!'

George Pollard

George Pollard was a family doctor in Midsomer Norton for 43 years. He retired in 1929, when he was 70. From 1916 to 1919 he was with the RAMC at the Taunton Military Hospital. He served on dozens of committees, from mining and education to farming and football. He was a County JP and the Medical Officer of Downside School but nothing that he ever did meant more to him than his beloved 1st/4th Battalion of the Somerset Light Infantry, and it was that for which he would want to be remembered.

LESLIE POLLARD

'He stayed in India for the whole of his military career and retired as a Brigadier in 1939 - did you know, the Indian Army's Corps of Signals still holds its reunions at the Pollard Arena in Jabalpur, Madhya Pradesh? At the outbreak of the Second World War he went back into uniform as Commandant of Catterick Camp, the garrison town in Yorkshire. After that war he and his wife Patricia settled here in Stone Allerton with the Brigadier's batman, MacDonald, and their much loved Jersey house-cow, Jemima. He died in 1983.' (Joan Stevens)

JOSEPH REGAN and ARTHUR DINWIDDIE

Joseph Regan (No:10431) and Arthur Dinwiddie (No:10430) first joined the Grenadier Guards in August 1902 and both left the army after three years. They were then mobilised on 5th August, 1914 and were in France six days later. The gunshot wounds that Regan had sustained rendered his right arm unusable and he was discharged on 14th August, 1915, unfit for further service. Arthur Dinwiddie, who was unwounded, left the army on the same day having completed his period of engagement.

STAN SMALL

'Dad spent the first few years after the war as Lord Strachey's chauffeur, but he couldn't afford to live on those wages so he went back to mining, this time up in Coventry. After that he became an aircraft engineer! First at Brize Norton - he used to cycle up there from home - and then at BAC in Bristol. He was there all through the Second World War and right up until his retirement in 1963. He died in 1983.' (Rachel Humphries)

GEORGE TAYLOR

'When Dad came back he gave his sweetheart an ultimatum. Either she married him or he was off to America. Well, they married, and they bred well 'cause they had ten of us: six boys and four girls. He went back to the mines when he came home and worked there pretty-well all his life, apart from when he was injured by a rock falling on him underground, and a spell in a factory during the second war. He was 92 when he died. The story he told you about swimming across the river to get away from the Germans? Well, he could never swim. He hated the water. Dad reckoned it was the pack on his back that kept him afloat just long enough to reach the other side. He was scared out of his wits.' (David Taylor)

SAMMY TAYLOR

The final paragraphs of this book are self-indulgent. I grew very fond of many of the people I interviewed but none more so than Sammy Taylor. On my office wall hang two of Sammy's tin whistles from the trenches, together with a framed, tinfoil Coldstream star that he made and gave me. He was the gentlest of men. On a couple of occasions Torquhil Matheson brought Major-General Sir George Burns, KCVO, CB, DSO, OBE, MC, BA, Colonel of the Coldstream Guards and Lord Lieutenant of Hertfordshire, to my home to meet Sammy, and I have happy memories of the former coal miner patting the General on his knee and asking, 'Are you all right, my dear?'

On his hundredth birthday, in 1991, Torquhil and I arranged a surprise for Sammy. His family was invited to my house for a celebration drink and at noon we put a seat in the porch for Sammy, who sat there - unwitting and uncomplaining - with a rug over his knees. At the same moment, from 100 yards away, a small corps of Guardsmen Drummers, drawn from all the Guards Regiments and led by the Senior Drum Major of the Household Division, marched up the road playing the regimental tunes of the Coldstream Guards. They were followed by half-a-dozen officers and men of the Guards' Association. Sammy loved it. We gave him his whistle and he gleefully played along with the flutes and the drums. Then he grinned and teased the musicians - especially the Grenadiers who were with them: 'Always the Coldstream. Second to none. Second to none.'

Thank you, Sammy

Index

We never spared a thought about why we were there. It was just a horrible fact of life.

Herbert (Tommy) Atkins